D1590873

The Book of Neptune

The Book of
Neptune

by

Marilyn
Waram

International Standard Book Number 0-917086-84-8

Cover Design by Maria Kay Simms, San Diego, CA

Printed in the United States of America

Published by ACS Publications, Inc.
P.O. Box 34487
San Diego, CA 92103-0802

Dedication

This book is dedicated to the Astro-gang in Terrace and Kitimat, British Columbia: Elaine Maikapar, Marianne Brorup-Weston, Debbie Taphouse, Irma Dube, Joanne Batjer and Elaine Farina, as well as to Anne Twidle, because we grew together and stood together through good times and bad. I love you all so much!

Acknowledgments

First and foremost, I'd like to thank Maritha Pottenger from the bottom of my heart for asking me to do this book, and then for offering such enthusiastic support and encouragement at various stages. I couldn't have asked for a kinder editor.

Dr. Zipporah Dobyns and Maritha, through their astrological intensives and the *Mutable Dilemma*, together opened up so many doors it took me years to walk through them all! Their unique psycho-spiritual approach to astrology gave me the tools I was desperately searching for, and gave me the ability to change what I didn't like in my life and create something better. Zip, Maritha, thank you!

My parents, Pat and Seff Wilson, who wanted a daughter they could be proud of and ended up with an astrologer. They care about me even though I'm a little odd!

Vic believed I had talent from my first tentative beginnings, built the desk of my dreams and paved the way for me to teach my first astrology classes, from which everything else bloomed.

John McCormack listened patiently while I chatted about the ego risk involved in actually writing a book. Like Tigger in "Winnie the Pooh," I thought I could if I really wanted to, but when faced with the opportunity, I suddenly wasn't so sure. John understood, and supported. He still does, bless him.

Collin Sansregret made dancing lessons such a joy that I was able to keep my head above water during a very difficult period in my life **and** continue to write this book. He has, therefore, contributed to the success of two life-long dreams of mine— dancing and writing. Thank you, Collin!

Every client I've had and every friend I've shared conversation with has contributed to my understanding and helped me grow. Because of their responses, I have learned that love links to love, and that love is the natural state of our spiritual selves, which is, I believe, one of the essential lessons of Neptune.

Contents

CHAPTER ONE

CLEARING UP NEPTUNE

Getting in the Mood

How does one begin a book— which is essentially geared to the conscious, logical, rational mind— about the planet Neptune— which represents issues and drives that are usually unconscious, alogical and arational? How does the conscious mind and ego come to grips with a complex of concepts which cannot be defined in concrete terms? Neptune represents the **non**-concrete, the ethereal, the watery, the spiritual aspects of experience, all those matters with which the scientific, orderly conscious mind is ill-equipped to deal.

Our minds are trained to function with words, words which actually help to shape our experience of reality. Our unconscious mind, in contrast, functions with symbols; pictures, shapes, colors, using people who represent some part of ourselves in dreams, and so on. Each of the symbols carries a meaning or a complex of meanings, which may be important to a single individual or universally accepted. The unconscious mind uses these symbols to draw the attention of the conscious mind to something important. It is up to the conscious mind to accept the symbols and get in touch with the gut-level feelings engendered by the symbols because that is the message. Then the feelings or new insights can be worked with, consciously.

Experiencing Neptune

Yet all those who try to translate the experience of Neptune, whether they do so through music, poetry, art, meditation, psychological insight or some other medium, know that the experience loses a great deal in the translation. Anyone who has ever awakened from a beautiful dream and tried to convey the sense of peace and love and harmony of that dream to another person will understand how difficult it is to bring the world of Neptune (dreams) into the physical world. It seems we can only capture parts and pieces of it, at best.

In order to truly comprehend Neptune, perhaps one must experience Neptune, and be able to perceive that experience as something valuable and valid, even though it is apart from the usual linear scientific/technical/rational experiences of which our Western world is so enamored. An ability to list Neptune traits and key words is only a preliminary step, albeit an important one. Knowing the things, and in many cases the non-things, which Neptune represents can help the rational mind categorize experiences: "Oh, dreams are Neptunian, daydreaming is also Neptunian...**that** is what a Neptunian experience feels like!" The acceptance on an intellectual level of certain issues and experiences as Neptunian can help a person recognize those issues when they arise; it is still the experience which brings the knowledge to life for that person.

Open-mindedness

An important prerequisite to understanding Neptune and all that it represents is an attitude of acceptance. When Neptune is judged negatively, acceptance is difficult. If an astrologer's view of Neptune is largely negative, it is a good bet that the astrologer has not learned to accept the Neptune in her chart, is, in fact, out of tune with it and experiences it as negative. Such a person will have a difficult if not impossible task to present Neptune in its positive possibilities for clients.

If the view is totally positive, it is an indication that the astrologer is overly Neptunian and views the world with rose-colored glasses. Such an astrologer will find it difficult to cope with the negative manifestations of Neptune and may not relate to the questions and concerns of a client who desperately needs

perspective on his Neptune nature.

When the view of Neptune is balanced, it is likely that the astrologer has mostly come to terms with the Neptune part of her nature and is at peace with it. This astrologer will be free to recognize destructive Neptune manifestations in clients and will also be able to see many possibilities for the client to express Neptune energies in constructive ways.

Incidentally, astrologers who are out of sync with Neptune tend to either have too much or too little compassion and sensitivity. The former can lead to a great deal of confusion in the astrologer's mind about how much to help and get involved in the lives of clients. The latter can lead to a lot of frustrated clients, many of whom consult an astrologer in a desperate search for understanding, having been unable to find anyone in the conventional world who can accept them **as they are**.

Obviously, in order to deal with Neptune in such a way as to recognize both its negative and positive tendencies, it is important to have a nonjudgmental view of the concerns represented by the planet. Perhaps it is a good idea to take a moment right now, as you read this, to relax, take a deep breath and let your current ideas about Neptune, positive and negative, simply slide away, not because they are wrong, but in order to open up your mind for new impressions. After all, that is the Neptunian approach!

Understanding Neptune

So here we are, trying to fit our logical, rational, linear-thinking minds around Neptune, which represents experiences that are wholistic and pervasive, spiritual and universal yet deeply personal, ecstatic and agonizing. We are trying to use words, which relate to objects or objective qualities, to describe what may be the ultimate inner experiences. The words can tell us that Neptune is associated with such **things** as water, gases, cosmetics, stage magic, television, drugs; and such **experiences** as empathy, inspiration, bliss, romance, mental confusion, spiritual yearning or the desire to escape from the harshness of the world. Immediately questions arise: "What do water and television have in common?" "How can drugs and drug-induced 'trips' or escapism be related to spiritual development?"

What do water and television have in common? Neptune. Water is a universal symbol for the unconscious as well as the illuminated consciousness, both of which are clearly Neptune's domain. Television is associated with both artistic expression, in terms of acting and stage work and staged illusions, and with escapism, when watching TV becomes a way of life, or more accurately, a way of avoiding life— all of which relate to Neptune's meanings.

Indeed, the variety of issues and objects and experiences associated with any given planet can be a source of confusion and misunderstanding unless the essence of the symbolism is clearly understood. Essences in general are, however, difficult to agree upon because they require a depth of vision not everyone has developed. What seems an essence today is tomorrow only one more manifestation of yet a deeper essence.

Neptune's Essence

The essence of Neptune, as I see it today, is that drive within which seeks to find, understand and (re)unite with that which is larger, more spiritual and more perfect than anything which has yet to be found on Earth. It is our need to be in touch with, or at the very least to search for, Something in which we can wholeheartedly believe, Something— or Someone— in whom we can place our faith and whom we can trust to never let us down. It is that sense that somewhere there is an experience of total, unconditional, infinite Cosmic love of such magnitude that all human experience pales before it. We yearn for this, whether we are aware of it or not.

Now, what different people do to try to satisfy this craving can vary greatly. Much of life appears to be a series of pitfalls or tests for the unsuspecting— as if only those with the purest of hearts can see which choices will truly lead us to the Neptune experience we seek, and which are false leads. Neptune itself is associated with both, the path of clarity and illumination and the path of confusion and dishonesty or illusions.

From this essence of a yearning for a spiritual absolute, then, come the two paths, one which leads us in the direction we want and one which only appears to lead us in that direction. The former tends to bring to mind the positive manifestations of Neptune: idealism, empathy, vision, inspiration, acceptance, healing, transcendence, spiritual illumination, artistic/creative ability. The latter tends to make us think of the negative manifestations: escapism, drugs, alcoholism, mental instability, chronic confusion, illusions.

Reality

An important issue which needs to be included in this discussion of Neptune and its meanings is that of reality. As astrologers we customarily assign reality to Saturn. It fits well. Then along comes Neptune with its surrealistic experiences and we begin to question, what **is** reality, anyway? A vivid dream **feels** real enough at the time it is experienced.

Have you ever had the experience of waking from a dream and not being sure for several moments if it was a dream or if it all actually happened?

There may be no better way to actually convey Neptune's relationship to reality than to relate this enchanting little story from China.

A Chinese Vision

There were two friends who went for a walk in the woods, and in the course of this walk they came upon the ruins of an old temple. Amid the ruins an old monk had set up residence. He came forward to greet them and began to show them around the temple. There were many magnificent statues of gods, but what really fascinated the two friends were some unusual paintings on some of the walls, paintings of lovely scenes.

One scene in particular captured the attention of one of the friends, Chu; it was a delightful rendering of a small city. In the middle of the city stood a lovely young girl, with her hair unbound as was the custom among unmarried women. Chu was completely smitten and fell in love with the image of this girl. Now the old monk decided to teach Chu a lesson and through his magic transported the pining youth right into the city in the picture, where he immediately met the very girl with whom he was so smitten. She was, to Chu's delight, just as taken with him and they went off and enjoyed a rapturous love affair. The girl's friends, noticing her involvement, came over with beautiful combs to pin up her hair. Chu was, by this time, more in love than ever.

Several days later, however, a terrible commotion was heard outside their house. When they went to see what was going on, they saw military men going through the houses, looking for aliens, for people who did not have the correct registration papers. Terrified, Chu hid under the bed. However there was soon more noise than ever outside and he could not resist going to the window to have a look. Suddenly he found himself floating out the window and a moment later he was back in the temple with his friend and the old monk, and indeed he found that only a few seconds had passed since he had disappeared. Amazed, Chu and his friend turned to the monk for some sort of explanation.

"Visions are born and die in those who behold them," he said. "What can an old monk say?" But then he raised his eyes back to the painting, and following his lead, so did Chu and his friend. The girl's hair was no longer down, but pinned up by beautiful combs.

And now, while the small shiver of awareness slips over you and your hair struggles to stand on end, close your eyes for a moment and ask yourself: Which was real, the temple and the monk, or the girl in the town? What difference does it make?

Assimilating Neptunian Concepts

Perhaps the best way to learn about Neptune is to go on a meditation retreat for a week. Not all of us have the time or the inclination, and many of us need inspiration when it comes to putting appropriate words to our experiences. That is part of what this book is all about— words to describe Neptune. Those who take the experience deeper for themselves, those who relate the words and ideas in this book to experiences they themselves have had, will find their understanding of Neptune is brought to life. That is why little meditations are included at intervals throughout the book. Neptunian concepts take time to assimilate.

Exploring Some Key Words

Key words are a favorite device for teachers to convey some of the major meanings of various planets, signs and houses. Some of the key words commonly applied by a number of authors to Neptune include: artistic, mystical, sensitive, idealistic, confused, deceptive, dreamer. We will take a quick look at these words, to see if and how they fit into the Neptune picture.

Artistic— the meaning here, usually expanded upon in the texts, is that the planet Neptune is associated with artistic ability. This is usually borne out in experience with charts, where individuals with a strong Neptune[1] can be asked about their artistic ability or expression. Perhaps a better word might be "creative," because many Neptunians are creative musically, some with a very practical chart orientation are into handicrafts rather than pure art, and some, busy with other pursuits, have not developed their own talents but have a fine appreciation of art, music and other activities which seek to bring visions into a form that can be shared by the world. It is amazing how much creativity is associated with Neptune. In the sixth house of work, for example, it can indicate a hairdresser— not usually someone we think of as artistic unless you understand that they, no less than formal artists, must visualize their creation and then bring it into being. Their medium is simply human hair rather than acrylic or watercolor or clay!

Mystical— a mystic is someone who believes that there is much more to life and reality than that which can be measured and described by science, and that these apparent mysteries can be and perhaps can **only** be experienced subjectively, within each individual. This sounds very much like Neptune's essence, as described earlier. Again, this is generally borne out in charts, even in those in whom it seems most unlikely. People with a strong Neptune have often gone through school secretly refusing to accept in their heart that what they learn in science class is all there is to life. In the face of a technological world, they silently persist in searching for deeper answers, certain that those answers do indeed exist, if only they can find the right

---

1. Strong means an angular Neptune, a highly aspected Neptune, or a strong repeated Pisces or 12th house theme or in this case, a Neptune placed in an artistic/creative house: 2, 5, or 12.

doors to open.

Sensitive— this particular word is applied in two ways. First, it can mean an extraordinary emotional sensitivity, that is, the tendency to be easily hurt by cutting remarks, or to easily pick up on the distress or hurt or other strong emotions being experienced by others. This sensitivity borders on and is very often accompanied by psychic openness, the ability to see auras or visions or to know about things by means other than the ordinary. This slides us into the second meaning, which means psychic or mediumistic sensitivity. Many Neptunians are aware of other "presences," and may feel the existence of entities or ghosts or discarnate spirits. Some can allow these entities to channel messages; others "hear" or "feel" the messages and pass them along.

Idealistic— this refers to a tendency to consider ideals more important than practical issues. Idealistic parents who decide that love and kindness are most important in childraising may equate all discipline with punishment and refuse to set any limits for their offspring. Idealistic politicians may decide that democracy is more important than progress and will opt for chaos and lack of accomplishment as long as the democratic ideal of one vote for every person is adhered to. In other words, these people take a purist view of whatever they consider to be important concepts and may not be able to contemplate sullying those concepts in any way. This may be used as a reason/excuse— depending on your viewpoint— for lack of accomplishment: the person who refuses to have children because he couldn't be a perfect or ideal parent; the person who avoids politics because he couldn't enjoy anything less than pure democracy or pure autocracy; the person who refuses to develop a latent talent for music because he can't find the ideal teacher or the perfect instrument; the person who can't find a satisfactory lover/spouse because no one quite meets his vision of the ideal mate, and so on.

Confusion— it is amazing that this planet which symbolizes the most inspired visions and human spiritual experiences also symbolizes the ineffectual and misguided— gullibility, inattentiveness, lack of focus and clarity, bad drug "trips" and self-delusion. This probably stems from the action of the energies represented by Neptune, which strive to dissolve the boundaries of perception. In order to experience spiritual— or psychological— growth, a person needs to let go of her current perception of the way things are, and grow into a new, larger, more encompassing perception, which means the old perception must disintegrate. For those who encourage and cooperate with this process on a conscious level, the new insight and illumination arrives to fill the void. For those who fight it or refuse to acknowledge that it is happening, who cling to outmoded ideas and desires, the void seems to swallow them up, to a greater or lesser degree. Sometimes it is only a momentary dip into the pool of unconsciousness, which results in absentmindedness. Other times it is a longer swim, at least in some area of life, which results in a blind spot, an inability to see issues clearly, a recurring confusion and lack of direction. Occasionally it is more pervasive, where the waters of the unconscious seem to overwhelm the individual until she loses touch with what the rest of us see as reality.

Deceptive— this can be seen to be partly a result of confusion. That is, the Neptunian himself may be confused about issues and may give out conflicting messages. Moreover, Neptunians tend to want to do the right thing and usually hate to disappoint others (since they are often disappointed themselves). And they are commonly seduced into trying to be all things to all people, into making promises to keep another person happy or to fulfill another person's belief in them, rather than facing realistically what they can actually do. Other times, the Neptunian has opted for illusion, self-deception, dreams and promises rather than accept that what is yearned for must be earned and grown into. This Neptunian has an amazing ability to lie to himself and will try to seduce others into supporting the lies— at least to the Neptunian's face. Sometimes this key word also refers to the Neptunian ability to seem calm on the surface when all inside is roiling about at a furious and painful pace.

Dreamers— this key word alludes to both the Neptunian tendency to daydream and the tendency of the Neptunian to settle for daydreams and poignant wishes rather than doing anything constructive to give those dreams form. The Neptunian may be able to entertain others with stories and music and acting and thereby make use of her daydreams. Many, however, spend their lives talking about their big dreams, how they are going to do this and that, and will do it just as soon as circumstances are right. But after a few years it becomes obvious that their plans are always changing, their commitment to any plan lasts just as long as the illusion of "someday" can be maintained and then they are on to the next dream. They choose the dream over action.

Neptune's Domain

You will already, hopefully, have gotten the picture that Neptune is associated with the non-earthly, the spiritual, the imaginative, and the illusory. Yet like all the planets, Neptune manifests at different levels: physical, psychological and spiritual.

PHYSICAL MANIFESTATIONS
On the physical world plane, the Neptune essence is manifested through creative arts. Visual and musical works can be evocative, stirring, disturbing and generally take the viewer/listener out of present reality into some imagined realm. Music is a way of reaching the soul; played sweetly and purely it is not only uplifting but restorative. There are systems of healing, both physical and psycho/spiritual, which focus heavily on the healing power of music in general and certain notes in particular.

Typical of its nature, Neptune rules more experiences and activities or actions than actual **things** on the physical plane. Most of the things have to do with liquids and gases. This means Neptune is associated with all that is watery: rivers, lakes, streams, the great seas, and the lowly mud puddle. How symbolic!

Gases include clouds, fog, anesthetics, and the air we breathe.

Gases and liquids demonstrate beautifully the qualities represented by Neptune— difficult to contain, they take on the shape of whatever holds them, if anything can. If there are cracks or holes, the gases and liquids seep through and escape. Frequently, gases and liquids simply dissolve the boundaries of that which surrounds them.

Neptune is also associated with places of confinement, strangely enough. Prisons and hospitals don't seem to share a common meaning until we think of seclusion, of withdrawing from the world, enforced or otherwise. Retreats and ashrams fall into this category, too, as places where one can contemplate inner realities and truths without the need to cope with the hustle and requirements of the world at large.

PSYCHOLOGICAL MANIFESTATIONS

On a psychological level, Neptune is associated with thinking processes of either exceptional clarity and insight or exceptional muddle, confusion and "magicthink." Here the boundaries which are dissolved are those of the rational mind, which effectively help us to cope with the real world, but also limit our perceptions to that which is generally acceptable to society at the moment. Neptune leaks into our minds the realization that there is much more going on in the universe than that which we witness with our physical senses.

Expanded Awareness

In its positive manifestations, Neptune represents an urge and need for development and maturation and understanding which does not settle for ordinary answers. As the awareness of greater truths becomes more compelling, perceptions expand. It becomes possible to "see" energy and perhaps colors surrounding other people. Ordinary objects may become transparent—and where there appears to be only empty space, the developing Neptunian may see an object. Visions may occur, or sensations which are experienced but known to be from outside oneself. Meditations can be very symbolic or very dissolving. Some Neptunians lose all conscious awareness during meditation; others are quite aware but experience an unconscious filtering out of extraneous noise or light or occurrences, afterward being surprised to find out how intrusive those disturbances were to others.

Throughout it all, the Neptune awareness expands and insights are gained, insights which bring deep inner peace and acceptance, not just simple intellectual understanding and satisfaction. There is often a strong sense of understanding that we humans deliberately limit our own possibilities through fear and ignorance, on a scale which can hardly be imagined. The Neptunian suddenly realizes, though he may have to repeatedly recapture the realization, that all things are indeed possible.

Wishful Thinking

In the negative manifestations of Neptune, the boundaries of logic may never have been accepted. In their place is a strange "system" of "magicthink" roughly defined by the rule, "Whatever I want, is." That is, the individual sees only what is personally desired and personally acceptable. It is a twisted interpretation of the "all things are possible" realization. This leads to selective amnesia, selective listening, the ability to ignore signals which are meaningful to others, evasion or denial of facts which do not fit one's particular pretense, and self-delusion in order to preserve the chosen pretense. This all sounds like madness, which is also a manifestation of Neptune. Madness is, perhaps, an extreme version of "magicthink."

Some psychiatrists, such as R. D. Laing, suggest that there is a special type of madness which is akin to and may be identical to, the chaotic inner journey undertaken by a shaman or medicine man who is in "training." Perhaps there are many natural shamans in our hospitals, with no one to guide them safely through their torturous inner journey of self-discovery. Those who would have sway over the most potent magic seem to have to encounter that magic power within and learn to master it. Those with a guide, a mentor who has herself taken this often perilous journey, have a considerably higher rate of return to "sanity" than those who languish— drugged, shocked and isolated— in our institutions.

SPIRITUAL MANIFESTATIONS

On the spiritual level, Neptune is at its most expansive, for better or worse. Positively expressed, there can be a constructive dissolution of the boundaries of the ego, where the sense of personal importance is not lost, but is transcended by an awareness of the true meaning of at-one-ment. In other words, there is a gentle and loving coming to terms with the connection each one of us shares with every other of us. This sense of connection brings with it a vastly different outlook on life and on other people. Inner values change, often quite drastically. Generally, pursuits valued by those firmly rooted in the world, such as ambition, "getting ahead," "establishing yourself," "having a good time," all suddenly seem empty and meaningless when viewed from Neptune's dimension. None of these will bring deep or lasting satisfaction, or inner peace, and this is so abundantly clear that the Neptunian who reaches this stage consciously has little or no trouble abandoning these pursuits.

While others strive for worldly goals and achievements, the Neptunian envisions and yearns for increased inner connectedness to Spirit, God, Heaven, and all that is now seen to be the Source of human life, of all life. Curiously, while worldly ambitions have to be worked toward with physical effort, Neptunian visions need a different kind of effort all together. As always, Neptune is connected to dissolution, to faith, to letting the energies of the universe flow as they will, without attempting to direct them with ego demands or ambitions. This can sound like simple floating and even apathy, both of which are often mistakenly accepted as the path toward Neptune's enchanting, seductive Nirvana. Yet these are deceptions, and if the great gurus of the world are to be believed, they are not even deceptions of Neptune but of an immature ego eager to avoid responsibility and perhaps also eager to avoid its own dissolution. Such dissolution seems like a terrible threat to the ego, which is incapable of understanding that it is not annihilated by Neptune's process but actually enlarged. The ego is unwilling to give up its job and its control and will throw up all manner of roadblocks to Neptune's process. Some of these roadblocks are obvious, such as deliberate repression of Neptunian experiences. Others are extremely deceptive, such as **seeming** to accept the way of Neptune, **looking** very spiritual on the outside yet behind all the right-looking actions is an ego still very much in control and unwilling to let go. This, then, is the negative manifestation of Neptune at a spiritual level— which really isn't Neptune after all, but a negative reaction to Neptune, and really isn't spiritual after all but the illusion of spirituality.

How difficult it can be to tell the difference between Neptune's positive and negative expressions!

The Unconscious

Each of us has a personal unconscious— that dimension of ourselves which retains memories of personal experiences which are not held in the person's conscious mind, which can, after all, handle only so much data. Some regions of the personal unconscious are more accessible than others; we have all had the experience of having someone "jog" our memory, to relate a sequence of events until we remembered an occasion which we could not reconstruct on our own. We all have little things to which we react with memories— the smell of turkey cooking at Christmas may bring to mind a particularly special Christmas celebration, for example.

Some dimensions of the personal unconscious can be reached through meditation or through various forms of therapy. Others may only be accessible to hypnosis, or to indirect interpretation based upon use of language, dream symbols, body language, or a pattern of behavior which shows up repeatedly, all of which reveal important information about what is going on in the unconscious.

Different schools of psychological thought have different attitudes toward the unconscious. Freud saw it as the "subconscious," as the source of bestial drives and desires and the repository of repressed memories. Freud's subconscious was no friend!

JUNG'S UNCONSCIOUS

Carl Jung had a far more positive view, seeing the personal unconscious as active, dynamic, creative and perhaps the best guide and friend an individual had. Jung was aware of repressed memories and strange, perhaps unacceptable drives, but he perceived also that the unconscious was a source of constant prompting, constant hinting that the conscious mind needed to pay attention to certain issues. He saw that the individuals who did pay attention to whatever the unconscious was revealing, who took the unconscious seriously and worked to resolve the issues raised by the unconscious became happier, healthier and more at peace with themselves. Those who ignored or repressed those promptings from the unconscious got increasingly tense and unhappy as they had to work harder and harder to pretend the promptings were not happening.

Collective Unconscious

Jung also postulated the existence of a collective unconscious, a dimension of the unconscious which is shared by all, with memories common to all humans. He came to this conclusion after much travel to foreign lands and cultures, where he observed rituals and customs and where he interviewed many people about their inner experiences such as dreams, visions and so on. He began to see that there were some concepts and some symbols which seemed common to people everywhere, regardless of their culture, education or early-childhood experiences.

These common concepts showed up in rituals, in cultural attitudes or in individual dream experiences, but they were widespread, far too much so to be accounted for by the idea of "contact." In other words, Jung felt that these ideas were integral to human nature, that they had not been spread with the burgeoning of "civilization" but already existed in the unconscious minds of people everywhere. He produced his theory of a collective unconscious to explain this phenomenon— the existence of a dimension of the unconscious which is common to everyone, which contains collective memories— memories of all that has happened and all that is known. His collective unconscious theory also allowed Jung to account for the existence of psychic phenomena. If the collective unconscious did indeed exist, as his experience certainly indicated it did, then it followed that some individuals could possess the ability to "tap" into it, thereby having access to the information contained therein.

Spiritual Dimensions

Carl Jung envisioned the unconscious, personal and collective, as vital, full of energy, ideas and desires of its own, which were the source of the energy, ideas and desires of the conscious mind. Because he himself experienced psychic phenomena, he was open to and interested in ESP, and went to a great deal of trouble to open up the occult to psychological understanding. He saw in alchemy, astrology and the I Ching, systems designed to gain access to the knowledge of the unconscious. He did not, however, admit to a specifically spiritual force in human life. He found the unconscious an adequate source of power and inspiration.

Author's Viewpoint

Personally, I find Jung's work wonderfully illuminating and exciting. He and his followers open up so many dimensions to human experience and make sense out of so much that seems unconnected. But I miss the spiritual dimension. After I read a Jungian book, I feel something important was omitted and that something is always the sense of connectedness to spirit, to an inner Self who is me but is also much more than me. It is this Self within who seeks to be heard above the clamor of the conscious mind and around the insistent symbolism of the unconscious mind. I wish to make it clear that I accept that there is a Divine element in this universe, and that we are all part of this Divine element. I can say little more about it except that I believe we all have a thread of Divine nature within us, and astrologically I believe that thread is symbolized by Neptune.

Consequently, at the foundation of my understanding of Neptune is a conviction that we are creatures of Spirit, and that Neptune symbolizes our relationship to our own spiritual nature. Behind all talk about the unconscious is, to me, the understanding that our essential, spiritual Selves stand at the center, more powerful than the unconscious, yet less intrusive. To find our way back to our own center, however, seems to require that we accept our unconsciousness, try to bring as much as possible into our conscious awareness and accept responsibility for it, and learn to direct it constructively. In other words, we learn to re-own and use those parts of ourselves which we have denied. The journey to Neptune is a journey within.

Neptune, Pisces, the Twelfth House

Many of the comments which apply to qualities associated with Neptune also apply to Pisces and the twelfth house. An experienced astrologer can often pick up Neptunian attributes in a person whose chart is unknown, but it is not nearly so easy to say accurately how those attributes will be symbolized in the chart. It may be by the placement of Neptune conjunct an angle, usually the strongest statement of Neptunian motifs. It may be by Neptune involvement in a close major aspect to a personal planet: the Sun, Moon, Mars, Mercury or Venus. It may be by a stellium in the twelfth house or in Pisces.

SIMILARITIES
The similarities tend to outweigh the differences. All will have a tendency to value otherworldly goals more than mundane ambitions. All will have experiences with intuition which border on the precognitive. All will understand the expression, "Divine Discontent," for they will have experienced it. All will at some time have struggles with feelings of overwhelming vulnerability, confusion, escapism and feeling unable to make the very vital connection between their reality and their dreams. All will have some kind of artistic sensitivity; most will have definite talent, whether latent or developed. All will possess a gentle, emotional and easily wounded side, regardless of what else in the chart makes them appear otherwise. All will need quiet times to themselves in order to recenter and rejuvenate. They get scattered too easily, dragged outside themselves, are too easily influenced by the moods and emotions of those around, and need peace and quiet to regather their own forces.

DIFFERENCES
The differences are harder to define. Neptune strongly conjunct an angle tends to represent the purest expression of this planet, a placement which indicates that Neptunian issues will tend to affect most areas of life. A personal planet with strong aspects to Neptune also shows major Neptunian traits, but the areas of life affected are more narrow, more connected to the issues of that planet. For example, Neptune closely square Venus in a chart can indicate a person who, while otherwise practical and sensible, has a difficult time being realistic about love and romance.

Stelliums are even harder to differentiate. I have seen clients with Pisces stellia and clients with twelfth house stellia. Generally the ones who are most obviously Neptunian are those with twelfth house stellia. Those with Pisces stellia also have many Neptunian traits and experiences, but it tends to be a somewhat private part of their lives. It is rare to find a sign position expressed as strongly as a house position— both operate and both must be considered in interpretation, but generally the house position is stronger.

TWELFTH HOUSE VERSUS PISCES STELLIA

I think back to two clients, one of whom had an Aries stellium in the twelfth house and one of whom had a Pisces stellium in the first house. The one with Aries in the twelfth was the obvious Neptunian— quiet, unassuming, peaceful, loving and accepting, even after her conversion as a born-again Christian. The one with a Pisces stellium in the first house was very independent, assertive and determined to live her own life, although bothered by her inability to deal with large groups of people due to psychic openness. Both displayed Neptunian traits such as sensitivity, strong compassion and interest in spiritual subjects, yet the one who was easily recognizable as Neptunian was the one with the twelfth house stellium.

All of this means that much of what is discussed in this book is applicable to those with strong stellia in the twelfth house or in Pisces, those with Neptune conjunct an angle in their chart and those with Neptune in close aspect to a personal planet. It may also apply to people who have Neptune involved in a large number of aspects with other planets.

Then again, it might not! We are, after all, discussing Neptune. And one thing is certain about Neptune— you just can't tell!

CHAPTER TWO

COMMON THEMES WITH NEPTUNE

Neptune frequently gets a bad press. In the older texts, particularly, chapters on Neptune drip with condemnation over its association with demon alcohol, illicit drug use, and the general inability to live an upstanding sort of life. Where does this fit in with the planet which represents our most spiritual orientation?

Self-destructiveness

Nearly every author who has addressed the subject of Neptune has had to deal with the easily observable phenomenon of the Neptunian tendency toward self-destructive behavior. Many people cannot reconcile themselves to this; they find Neptunian behavior incomprehensible, sometimes immoral and more than a little frightening. Anyone who has had to deal with a negatively expressed Neptune on the practical level, living with a drug addict, an alcoholic or a victim who seems immune to suggestions for self-improvement, will readily agree that Neptunian problems can certainly seem bewildering at the least. At their worst, the problems are tragic, perhaps the more so because they are usually so unnecessary.

The Neptunian who is committed to self-annihilation cannot easily be redeemed from her chosen path, yet that chosen path looks miserably chaotic and painful to others. Then, too, there is the Neptunian fixation on suffering, a fixation which can reach mind-boggling proportions. Those who try to help, who try to understand **why** the Neptunian is so actively engaged in self-torment, inevitably end up frustrated and even angry, because it seems impossible to reason with these often gentle souls who can be so blind to the role they play in their own pain. While it is often possible for an outsider to see **what** the Neptunian is doing, and the destructive attitudes behind the behavior, it is not a simple matter to understand **why** the Neptunian believes what she does.

Seeking the Highest

While Neptune refers to that drive within us which aspires to the highest we can imagine, somehow it often gets expressed in strange, convoluted ways. The most basic mistake with Neptune seems to be that of looking for Heaven out in the surrounding world. "Heaven" in this instance refers to the highest ideal, the incredible, harmonious, loving perfection dreamed of and yearned for by every Neptunian. Many Neptunians are somehow convinced, on an unconscious level, that absolute perfection is waiting for them out there, somewhere, and all they have to do is find it and move in; all they will have to do is take up residence. These people do not fully understand— or cannot accept— that we make/create perfection within ourselves by transforming and perfecting ourselves. Then we will carry that perfection with us, always. Those who look for "Heaven" outside themselves, in a parent, a mate, children, a job or so on, are doomed to disappointment or to a life of glossing over the imperfections and pretending that all is well.

Honesty versus Illusion

Lack of inner honesty is another fundamental mistake in handling Neptune's complex issues. It is ironic that this planet which is associated with the expanded vision and clarity of the psychic is also associated with self-delusion. The former could be compared to a ray of light, straight and pure; the latter is then seen as a ray of light which has been bent and perhaps splintered. The resulting rainbow may be seductively beautiful, but it is no longer complete. Those who would stand in Neptune's light need to be rigorously honest about themselves— what they are capable of and what they are not capable of, what they are willing to do and what they are not willing to do, what their true talents are and where they have weak points, what their inner conflicts are and what impact those conflicts tend to have on their lives. Those who cannot be completely honest are living with illusions, and to the extent that illusions are harbored, to that extent a person is neither free nor capable of manifesting Neptunian energy constructively.

Those who live with illusions must expend a great deal of energy to maintain them. To walk with Neptune demands that illusions must be torn away. The difficulty lies in the fact that Neptunians usually want to please others and can fall into the trap of behaving as they have been told they should, rather than finding out what is authentic for themselves. This propensity makes it particularly easy for Neptunians to live illusions, and particularly difficult for them to work their way out of those illusions.

Self-acceptance

Lack of self-acceptance is the third common misapplication of Neptunian energy. Many Neptunians who insist upon suffering are those who are not willing to accept themselves as members of the human race. They are a race of superior beings, they are certain of it, only they are constantly confronted with the evidence that they they are, after all, merely human. The gap between what they believe and what the world keeps showing them is painful, sometimes excruciatingly so.

Many of these people choose the path of illusions in order to stop the flow of unpleasant input from the outside world. All information which does not actively support their generous view of themselves is denied or twisted around or dismissed as irrelevant. The Neptunian on this path will usually do almost anything to maintain the chosen illusion, and is capable of immense cruelty when the illusion is in danger of being exposed. The cruelty is usually on the emotional level, however, rather than the physical, and is often indirect. That is, the

Neptunian will interpret some perfectly innocent or actively loving behavior as somehow threatening or hurtful and will withdraw in abject misery. The individual on the receiving end of this treatment feels bewildered and guilty at first, and then hurt and angry at the thinly veiled rejection and twisting of what they offered.

Intertwined Attitudes

These three basic attitudes (quest for absolute perfection; lack of inner honesty and lack of self-acceptance) seem to be the ones most often associated with a destructive Neptune pattern. While they have been discussed here individually, in real life they are often intertwined in a complex manner. The Neptunian usually embraces all of them, at least in some areas of life.

While the basic destructive attitudes may be few, the actual way in which a negative manifestation of Neptune will be acted out varies a great deal. Some of the more commonly encountered ways can, however, be discussed here, along with their relationship to the various fundamental traps into which Neptunian drives are easily misdirected.

Sacrifice, Surrender and Suffering

Pisces and the twelfth house have frequently been summed up in the phrase, "Serve or suffer." It applies no less to Neptune. Those who walk with Neptune often bear the cross of an agonizing openness and vulnerability to everyone around them. Empathy unrestrained becomes unity. If you hurt, I hurt— the experience cannot be shut out or differentiated without many painful experiences. It is as if the Neptunian has to experience incredible pain repeatedly in order to learn how to survive it and to have the faith that he can survive it, and also to learn how to not be so open that he is dragged into other people's misery. The learning experiences are painful only because one after another, illusions are exposed and torn away, usually illusions about the function of pain.

ROMANTICIZING PAIN

Many Neptunians are convinced that suffering is somehow noble, or a demonstration of extraordinary love. They do not see or understand that it is very often a waste of time and of a precious resource. They waste a great deal of their empathy this way— feeling other people's pain and agony and fears, and allowing themselves to be dragged into it all, rather than using their empathy and compassion to understand others and then to uplift them, to inspire them. When something such as pain is romanticized, it is also valued, put on a pedestal. The Neptunian will continue to seek out these experiences until she gets sick and tired of hurting and starts to take an honest look at what she actually achieves with her pain. The longer she has been locked into a loving/giving/victim role, however, the harder it is to admit that it has all been a self-perpetuating illusion. She **may** also have to admit that it has been a self-serving game, a dishonest but frequently effective way to bind others to herself.

If victimization and martyrdom are carried far enough, they begin to slide into a drive for self-annihilation. Sometimes this is a progressive process— the person starts out giving too much to others who do not appreciate the gift. Instead of learning the lesson about casting pearls before swine, the Neptunian may simply conclude that he himself is lacking. Other times this need to negate the self completely is apparently there from early in life, perhaps the result of an abusive upbringing.

"KILLING" THE EGO

Self-annihilation is sometimes a mistaken interpretation of the need to transcend the ego and self— attempts to overcome and "kill" the ego rather than growing beyond it gradually. This misconception is helped along by the lack of semantic clarity of many gurus who loudly proclaim that it is necessary to kill the ego in order to make real spiritual progress. Careful reading of their meaning, however, reveals that they do not actually mean that the student has to achieve this in a massive act of self-hatred and incredible will power. Rather they refer to an inner battle which is, over the long haul, arduous and demanding, but consists not in killing outright the ego, but in gradually gaining its acceptance of second place, gradually transcending or outgrowing the ego's need for security and safety.

Those who try to "kill" the ego by an act of will are usually those who are least comfortable with their own ego, whose ego is in active conflict with their spiritual aspirations, and who wish to achieve the wishes of one part of their personality at the expense of some other part. This is psychological rape, for which the abused psyche will surely seek revenge. Generally these people convince themselves that they have destroyed their own ego, when in fact they are merely ignoring it.

Nearly every psychological theory around has repeatedly shown that only a sturdy and well-developed ego can hope to attain psychological (and therefore spiritual) maturity. Yet this concept of ego-annihilation seems a common misunderstanding and misinterpretation among another group of people, those with less than sturdy egos, who may harbor an unconscious self-hatred. It can seem— this idea of killing the little self which after all, is the locus of so much inner agony— the answer to their problems. They do not accept responsibility for their own suffering and therefore do not see that they must work through their problems, rather than simply pretend or wish them away.

HIDING

Many times Neptunians, especially those who have severe conflicts in their charts, wallow in a pit of self-condemnation which is so deeply rooted and so severe that they literally cannot face themselves. They feel they must, to survive, hide from themselves and their inner pain. These people have succumbed to Neptune's apparent weakness and lack of energy in handling worldly issues; they do not feel able to stop their inner suffering in any way except to ignore it. What they are hiding from is often significant— enough pain to cause them to label themselves harshly and hatefully.

Sometimes this pain is connected with a traumatic event, such as abuse or some other shocking event which happened in childhood and has left a festering wound buried under layers of fear and confusion. Children, lacking the experience and/or knowledge to gain a perspective on severe problems, frequently cope by either suppressing the memory of the event, or assuring themselves that it didn't matter, that they haven't been affected. They do this for their own emotional survival at the time, but they pay an increasingly heavy price as they grow up if they continue to employ these defense mechanisms. The issue which never got resolved, only glossed over, invariably affects their attitudes and beliefs and these in turn affect their behavior and self-image. Unresolved psychological issues are like undigested food: they sit around long after they can be useful and begin to rot and poison from within rather than nurture.

INNER CONFLICTS
Sometimes Neptunian self-condemnation occurs because an individual cannot integrate an inner conflict, and the resulting pull between two strong desires makes her feel as if she is being torn in two. The most emotionally damaging kinds of inner conflicts seem to be those where the person has a strong natural inclination to engage in some behavior which she has been effectively taught is somehow taboo. For example, people who have great difficulty doing things on their own may have somehow picked up the idea that independence is very bad; this can occur when a parent has prevailed upon the child that she cannot do anything on her own. For a susceptible child, independence can then become taboo— too dangerous to even contemplate. If it is so deadly a concept, even entertaining it can seem dangerous, so that by the time such a child reaches adulthood, all impulses toward independence have been successfully ignored and repressed.

If the whole chart indicates that this person leans toward conventionality and placidity, the suppression may result in little, if any, inner conflict. If, however, such suppression occurs in a person whose chart indicates a strong drive toward and need for personal independence, the result is a personality at war with itself. From within come urges and demands which seem terribly "bad," which makes him call himself bad. He can easily begin to condemn himself and become subtly or actively self-destructive in the belief that he must be punished.

"BE PERFECT"

Often self-hatred is connected to some impossible-to-maintain world view which has been fostered by parents. For example, parents may instill in their children the idea that they (the children) must be better than everyone else, must live up to higher standards. This can be very constructive, in the sense of encouraging the children to find their inner strengths and develop them. It is, however, often profoundly destructive as the children find themselves trying to live up to impossible standards. They cannot; they do not have the inner resources, the experience, the knowledge, etc. Yet they are caught in the trap of trying to please their parents.

If there is a strong and influential adult around who is respected by the children, who can point out kindly that the parents are being unrealistic, the children will have a realistic standard to measure themselves (and the parental expectations) by. If there is no such person, the parental power may seem absolute, and the children become accustomed to always trying to win approval when the deck is stacked against them. In this, they also become accustomed to failure.

DEFENSES

Some children react by deliberately courting failure. The pressure to live up to parental expectations is too painful; they would rather simply fail and do so in the hope that the parents will stop demanding so much.

Others react by rationalizing their inability to meet the high standards— something else prevented them from doing their best. The teacher was unfair; they didn't feel well at the crucial moment; whatever the excuse, it is important to place the blame somewhere other than on the self or the parents.

Still others chose to ignore their failures, lie to themselves and simply pretend that they have met the required standards. This involves a betrayal of what is known to be right and true, however, and once again self-esteem suffers. That this is seen to be preferable to an admission of failure and/or a recognition that the parents were unrealistic or unfair gives some indication of how important it can seem to win parental approval.

And of course, sometimes all three of the above, and more besides, will be involved in the self-hatred.

NO BOUNDARIES

Beyond self-hatred, which is a common theme underlying attempts to sacrifice the self and/or the ego, there is the simple association of Neptune with dissolution. Neptune's mode of operation is to dissolve solid boundaries or obstacles. The ego is, in a sense, an obstacle to spiritual growth, although it can be won over to support the cause. Neptune weakens the ego by simple disinterest. That is, under Neptune, ego issues seem ridiculous, trivial and not worth the investiture of any effort. Worldly ambitions and concerns do not motivate the Neptunian— she is apart from them. The ego itself seems unimportant, so it is doubly difficult for the Neptunian to spend the time and energy required to develop a sturdy ego, and many do not. These people often merely drift onto Neptune's deceptively undemanding path, without the inner resources to deal with its challenges. Those very necessary inner resources can only be developed as people work toward developing a healthy and sturdy ego!

REAL LIFE

When it comes to suffering, Neptunians seem to attract more than their share, but upon close examination a great deal of it is caused by their own refusal to accept the physical laws of the universe. Perhaps one of their crosses is a vague awareness that this is not how it is supposed to be in heaven, their natural environment. Their special task may be to live with this awareness and yet still cope with the world and live according to its laws. They have to accept that no matter how much they may want to walk on water, they cannot do this without a great deal of growth.

A fully blown, overdone Neptunian **wants** desperately for the world to be as perfect, flowing, harmonious and loving as his inner self knows is possible. So strong is this desire that he misses the rest of reality— that the world is **also** cruel, harsh, demanding and often miserably unfair. Learning to cope with the harsh side of life is only possible when you admit it exists, and the Neptunian has built-in defenses against such an admission. Thus he may drift into the world totally unprepared for the cruelty, defenseless against the pain and demands, living on dreams and "should be's" and virtually incapable of dealing with reality even when it hits him in the face.

Every planet has its gifts as well as its crosses. Certainly one of Neptune's major crosses is this tendency to subtly demand that the world conform to the inner vision of perfection, and to attempt to live life **as if** it did conform to this inner vision. A Neptunian may want to play the game of life by her own set of rules, and those rules simply and plainly do not work unless and until the Neptunian truly has acknowledged and worked through all her own problems and conflicts. Attempting to live this way, with her own set of rules, asking the world to pretend along with her, she inevitably sets off into life unprepared. If you refuse to acknowledge the existence of a wall, slamming into it headfirst is still painful. Neptunians suffer doubly because in their minds the wall has no business being there!

Neptunians hit many, many walls, mainly because they simply won't admit that the walls exist. They may suffer much pain until they learn to acknowledge not only pain but their own part in bringing suffering upon themselves. Then they learn some world-coping skills; they learn to say no when that is appropriate, learn to say yes when it isn't the easy thing to do but will bring the most long-term benefit. They learn to let other people live their own lives without taking on their problems. They learn to toughen up, to harden their hides against the small wounds life may deliver on a routine basis. They admit that life is not a version of heaven on earth. They learn that their vision is not a reality which is already present and all other issues can be safely ignored, but that it is a goal for which to reach.

The Neptunian learns, gradually, to accept life as it is and how to cope with that most effectively. This Neptunian will then attract no more suffering and pain than the average person. Self-acceptance is often the key. That is, the person who does not like himself will usually fight accepting the world much longer than the person who is generally comfortable with himself.

INSIDE = OUTSIDE

Our world in many ways is a reflection of our inner state. If we like ourselves, the world doesn't seem like a bad place, but a place of opportunity, things to be tried. Mistakes will be made but are not the end of the world, only mistakes. Life goes on and the person who likes herself will carry on. The person who has severe inner conflicts, such that she doesn't like herself finds the world a miserable place, a place of constant tests and failures, pressures and impossible demands, false promises and letdowns. The person who doesn't like the reality of herself will not accept it, nor the reality of the world. She must therefore create a visionary or pretend world, and try to live in that. Some do it to such an extent that they are declared insane and are institutionalized. Most simply live on the threshold of the real world, not involved enough to cope successfully, but involved enough to feel battered. That is, they haven't denied reality to the extent that it no longer has an impact on them, only enough to fail to perceive their strengths and ability to deal with issues.

SKILLS TO LIVE THE VISION

We may well ask why anyone would set themselves up for such agony. It is important to realize that no one sees at the outset that they are doing so. The equation looks something like this: "I am aware of energies that flow between people, of the unity of all, of the true, wondrous magnificence of the universe. I know that we (as spirits) are not meant to suffer, to work hard or to struggle so much. I **know**, I deeply know and accept that life simply flows, that love flows, if only we don't confuse it with worldly ambitions. We are surrounded by immeasurable, unconditional love and beauty. All pain and suffering is a mistake. Therefore I will not get involved in worldly ambitions, nor in worldly pain and suffering. I will live life as it is meant to be lived— flowing and harmonious."

There, suddenly it makes sense, doesn't it? The Neptunian sees the misery and hardship of life as mistakes, and refuses to participate in those mistakes.

Unfortunately there is something missing from this simple equation and that is that it does not and cannot work for "ordinary" humans. It is a vision of enlightenment and awareness and it cannot be used successfully by the unenlightened and the unaware. Though they can see the vision, they do not know how to live it successfully. This is because they do not know themselves on deep levels, they have not mastered themselves. Consequently they are not only refusing to participate in the world's mistakes, they are refusing to participate in the solutions to those mistakes. The Neptunian assumes noninvolvement is a solution, and fails to see that he has not acquired the skills to live the vision he sees.

Heaven on Earth Please

The Neptunian is blessed with a vision of heaven, of perfection, of the ideal. Every person and every process is, to the Neptunian, a reflection of the Divine, therefore already perfect within itself. Neptune naturally gravitates toward loving harmony in all people and processes, and this tendency creates within the Neptunian the ability to see the loving and harmonious way to live, the flowing and easy way to do something. Moreover, anything connected to Neptune is valued highly, perhaps to the point of being overtly worshiped, but more likely the process is unconscious— that is, the thing or process or goal is valued greatly but the person often is not fully aware how much importance is so invested, nor to what lengths she may be willing to go to protect that investment.

VALUES
The important role of values can be seen when it is realized that values color perceptions, the way we interpret the meaning and importance of events, and perceptions influence our feelings and emotions. All of these can influence our behavior.

As an example, look at people who place a high value upon harmony in human relationships. Such people will look upon arguments and disputes with horror— the degree of horror increases directly with the degree of value assigned to harmony. These people will react to quarrels as if they were extremely threatening, ghastly experiences to be avoided at all costs. Their behavior will tend to be placating, conciliatory and calming. If they find a weak spot in another person, they will carefully avoid it, in order to avoid upsetting that person.

Now look at people who value lively challenge and debate. Such people will thrive on disputes, seeing them as an arena in which to flex mental muscles. Peace may be seen as downright boring. These people may well deliberately provoke quarrels just for the sheer exhilaration of providing themselves with a contest. Their behavior will tend to be assertive, contentious and provocative. If they find a weak spot in another person, they may deliberately poke at it to get a reaction.

It is obvious that these are two vastly different reactions to disputes, and that these reactions are based upon the value assigned to harmony. Because the former group greatly values harmony, quarrels are usually upsetting; to the latter, they are often fun and interesting. This explains why two people can clash, can "rub each other the wrong way" and can fail to understand each other. At the back of their vastly different approaches to life is often a different value system.

ALREADY PERFECT

Just as Neptune is connected with values, it is also connected with tendencies to idealize, to see the perfection in something. What or who the Neptunian will tend to idealize is often clearly indicated by the house position or by planets to which it makes a close aspect. With a trine or sextile, the idealization flows naturally and easily and rarely is the source of **inner** conflict, though they may annoy others by overidealization of something. With a square or other challenging aspect, the idealization could lead to a loss of balance and perspective, or to conflict with some other part of life.

Idealization is, in many ways, the ability to see the best as if it already existed. The ability to envision better possibilities is the essence of inspiration, whether artistic or moral. It is a necessary prerequisite to growth, for growth is toward something, a goal, a dream, toward completion. Those who are idealistic provide a vision of something just a little better, they say, "how nice it would be if only..." and they stretch their own minds to include just a little more, something a little nicer, more peaceful, more lovely, more flowing. In so doing, they inspire others who may not have conceived of such a vision on their own.

This capacity to dream and envision helps us to cope with the often painful and often dreary parts of life. The dreams may lack substance to begin with, yet they are just as real as any other experience which has an impact on our lives.

So Neptune is connected to visions of the ideal, something better. Some Neptunians are aware that these are "visions," or as yet, potentials rather than actualities. They are quite clear that the ideal is a goal to be worked toward, but it may not always be possible to achieve.

Other Neptunians focus only on the goal, on perfection. They do not seem to be able to accept anything less. To these people, "good enough" is a betrayal of their deepest values, and is not to be tolerated. Those who employ this attitude at work will drive themselves or their employees to the point of exhaustion, or feel defeated before they begin, knowing they can never really reach their own standards. Those who carry this attitude into relationships are bringing with them a monstrously heavy ball and chain— whether they expect themselves or their partner to be perfect, they are asking for "Heaven" to be made manifest on Earth.

POISONOUS PERFECTIONISM

Perfectionism is a true curse to the carrier of the trait and to those nearby. The perfectionist has allowed the goal itself to become more valuable than any other consideration; time, money, energy, love, other people, joy and so on all fade in significance before the god of faultlessness. Those who cannot let go of the dream of perfection may find the dream is all they are left with as they sacrifice their inner resources to it, and lose the respect and love of those around them.

BALANCE NEEDED

Idealism and the ability to envision an ideal, a perfect dream, is truly inspirational, but those who cannot keep their perspective on this vision, who are prepared to sacrifice all for the sake of this vision, usually have their wish granted. It is a pity that most of them do not realize the cost of their dream, for they are never truly happy within themselves. They live with endless dissatisfaction rather than challenge or rein in their own ideals.

It is easy to see how this Neptunian is looking outside for "the answer," for the means to satisfy that inner yearning for a far better quality to life. As with many of the seductive Neptunian paths, it is one which leads only to inner pain. One of the important life skills to learn is when to accept that one has done enough, and to let go of the dream of perfection in the outside world.

Chaos and Creativity

Neptune is associated with inspiration, and therefore it holds a special key to creativity. The Neptunian is often unusually open to promptings from "other realms," whether these are from the deepest unconscious or from some outer source. In fact many Neptunians experience these promptings as coming from outside themselves, as if they are providing, like the psychic, a channel for energy to manifest. The Neptunian who listens to the small voices within often comes up with the most insightful writings, the most heavenly music, the most stimulating artistic creations.

There can be another side to these inner promptings, however. Many Neptunians get caught up in them, not in the sense of madness but in the sense of being absorbed in flowing impressions. These can be so soft and gentle and seductive that the Neptunian is unwilling to give them up even to a small degree. To such people, the discipline needed to accomplish goals seems too intrusive, too harsh and demanding and too cold a rule to impose on their lovely inner world. Other Neptunians are simply too weak-willed to take on the tasks of the world. These may well be the most purely creative Neptunians, yet they are the ones the world looks at in despair for they do so little with their talents.

"GO WITH THE FLOW"

These Neptunians may simply be unable to employ organization and discipline, or they may be unwilling to do what is necessary in order to have a sense of order and control. If the flow of creativity is valued more than achievement and deadlines, the Neptunian will complain that deadlines and demands crimp his style. If the delights of imaginings and daydreams are valued more than order, then the Neptunian will daydream and cheerfully leave his affairs in a muddle. Some Neptunians use this as an escape.

Neptunian energy is diffused rather than concentrated— many Neptunians experience a distinct lack of energy and may also experience difficulty sorting out their values and inner priorities. This, added to their natural preference for experiences which flow and are harmonious and loving, may make them all but allergic to work. Do not laugh— the comment is quite literal. Neptunians have a positively awesome ability to come up with reasons why physical or dreary jobs cannot be accomplished— and becoming allergic to some chemical routinely encountered in their job is one way out of the situation.

Some Neptunians, therefore, use their propensity for vagueness and confusion as a good excuse to get out of whatever they do not want to be involved in. This extends as well to their own inner processes, if these are painful and difficult. It may seem easier to fall asleep or forget or get distracted or simply be befuddled than it is to do the dreary and emotionally exhausting work of inner psychological refinement. Many Neptunians seem to be out of control of these reactions, that is, they are not making a conscious choice to adopt these behaviors. The choice is theirs, however, even if it is on an unconscious level. While this realization may bring some feelings of guilt, it also brings power, the power to change, if the Neptunian will only accept the responsibility.

CULTIVATE NEW SKILLS
Before we get too judgmental, however, it might be well to realize that discipline, order, logic and responsibility are just plain **foreign** to the flowing nature of Neptune. It is no more fair to expect Neptunians to naturally express traits which go against their nature than it is to expect Saturnians to possess a natural talent for music. Each can certainly cultivate new talents and abilities, and indeed this is appropriate for meeting the varied demands of daily life. There is a place for Saturn's sense of order and discipline in handling bank accounts, and a place for Neptune's ability to float and drift and be open to inspiration in creative pursuits.

The important point here is that if left to follow the path of least resistance, one planetary energy can be applied to all life situations. This is neither helpful nor effective. Neptunians need to take a look at their characteristic approach and determine honestly if it is serving their interests well, or if they could possibly develop another planetary approach which would better serve their interests in some situations.

Of Clouds and Clay Feet

Neptune's proclivity for being able to see beyond day-to-day reality often leads people into an attitude whereby they assume they do not have to deal with that reality. Their focus on the world of spirit may seduce them into believing that it is the only world which matters, the only one to which they need attend. They may resist the calls to pay attention to the world in which the rest of us live and work and play. Such people are often referred to as having "their heads in the clouds."

It is an interesting phrase; Neptunians always seem to be reaching for Heaven in one way or another. Yet as uninvolved in the world as they can become, few Neptunians succeed in eradicating their enormous emotional sensitivity. This sensitivity is part of their openness to outside input. It is, therefore, part of their ability to empathize with others and part of their ability to receive inspiration. Neptunians find it extremely difficult to contemplate fettering this sensitivity because they fear they will also lose their receptivity, which they cherish dearly. With Neptune's tendencies toward sacrificial behavior, many who have this planet emphasized in their charts will choose to suffer from their sensitivity rather than give up the openness. How can such people repeatedly get themselves into painful situations?

NO DEFENSES
Neptunians are, in general, a gentle and peaceful lot, accepting and tolerant. They shy away from disputes, challenges and competition. They have little appetite for games, of the social or sporting variety. Most Neptunians feel very loving and they prefer to think the best of others. In the world in which they exist, there is no need for defense because peace and harmony

are the order of their day. Consequently Neptunians have few inborn defenses, other than avoidance, against the slights, offenses, teasing and outright attacks which are a part of human experience. Neptunians prefer not to deal with that part, and are ill-equipped to handle it. They usually react by feeling hurt and withdrawing. Such behavior brings out the protective instinct from some people, and the urge to kill from others. Either way, the Neptunian usually ends up looking like the victim, a role they assume with ease and sometimes with a thinly veiled satisfaction.

VICTIMS AND VICTIMIZATION
It is a psychological truism that there are no victims who are not also victimizers. This can sound shocking— think of all the poor people you know who have been unfairly treated by life in general and other people in particular. How unfair it seems to say that these obvious victims are, in their own way, cruel and/ or abusive. We are accustomed to thinking in black and white terms; the spouse-abuser is a beast, and the abused person is a victim. In reality, relationships are seldom, if ever, that simple. Many abused people are masters at subtle psychological abuse, at making their spouses feel inadequate, powerless or unworthy. Others do this openly. Still others make demands on their partners which are emotionally burdensome and terrifying, yet the partners cannot refuse because the "victim" seems so helpless, so needy. Such "victims," so mired in their own needs, are usually excellent at selective listening, at ignoring whatever their partners need or ask for. The partners eventually crumple under the pressure and may well strike out at the quiet monsters with whom they live.

FEELING WEAK
Last but not least, Neptunians are so good at seeming helpless and fragile that they usually believe this to be true themselves. They therefore interpret any situations which they find upsetting as too difficult to handle and they may opt out altogether. In so doing, they leave someone else in the lurch, a fact they blissfully ignore. If confronted with the situation, they patiently explain how it is unfair to expect them to handle it in the first

place and nasty to hit them over the head with the results of their behavior in the second place because they can't cope with that, either. It is all unpleasant and they cannot be expected to deal with unpleasant issues, don't you see?

Sometimes Neptunians simply evaporate from the scene altogether to avoid issues. Other times, they utilize a selective sensitivity; they see only the side of an issue with which they are at home:

As an example, many people are intrigued by the idea that our thoughts have creative power. That is exciting, and many people anticipate better conditions for themselves through creative visualization and affirmations, etc. Yet many of these same people never stop to think— and accept— that destructive thoughts such as anger and hurt are equally "creative," that is, that if thoughts can affect our world, then destructive thoughts are having a destructive effect. There are many people who are quite self-disciplined about positive spiritual practices, yet who completely forget themselves and their supposed creative power when they feel insulted, or angered by something. These people can pour enormous negativity out into the world without any thought whatsoever for its effect, and they are certainly strongly resistant to the idea that they may be having such a negative impact.

One last issue here is that of dreaming the impossible dream and refusing to deal with one's practical responsibilities. It not only makes trouble in one's personal life, but in the life of loved ones and friends as well. The Neptunian dislike for responsibility makes denial and glossing over a favorite response here. "It isn't really important," they say, and subtly beg others to agree. They may charm their way out of many situations, never noticing that others have to deal with the consequences. Neptunians often do have a special clarity of vision about what issues are not really worth the expenditure of vital human energy, but they can abuse this talent and think that no worldly matter is important. In so doing, they may cheerfully ignore deadlines, promises, standards and often, the very real needs of other people.

It appears that even the gentle Neptunian can inflict great hurt on others, yet this may be the most threatening truth of all for this mystically minded soul to face.

Summary

The Neptunian must, it seems, struggle with too much of a good thing. The very gifts she enjoys, of vision, inspiration and idealism, can be her downfall unless used with the greatest humility, honesty and genuine love. Perhaps the Neptunian suffers because she can see what others cannot, the perfection of which we are capable, and yet she must face the same struggle most of us face. She must learn to recognize herself fully before she will be welcomed in Paradise.

Meditation

Why doesn't it work, ultimately, to look for answers outside of oneself?

CHAPTER THREE

STORYTIME: NEPTUNE AND MYTH

It seems there are many ways to get into difficulty with the expression of Neptune. There are also many ways to get out of those difficulties. One of the primary struggles we of a Western culture have with this energy, which is enticing yet elusive, real enough to have an important impact yet difficult to describe and harder to make sense of, is that we want to impose all our standards of "proof," "realistic," and "scientific" on experiences which are essentially inner, psychological and spiritual. We ask specific questions and we cast around for specific answers. If ever there was a planet made to frustrate specifics, that planet is Neptune. It rules the sign Pisces, the polar opposite of the sign of specifics, Virgo. The harder we try to define precisely the qualities of Neptune, the further we drift into the teasing language of indistinct inner experience.

How then are we to deal with Neptune? Must we accept that it is the planet of the unknowable, and leave it at that? Many astrologers do stop there, and are hard put to understand this planet and the energies it represents. Some dismiss Neptune as not important in an individual chart unless it is in an angular house, and then they assume it is likely to turn the individual into a drunk, a drug addict or, for a fortunate few, a peculiar but essentially sane psychic of one sort or another.

Many are not content with this view. Those whose experience of Neptune is deep and personal have struggled with their experiences and have tried to clarify them, not an easy task for people whose usual mode of expression is a confused sort of shrug as they realize they are almost powerless to fully translate the richness and meaning of Neptune to someone who hasn't experienced it. Yet these experiences are not only very real and deeply felt, they are extremely important because they reveal the depth and breadth of the spiritual side of human nature. They open the door to new possibilities, to a much wider scope of potential than was previously accepted. They reveal, to those who pay attention, that human nature is far more than ego and mind, has needs far greater than technology and accomplishment, and has talents far more diverse than those allowed for in most fields of science, business or education.

Dissolving Worldly for Spiritual

But the meanings of Neptune reveal themselves in ways that are foreign to the experience of the logical mind. That part of human nature symbolized by Neptune speaks the language of the unconscious, making use of symbols and representations, feelings and urges, or lack of interest in areas where a person is "supposed" to feel dynamic drive. Neptune has a tendency to represent dissolution of worldly values. This can be quite frightening for those who formerly subscribed fully to concepts such as ambition, "getting ahead," acquiring wealth or at least security and comfort. Neptune symbolizes a state of awareness in which worldly values recede markedly in importance as the temporary nature of such achievements becomes obvious. In this state of awareness, only inner achievements are seen as important because they are the only ones that last. It might be wise to mention here that those in touch with Neptune tend to take for granted some kind of eternal life, whether that is defined as reincarnation or some other kind of lasting spiritual existence. Neptunians are often willing to take on faith that which others want proven absolutely. They "feel" the rightness of developing inner sensitivity and awareness.

Neptune's Language

So, given that Neptune represents a need for individual spiritual development, and given that the path is not at all clear and the directional signs are all in symbols, how does one learn to speak the language of Neptune?

The language of Neptune is all around us. As usual, it is neither obvious nor even what it seems.

Many people would place whimsical art, fairy tales, poetry, religious epics and myths into the same category as stories: they are all fiction. Perhaps they are noble, or entertaining, or contain threads of historical truth, but they are essentially unreal and often unrealistic. Many contain elements of magic or miracles, and it is easy to suspect that the creators of such works simply let their imagination run wild until what was wished for could be represented as if it actually happened.

Such a view of a wide range of creative works— that is, as fiction with little value beyond the entertainment— is not only limited but limiting. Truth dresses herself up in many costumes and is not always easy to recognize. Furthermore, only the logical conscious mind is able to deal with a constant diet of facts and information. The "soul" and the unconscious mind do not thrive long on such fare. Those people who try to eradicate all traces of whimsy from their lives end up as dry, joyless creatures who seem devoid of emotion and who also seem to understand little about their fellow humans.

Art Reflects the Future

A single creative individual may well be capable of losing himself in self-indulgent expression, but the river of human creativity does not spend itself uselessly in unproductive pursuits. The group of creative people, as a whole, have something important and compelling to say to the group of humanity as a whole. That something is not, however, particularly deliberate nor particularly specific. Rollo May, in his book *Courage to Create* made the point that artists as a whole seemed, in any era, to be painting the story of the future direction of the human psyche. That is, the artists seemed to be able to express on canvas, in symbols and colors, the future of their culture.

As a quick example, those artists who participated in the

movement toward abstract art were often accused of being unable to actually draw anything "realistic." They were, in fact, quite capable of producing traditional art, yet they felt compelled to express their messages in broken, jagged lines. Most people were not ready to see, nor capable of understanding, how Western culture, so dedicated to science and technology, was fragmenting human nature. The growing influence of and dependence upon logic and "proof" fed only the conscious mind and, to some extent, the ego. It did nothing to nurture the emotional, psychological and spiritual parts of people's natures, yet these were being downplayed and denigrated, made worthless. The artists had a vision of the results of this one-sided view— and they put their fractured visions on canvas for the world to look at.

At the time, the artists themselves knew they were exploring their own perceptions, but the social significance of their work was not fully appreciated. It is easier now to look back and see that they preceded by many decades the cry of psychologists and others concerned with the mental and spiritual health of individuals, a cry of warning that we, as a race, were cutting ourselves off from ourselves. The warning of fragmentation was clear, but who understood clearly the actual message? Only those who responded to the new art; perhaps their unconscious minds recognized and gave credence to what the artists portrayed. These were the minds which were open to the message of Neptune.

Movies Carry Messages

Creativity is not limited to art. There are those who create stories in many forms. Today, there are those who make movies. It is undeniable that many stories and movies are an expression of the basest sides of human nature, but many are also inspirational. Some manage to be wonderfully entertaining and yet carry a vital message, perhaps on the healing value of love, or on the necessity of having a goal in life. Those books and movies which are meaningful to a great number of people, we call "classics." The names or favorite expressions of their characters may become part of our current language. It is as if they express something which we all feel or identify with, and if they do this successfully, we honor them by repeating and keeping alive their main characteristics. They become symbolic of a whole complex of experiences.

Fictional Characters As Symbols

Take, for example, a man who is having difficulty keeping his perspective on Christmas. He wants to return to the delights of childhood experiences, but he is vastly disturbed by the commercialism so prevalent today. Furthermore, as a child, Christmas "happened" all around him, without any effort on his part. Usually mother was the one who made it all happen. Little girls see this and grow up and slip into the role of the person who makes Christmas happen. But a little boy may not know where he fits in once he grows up. He can easily become a man who is thoroughly uncomfortable with Christmas, caught between a desire to experience it all again, and the adult awareness that it takes effort, which seems to take away from the magic. He can become resentful at the same time he still harbors hopes, cynical and uncooperative while wishing it could be as wonderful as it used to be. The woman married to such a man can be bewildered and disappointed by his behavior, especially if he is unaware of his struggle and does not communicate with her. If, however, he turns to her and mutters, "Well, bah! Humbug!" just like Scrooge, he can express to her in one short phrase that he is having trouble with a selfish, miserly undeveloped part of himself. If she also has been exposed to Charles Dickens' *A Christmas Carol,* she will understand what he means, with no need for lengthy explanations. In such a way, characters become symbolic of parts of ourselves, and can function as a shorthand way of describing some of our very complicated inner experiences. **These are Neptunian messages.** A symbol carries much meaning.

Universal Archetypes

Myths and fairy tales and heroic epics, and some religious epics, also carry much symbolic meaning. They are not created by a single person but grow from a variety of sources, fed by a stream of creativity which gradually grows into a river. The more universal the story, the more people can identify with it, the more it will take a grip on their imaginations and hold their interest. And they will, in turn, hold on to it. They will tell the story with reverence, celebrate it with song and write plays around the same theme. It is not unusual for a myth to find itself expressed for a long period in verbal form only, then eventually a poet will set the story on paper, a playwright will feel it lends itself to the stage and he will interpret it for that medium. Perhaps a choreographer sees the play and thinks that she could express the idea meaningfully in dance, and these days someone is likely to try to make a movie or TV series around it!

The types of stories which strike a responsive chord in millions of people do so because they reflect back to us something important about ourselves, whether we are aware of what that something is or not. **These are the messages of Neptune.**

Dream Symbols

On a personal level, people who keep track of the symbolic content of their dreams usually come to accept that this is another way the unconscious passes on important messages to the conscious mind. Sometimes the messages are frankly precognitive, but more often they concern the individual's current, most pressing problems and issues. That is, the unconscious has something to say about what is going on in day-to-day life, whether the issue is outer, as in career or relationship problems, or inner, as in wrestling with some new concept or understanding. Actually, inner and outer life usually mirror each other, but we do not see this unless we learn to deliberately listen to the unconscious, and Neptune.

It seems then, that the unconscious has a variety of ways to communicate its concepts and concerns. It will use these ways— collectively through art, myth, epic stories, and so on, and individually through dreams and the acting out of personal myths— whether we open ourselves to them or not. It is, however, possible to deliberately open the channels of communication with the unconscious through such practices as meditation, yoga, the study of dream analysis, journal writing, or various forms of psychological therapy. These and other methods all reveal the messages of the unconscious, and some of those messages will be the promptings of the drives represented by the planet Neptune.

Those who want to get in tune with Neptune, who want to cooperate with the yearning it symbolizes and to learn to express it constructively, will need to open the doors to the unconscious and listen to the messages from within. Gradually, with patience and gentle honesty and exploration of various ideas and practices, they will find their own connection to this elusive yet pervasive drive for the highest ideal.

The Myths of Planets and Asteroids

There are other ways to insight, however. **Astrologers have a special "fast track" into the world of Neptune through the use of planets and asteroids.** Most are named after Roman gods or goddesses, who in turn were named after similar Greek deities. The pantheon of Greek gods and goddesses and their stories makes fascinating reading in and of itself, but it quickly becomes obvious that these supposedly divine beings were remarkably human. In fact, many of them seem to have been terribly one-sided, unable to develop balancing qualities or to temper their own amazing foolishness, pride or cruelty. For decades now, various psychologists have postulated that the Greek gods and goddesses who resided on Mount Olympus were in fact representations of various parts of human nature.

This puts a whole new light on the subject. No longer do the old deities look foolish, but they suddenly appear as representations of humanity's struggle with all its various drives, a god or goddess for each drive. There is a goddess of love, Aphrodite (Venus to the Romans), whose focus is on being thought attractive. Although she creates immense trouble for everyone by causing them to fall in love, she herself can commit to no one and she remains to the end a vain and self-centered figure. Is this the plight of the person whose focus is on **getting** love rather than giving it? There is a god of wisdom, Zeus (Jupiter), chief among the gods, who was powerless to stop Aphrodite's meddling, even in his own life. Repeatedly he fell in love with and seduced both goddesses and mortal women, forfeiting the love and respect of his own loyal wife, Hera (Juno). And Hera makes an interesting figure. She was a powerful goddess in her own right until she married Zeus. She seemed to give up all her strength and became an embittered and vengeful shrew when Zeus' frequent infidelities came to light.

Inner Gods and Goddesses

How much like us these divine entities seem. They struggled with jealousy, fought for supreme power, were devious in getting their own way, vengeful when wronged and yet were also capable of kindness and often bestowed favors with an open hand. They were also forces with whom to be reckoned. The Greek myths are full of stories about what happens when a human makes the mistake of ignoring or dismissing the importance of a particular god or goddess, or worships one far more than the others. If we accept the idea that the gods and goddesses are in fact personifications of different aspects of ourselves, it becomes clear from the myths that some aspects can get into disputes with other aspects, and that whatever else happens, the most foolish way to behave is to try to ignore an aspect of ourselves. The Greek myths tell us that **we cannot resolve a conflict by choosing one side (one god or goddess) over another**— we have to honor all or the rejected god will seek revenge.

If we look deep inside, we can often identify with one or more of the lofty Olympians. Most of us want to be liked and thought attractive, as did Aphrodite. Many of us like to chatter and have lots of stimulation, as did Hermes (Mercury). Some of us like to probe the deeper secrets of the earth and human nature, which was the realm of Hades. Many wives, having given too much of themselves to a mate who doesn't appreciate it, can readily identify with Hera. Many politicians have followed in Zeus' footsteps, willing to be absolute ruler yet unwilling to give up amorous pursuits; they end up looking self-indulgent and foolhardy, yet seem not to fully appreciate how the public views them.

Prominent Bodies

As astrologers, we can readily identify which gods and goddesses have special meaning for us, or for our clients. Those planets which are in high focus in the chart, especially those closely conjunct one of the four major angles, the Sun, Moon or Mars, are indicative of our own special "myths." That is, it is likely that the myths connected with the god or goddess after whom the planet or asteroid is named, will have a very special and personal meaning. It may even seem as if we are reenacting the myth down to very small details. This can be rather startling, to discover that one's own personal story was well known to the Greeks more than two thousand years ago, and in fact is such a classic story that it grew to the status of myth. Yet it can also be very illuminating, as can most of Neptune's communications, to find that there is a meaning to what may have seemed like a chaotic pattern.

Many of the keys to personal doors can be found in the planets and in their connected stories. It often seems as if just knowing about the tendency to act out certain myths is enough to free ourselves from the grasp of that myth. We can see in the story the larger pattern or "theme," in which we are usually too immersed to see clearly. It is easier to see it "out there" with some degree of objectivity. It is easier to see the patterns and the mistaken attitudes and the mistaken goals, and easier to let go of them when they are taken not as strictly personal, but as common elements in particular myths. It is easier to accept that we may be making those mistakes when we accept that we tend to live out a pattern similar to that myth.

CERES MOTIFS

Thus, a mother who is having a great deal of difficulty coping with the fact that her children are growing up may discover she has the asteroid Ceres on her Ascendant or otherwise emphasized. Ceres was Demeter to the Greeks. Demeter was the goddess of the harvest, and the mother of Persephone. When Persephone was stolen by Hades, god of the underworld, Demeter went wild with grief and abandoned her work to search for her daughter. People with a prominent Ceres in their chart may well find they must struggle to find a balance in their relationships, that they tend to invest too much importance in and/or are overly protective of others, particularly their children. They may even follow the myth to the point of actually having a Persephone-type individual in their own lives: someone who is dependent on the nurturing relationship and cannot grow beyond it unless torn from it by a compelling attraction to someone else.

If Ceres is in houses dealing with other relationships, for example, the seventh, these qualities may come into play with the spouse. In the eleventh, Ceres can pour a tendency to nurture into friendships or group activities, perhaps to the detriment of family relationships. It is worth noting that Ceres does not "cling" in the traditional sense; it is not particularly obvious that the relationship is unhealthy because Ceres always appears to simply be a devoted, wonderfully caring individual. She will almost always do what is best for her "daughter"; what she will not do, however, is let go voluntarily, unless she becomes aware of the myth and the need to let her daughter grow in directions of her own.

PERSEPHONE ISSUES

Just as each of the gods/goddesses had their failings, they had lessons to learn. It is possible for those of us who are living out a pattern similar to that of a deity, or any other larger-than-life character, to study their story and glean from it the lesson they— and we— are supposed to learn. That is, we can learn how to rebalance. In the myth, Demeter had to let go of her daughter. She did not do this willingly; the girl had to be torn from her by a dark, terrifying abductor. This suggests that the girl could not accept responsibility for accomplishing separation on her own, yet while in the realm of Hades she willingly ate some seeds of a pomegranate, an act which ensured she could never completely return to her mother.

Demeter had to accept that she could no longer bind her daughter to herself alone. Zeus decreed that Persephone would be allowed to return to her mother for a few months of each year, but the rest of the time she would spend with her abductor/husband. Those who find themselves living out the Ceres story just might find they have too tight a hold on those they love, a hold which, while loving, prevents the loved ones from growing as individuals. It is important to note that Ceres' downfall was also her strength, taken too far: her deep love and devotion. Ceres people can perhaps learn to let go when that is appropriate, and find others who need their care and protection. Their talent is to be practical in the expression of their love— they rarely have to be told what needs to be done to make another feel comfortable.

HELIOS THEMES

The Greek Sun god was Helios. He must have been widely worshiped because a huge statue of him which was erected near the harbor of Rhodes—an island just south of present-day Turkey—was considered one of the seven wonders of the ancient world. However the major story connected to Helios actually concerns his son Phaethon. Phaethon traveled far from his home to reach Helios' radiant palace in order to ask if Helios was indeed his father, as his mother claimed. Helios acknowledged this, then offered as proof to grant any wish the young man desired. What Phaethon desired was to drive his father's sun chariot across the skies that day. Helios tried to dissuade him, warned him that the way was steep and the horses dangerous, but in the end he had to abide by his promise. Phaethon could not control the horses and almost destroyed the world when the chariot went out of control. Zeus had to throw one of his thunderbolts to blow up the chariot and its hapless driver in order to save the world.

The Sun, astrologically, is connected to Leo and the fifth house, which are both associated with children. Helios is portrayed as a god who responsibly discharged his arduous duties each day, duties which demanded great courage, skill and strength. Yet he made a mistake when he promised to grant Phaethon anything the young man desired, for he could not grant his son the ability to be like himself. The whole story is ripe with deep meanings, such as the issue of Sun people's generosity accidentally sowing the seeds for someone else's destruction, but an issue which can be raised quickly is that of the parent literally outshining the child.

Many people with an angular Sun in their chart seem to be such radiant and outgoing people, to possess such dynamism, power, and strength of personality, that they may make somewhat terrifying adults. In the story of Phaethon, Helios had to remove his crown of blinding rays before his son could approach without harm, a rather obvious hint that Sun people just might need to "cool it" or tone down their energy output somewhat around children and quieter people. Further, although Helios sought to reassure Phaethon, he did so by displaying his power and magnanimity. It was certainly effective but it wasn't in Phaethon's best interests for it cost the youth his life! Sun parents might need to think carefully about the decisions they make regarding their children, to check out that they have really made a choice which will benefit the child, not prove how wonderful the parent is. Sun people, however, do usually light up the world of those around them with their confidence, exuberance and sheer joy in life. They have the ability to bring joy to others through the use of their creative talents.

ARTEMIS/DIANA
Artemis was the Greek goddess of the Moon. Close and thoughtful study of the stories connected to this virgin goddess lead to the conclusion that astrologers may have given very short shrift to the Moon and its meanings. Artemis was certainly the goddess of childbirth and all the feminine cycles and rhythms, but she was also a goddess who felt complete within herself and her femininity. She was goddess of the hunt yet she protected wildlife, the young and women, particularly those threatened by men. Even so she mercilessly killed, without regrets, those who offended her. It is as if she represents the essence of femininity in all its mysterious potential to absorb and comfort, yet to turn cruel when betrayed.

Artemis had many facets, as shown by the numerous myths in which she was involved, but she consistently held to herself. This quality of self-containment might bear examination by people who have the Moon prominent in their charts. Though such people can be wonderfully comforting with others, they may hold themselves just a little enclosed emotionally, to the detriment of true intimacy. Moon people, however, have the ability to make others feel "at home," nurtured and cared for to a profound degree, **if** the Moon person so chooses.

HERMES/MERCURY
Hermes, or Mercury, was the messenger of the gods. Although he was swift, he also had a dishonest side for he was less than a day old when he stole Apollo's herd of cows. A person who lives the Mercury myth could be one who takes advantage of inside information, who seems reliable and harmless yet who is crafty and self-serving. Hermes was also an eternal youth, and those who express this motif may find themselves not only youthful in outlook, but perhaps unwilling to grow up, in ways which damage their ability to live a satisfying life. Mercury people could possibly benefit from learning about honesty, integrity

and acceptance of responsibility. Their talent is speed, dexterity and a light touch.

APHRODITE/VENUS

Aphrodite, Venus to the Romans, the goddess of love and beauty, was married to the ugliest god in the pantheon, Hephaestus. She would not be loyal to him and enjoyed a succession of lovers, as the whim took her. In many stories she was portrayed as wondrously beautiful and generally kind but vain, self-centered and faint of heart. Someone who lives the Venus pattern may be one who is charming and rather sweet yet basically self-indulgent or simply too enamored of surface beauty and appearances. Aphrodite was unable to create an enduring relationship with any of her lovers, nor did she learn to appreciate any of the better qualities of her husband. Venus people might learn from the myth and try to develop appreciation of qualities other than beauty and harmony. Their talent is their ability to bring out the soft, gentle side of people's natures, to get them to drop their usual concerns and relax and enjoy life.

ARES/MARS

Mars was the Roman god of war, much admired by them for his courage and as a model of masculinity. His Greek counterpart was Ares, also portrayed in literature as a fighter, but the Greeks thought Ares was a pest and a coward when wounded on the battlefield. Both gods were primitive warriors, bloodthirsty and brutal.

Someone who lives the Mars myth could be too eager to do battle with others, too prone to asserting his own needs regardless of the effect on other people. While personal assertiveness is necessary and admirable, when taken too far it becomes obnoxious, single-minded aggression. People who live out the Mars myth could become loners who prowl restlessly, forever seeking the excitement of the next skirmish. The Romans seemed to have understood that Mars needed something soft to balance him, however, and in their myth, gentle Venus attracted his attention and love. Mars people might need to learn how to consider others. Their talent is the ability to stand up for themselves and fight when necessary.

ZEUS/JUPITER

Jupiter was king of the gods, mightier than all the other gods combined. In the earlier Greek myths, as Zeus, he appears to wield his power for the sake of power, but more and more he grew to become a god of justice. Although he was powerful and became associated with law and morality, which he imposed on others, he suffered little restraint himself. What Zeus wanted, he took. What he wanted was usually a woman, one who would later suffer mightily at the hands of Zeus' enraged wife Hera. Zeus was not much help to the women he seduced; most of them, although innocent, met miserable ends. Zeus, as the greatest of the gods, seems to display the best and the worst uses of immense power. He could often be prevailed upon to mercifully moderate or prevent the wrath of another god, yet he appeared to have little conscience about his own destructive habits.

Someone who lives out the Zeus myth could be extremely concerned about morality, ethics and justice in other people, yet unconcerned about it in himself. He might be shockingly aloof and unaffected when those he has influenced come to harm. He might feel, as an arrogant god who is above others, unwilling to restrict himself in any way. He might also be compulsively unfaithful to his partner, no matter how much he loves her, because he cannot really give all of himself to her. He might even find himself living with a woman who, although repeatedly hurt and angered by his behavior, will continue to stay with him, as Hera did with Zeus. Hera eventually left Zeus, as the myths tell us. Jupiter people may do well to learn to live according to their own rules and morality, to live up to their own values rather than telling others how they should live. Their strength is their faith and confidence in the rightness of the world.

CRONUS/SATURN

Saturn was the father of Jupiter, and king of the gods before him. In the Greek myths, Cronus (Saturn) knew that one of his children was destined to overthrow him, so he swallowed his offspring as soon as they were born. Zeus, however, was hidden successfully and did take the throne from his father. Cronus was a Titan, a race of enormous beings who were supreme in the universe before the time of the gods. The Titans were never given the clear characterizations which was typical of the later gods. In this way, perhaps, the Greeks communicated their feeling that the Titans were not symbols of traits which could become strictly personal, at least not in the sense of "personality."

There is no elaborate story connected with Cronus, only the motif of absolute power being overtaken by a creation of its own making. A person who lives out the Cronus pattern may find himself pouring most of his energies into the pursuit of success, power and control. He may also find himself alienated from his own offspring due to his tendency to overcontrol them, that they feel "swallowed up" by him and that they must overcome him in order to be free. It might well be necessary for the Saturn person to make a conscious effort to make a place in his life for relationships, hobbies, time for play and all the other qualities and pastimes which bring joy and depth to life. Their strength is their ability to wield power to bring about order and continuity.

URANUS

Even less is revealed about Uranus, the father of Saturn. Uranus was "Heaven" or "Father Sky," an entity formed out of the chaos that existed before all else, but he was never a distinct creature to the Greeks. He is represented almost as a monster whose offspring were the Titans, including Cronus, the Cyclops— one-eyed monsters— and three fifty-headed beasts which he imprisoned. He was eventually wounded terribly and deposed by Cronus. Uranus was not associated with any particular traits, but with a sense of immense presence and some vague quality of churning aliveness. There is no story of an organized rule, rather a feeling of awesome, impersonal, unpredictable and nearly uncontrollable power. People who have Uranus prominent in their charts do not seem to live out a distinct myth or pattern, but do have to contend with great restlessness and impulsiveness, which can only be harnessed and constructively channeled (overcome) by self-discipline (Saturn).

POSEIDON/NEPTUNE

As a god, Neptune, or Poseidon, has only fragments of mythology rather than a whole story of his own. The ancient Greeks were much involved with the sea, for fishing and for trading, and their Poseidon was second in importance only to Zeus, yet there is little mention of him in legend. Nor has he been written about in any great amount in modern times. Perhaps this is fitting, for Neptune seems to stand for an aspect of human nature that we understand rather poorly at this time. Our culture as a whole has provided for Neptunian needs in terms of churches, and artistic pursuits rather than in terms of providing encouragement for individual development of spiritual aspirations. In spite of the fact that there is little material available on the god Neptune, astrologers have noticed many patterns associated with the planet; this whole book is an attempt to explain and clarify those patterns.

Poseidon was revered not only as god of the great seas but because he gave humankind the horse. This is a remarkably significant event because it changed the face of civilization completely. Before the horse, small city-states and kingdoms could maintain themselves relatively well. It was extremely difficult for any kingdom to become too large because communication by foot was slow and any organization depends on communication for its unity and effectiveness. No army could travel far, except by sea. With the horse, however, armies could travel further, faster and with less fatigue. They could successfully defeat armies which were all on foot.

The horse meant messengers could be dispatched to distant destinations, making organization and defense of remote borders possible. Kingdoms could take over larger and larger territories, cities could no longer maintain their independence from each other, and trade was no longer dependent upon sea routes. Since horses could walk faster than oxen, farmers could till larger fields with horses, and the fields could be greater distances from where the horses were stabled. This led to the development of small towns, centers which existed for reasons of community rather than commerce or power. All this change occurred due to the taming of a single species. This could represent a facet of Neptune which has not been fully explored by the astrological community.

Neptunian people tend to be slightly confused by the demands of the world and often react by retreating into their mystical, magical world. They may benefit from rising above the waves occasionally, to take a breath of fresh air. Their strength is their familiarity with the spiritual aspects of human nature.

HADES/PLUTO

As god of the underworld, Pluto or Hades is yet another shadowy god. His major story seems to be as the dark abductor of Persephone. Thus he seems to represent the power of unconscious drives, which can suddenly erupt and seem to overwhelm us. Those who live out the Pluto story often seem driven by forces within themselves which they cannot seem to admit exist. Usually Plutonians are convinced that other people are causing their problems and troubles. With time and experience, often painful, they may come to accept the reality of these drives, and even to gain a measure of control over them.

Plutonian issues tend to be very complex and in the beginning, mainly unconscious, so that they tend to be threatening. For those who wish guidance on Pluto, *Healing Pluto Problems* by Donna Cunningham is an illuminating and very helpful book. Plutonians benefit from self-examination and illumination. Their strength is their resilience, their ability to withstand the seemingly overwhelming forces of strong emotions and desires and their ability to teach others how to heal themselves.

HESTIA/VESTA

Vesta was the Roman version of Hestia, goddess of the hearth. The Vestal Virgins, in Roman times, were responsible for keeping the flame sacred to Vesta burning; they were not allowed to have any other responsibility or relationship. If the flame went out, or if a sexual relationship with a man was experienced, the Virgins were punished by death. This seems the extent of the characterization of Vesta.

People who have Vesta prominent in their charts often bring a single-minded focus to the area of life denoted by Vesta's house placement, along with a reluctance to be deeply emotionally involved in a binding relationship or anything else which could interfere with work. While the powers of concentration are considerable, the tendency to develop a very unbalanced life is strong.

The Virgins who tended Vesta's flame were secluded from society and looked after, but a person today who is living out a Vesta myth needs to learn to participate in life— at least to some extent— with others. Such a person tends to hold herself deep within herself, which is probably a psychological necessity, but

to do so at all times is to deny expression to other aspects of the
personality; in such a manner do we unwittingly deny other
"gods." Vesta people particularly need reminders that all the
gods have gifts to offer, all the traits in a well-rounded personality have benefits. Their talent is their dedication to and
concentration on duty and productivity.

PALLAS/MINERVA

Pallas Athena was another virgin goddess, who, along with
Vesta and Artemis, remained untouched by the often lusty and
demanding gods of Olympus. She was a patron of artistic crafts
and also an upright warrior who stood in defense of justice. She
was a goddess who was rational rather than emotional; intelligent, assertive and independent, confidently considering herself the equal of any male, she presents an aspect of femininity
which seems startlingly modern.

Many people who have the asteroid Pallas highlighted in
their charts display the bright, even-tempered, equalitarian
nature associated with the goddess. As a virgin goddess,
however, Pallas never committed herself to another, and this
may be her theme: association without intense emotional
involvement. Such a person can seem very detached to others,
as if there is little or no "feeling" bond. She can be rational when
others need to talk about their emotions— a fine trait unless it
degenerates into insensitivity and outright coldness. Such a
person might take all the vital feeling of aliveness out of others.
Someone who is living out a Pallas theme may need to learn to
make room in life for strong feelings, in themselves as well as
others. Pallas' strength was her independence and self-confidence.

HERA/JUNO

Juno, or Hera, makes a fascinating study. As an early Greek
goddess she wielded a great deal of power, yet once wedded to
Zeus she quickly seemed to concentrate all her energies— and
all her hopes and dreams— on her hopelessly unfaithful partner. While Zeus was often portrayed as fearful of her scorn and
wrath, Hera did not really punish him for his infidelities but
usually took out her anger on his mistresses and their children.

A person who is living out a Hera myth may find she
commits too much of herself to the role of "wife." She may find

herself almost helplessly in the thrall of a very exciting masculine partner who either takes her for granted or who taunts her
with repeated evidence that she is not the only "one" in his life;
his mistresses may be human, or his work or his hobbies. Hera
will be jealous of all. She cannot afford to share her partner
because she has invested all of herself in him and expects him
to do the same. She does not accept that to do so is not
partnership but **absorption**. Like any polarized position, she
marries her opposite: Zeus, who cannot commit at all. His
oppositeness provides what she is failing to express, something
which she can learn to integrate into her own life and thereby
bring her life back to balance. Juno people might learn from the
myth the necessity of developing personal strengths and independence rather than devoting **all** energy to a mate. Their
strength is their ability to commit themselves emotionally to
another human being.

In many ways, the Zeus-Hera marriage classically portrays
the immense pain created when people attempt to express only
one side of a polarity. Hera was wife; she let her husband have
all the obvious (masculine) power and strength in exchange for
which she expected him to care for her and protect her. He never
did; he took the power she offered him and abused it. Zeus was
husband; he let his wife have all the (feminine) qualities of
support, loyalty and commitment, which he expected her to use
forever for his benefit. She berated and scorned him.

They were an unhappy pair who ruined a lot of other lives
until Hera eventually came to her senses and left him. She took
back her power and this is symbolic of trying to develop her own
strengths and the ability to look after herself, of trying to develop
a balance within herself. She healed herself by becoming
complete within herself, by developing both sides of the polarity
within herself. If we read the Greek myths thoughtfully as well
as intuitively, the gods and goddesses have much to teach us
about how to develop ourselves.

The above examples are only a superficial hint at the
richness of information available from the myths, information
which has direct tie-ins with astrology and the various planets,
and which goes well beyond the scope of this book. Beyond
simply reading the myths themselves, straight from the classics, there are numerous books in print which are written about
the myths from a psychological point of view. These shed even

more light on the way we modern humans live out the old patterns, and those that are written about the gods after whom the planets and asteroids were named give special insight to the astrologer about the possible way those planetary motifs could be expressed. A good New Age bookstore should have a selection of these books from which to choose.

Going Within

Ultimately Neptune's demand is to turn within, and to develop whatever we find there. Learning to turn within and listen to Neptune's promptings is not difficult, but it certainly does fly in the face of much of what we are taught in our technological and scientific culture. If we can accept that we as humans have more facets than just a physical body, an ego and a rational mind, then we need to look at what those other facets are and what other needs we have besides food, exercise, and perhaps some creative activity with which to occupy ourselves. Many people agree that we also have psychological needs and spiritual needs, in varying degrees.

Just as some individuals require a great deal of physical activity, some require a great deal of psychological and/or spiritual activity. These people are likely to have Neptune or Pisces or the twelfth house emphasized in their charts, and these are the people for whom personal dreams, myths, art, psychological studies, classic stories and even movies can provide much needed stimulation. They will have, quite naturally, intimate experiences of that which we are labeling "Neptunian," and will have compelling needs to grasp the significance of their experiences. For others, especially counseling astrologers, a deeper understanding of Neptunian experiences, methods of communication and learning processes can enlarge the scope of appreciation for the Neptunian side we all have, and expand their ability to offer insight to clients.

Many people have deep questions about the significance of their own lives, or they seek a meaning and purpose for their lives. They may sense something deeper, or simply something missing. They need to seek within for these answers, no matter how tempting it can be to seek outside. The ultimate journey is the one within, the one of seeking within oneself all the answers to all the questions. This is Neptune's realm.

We all experience Neptune in some way in our lives. We react with vast differences, one person perhaps taking dancing lessons while another experiences mental confusion and lethargy. In fact, it is normal to experience Neptune, and all other planetary motifs, in several different ways, some "negative" and some "positive." In our quest to fathom the differences, we need to turn to Neptune and ask questions. The answers will be forthcoming, but perhaps in a language with which we are unfamiliar. We can, however, learn to translate if we heed and honor those gentle methods which Neptunian energy utilizes. From the tiny voice within to the sweeping epic stories we treasure, all that is represented by Neptune speaks to those who can hear with their inner ears.

Meditation

You are a god/goddess and you have the opportunity now to tell the story of your own myth. Not many details are required; what is wanted is the broad pattern of your life. Turn deep inside yourself and compose your story in general terms. When you have your story, you may wish to write down its outline, and what it means to you, or what pattern you see. Does it illuminate anything in your natal chart?

CHAPTER FOUR

GENERATIONAL PATTERNS WITH NEPTUNE

Neptune remains in each sign of the zodiac for around thirteen years, during which time it tends to describe a "family" of issues faced by the world as a whole. This family of issues can only be described in general terms because various nations, cultures and groups of people deal with the issues in their own characteristic manner. People in the Orient or in African countries may react with patience and tolerance to an issue which brings enormous unrest to North America, and the reverse is also true. Just as individuals act differently during the same transit, depending on their level of understanding of and comfort with the issues raised during that transit, so various cultures, by their traditional outlook on and comfort with particular matters, are well or ill equipped to deal with those matters when they become focal.

Cultural Values

As an example, a culture which is comfortable with its older members, which honors them and makes wise use of their experience and wisdom, will not be particularly threatened by the prospect of a large increase in its population of older people.

Such a culture values these people and gives them a meaningful place in the community. Moreover, the mechanisms by which these people are cared for are already in place and fully accepted. Another culture, which rejects the aged, which prefers to keep them out of sight and mind, will naturally have a terribly difficult time coping with a significant increase in the number of older people. It will, quite simply, face a crisis of values, in which the people of the culture will have to see that the way they deal with their older members will not serve them effectively under the new circumstances. This process can rarely be undertaken without a great deal of resistance and resentment, social unrest, political seesawing and polarization.

In short, Neptune does point out some trends which are afoot right around the world, but it takes a large overview to see those trends as they are worked out in a variety of ways in different cultures. At the same time, care must be taken to avoid the tendency to notice only those historical events which demonstrate our conception of how Neptune in a particular sign **should** work. For example, Neptune is associated with fashion, and it is interesting to note that while Neptune was in the casual, sports-loving sign Sagittarius, very casual sports clothes became fashionable as street wear. But what are we to make of punk-rock fashions, which also became popular during the same time period? It is distressingly easy to overlook those events which do not fit into preconceived notions, but when this is allowed to happen, all we achieve is a fraudulent "proof" of our ideas, a proof which is easily demolished by others with more skepticism.

Achieving Clarity

Neptune in a sign tends to describe those issues over which the world as a whole has to achieve more clarity. Neptune is the planet of illusions, and also the planet of the clear vision which results when all illusions are finally dissolved. So Neptune in a sign indicates the matters about which the world as a whole harbors illusions. The Buddhists say that nearly all our perceptions about reality are, in fact, *maya* or illusions. Perhaps each time Neptune goes through a particular sign it is time for the world to try another step of growth, to try to unravel a few more layers of misconceptions which surround the issues of that sign.

The further Neptune moves into a sign, the more the people of the world, in their various ways, have to stop sweeping the issues of that sign under the collective rug. They find they must confront those issues, face them, define them, describe them and **do** something about them. Often the majority of the work goes on at an inner level as the values of many people are slowly adjusted, but inner changes are preceded by outward unrest and reflected by widespread movements and trends.

Dying Illusions

Whenever illusions are confronted, whether by individuals or by large groups of people, the usual reaction is fear and dread. When Neptune moves into a new sign, however, there is rarely much warning of what lies ahead. With Neptune, very little is in focus and the relevant issues seem to sneak up and catch almost everyone unaware. There may be few outward events typical of Uranus or Pluto, for the energy symbolized by Neptune flows like water, seeping into nooks and crannies and eroding weak spots. It is more a slowly dawning awareness than an explosive revelation. At first, people react by merely shoring up the sagging structures, some of which are material and some of which are internal, such as widely held values.

Repeatedly, however, people are confronted— on a variety of levels— over their dishonesty as a group about the issues which need reworking. A few people will seek to retain the status quo at almost any cost; some of these will even seek to glorify the illusion in order to preserve it. Some individuals will typically become victims, swallowed up by the illusion in its most flagrant form. They enact the tragedy which opens the eyes of those who begin to struggle to destroy the veil which hides the truth. Often these people become martyrs, who are all but destroyed themselves as they seek to expose the accepted dishonesty or fallacy for what it is and what it covers up.

Most people, caught in the middle, will remain vague, confused about the issue and unwilling to deal with it in concrete terms. Toward the end of the transit through a particular sign, however, many individuals and groups have heard the message, have seen the issue(s) more clearly and have made adjustments to their values.

A Sagittarian Example

The "spiritual" cults which became newsworthy while Neptune was in Sagittarius provide an excellent example of the points made in the above paragraphs. Sagittarius is a sign which is related to a restless search for truth. Neptune in the sign Sagittarius coincided with a period when the search for truth became elevated to an important, if largely unconscious, value for many people. While Neptune was in Sagittarius, many people felt a need for something to fulfill this restlessness and that something had to be "Truth." They weren't looking for more money or more status or other outward fulfillments; it had to be internal, and in fact, materialism was often spurned.

SPIRITUAL EXPLORATION

Many people were able to open their minds to new concepts and found meaningful truths for themselves in ideas such as meditation, Eastern spiritual concepts, deeper examination of the mystical aspects of traditional religions, psychology and the occult. There is much wisdom in each of these areas, and many others, and those who navigated the waters of Neptune in Sagittarius with the least pain were able to take the new truths they found and integrated them into their lives in a way which enriched their way of living.

Other people reacted to the spiritual uncertainty and restlessness by seeking out some certain truth, a truth they could nail down. In an attempt to solidify and pacify inner yearnings these people searched for a truth they could depend on, which wouldn't continually shift and demand that they challenge and reevaluate and constantly adjust. These people gravitated toward dogmatic religions which allowed for no dissension. Those of this group with relatively conservative leanings were drawn toward fundamentalist expressions of their cultural religion, while those with a need for something different from the norm were drawn toward mysterious new religions with strange and compelling demands. North American Christians and Middle East Moslems acted this out the most noticeably.

CULTS

It wasn't long before some of the mysterious religions were exposed as cults which flagrantly abused their members. In typically Neptunian fashion, the members of these cults largely accepted their treatment, even defending it as necessary for their own redemption. Then some cult members began to meet untimely deaths. More and more the cults were revealed as not only strange and abusive, but often as recruiting arms of subversive political groups or simply organizations run for the financial benefit of the leader. Some fundamentalist groups also came under scrutiny and were revealed to be equally rotten at the core.

Eventually there appeared some ex-cult members who were willing to go to extraordinary lengths to expose the reality behind the illusion of spiritual harmony of some organizations. Others took up the cause and there was a time when some real saviors appeared, men who would infiltrate a group to wrest from its grasp an innocent victim of group brainwashing. Some of the deprogramming which went on was horrifying, partly because of its own brutality and partly because it revealed to what extent the group had successfully broken down the egos and individual wills of its members.

DIFFERENT REACTIONS

So, there were those who attempted to retain the status of accepted "truth" by joining dogmatic fundamentalist groups, and there were those who attempted to glorify new truth by joining new religions. From these extremes came the victims, the abused and mentally tortured members whose treatment gave rise to the saviors, those who sought to make the rest of the world aware of what was really going on and how serious it was.

And, of course, there were many who simply opened their minds to the truths which could be found from other cultures' spiritual and philosophical pursuits. Throughout the period, there was a gradual acceptance of different expressions of truth, of different religions and philosophies. A businessman who meditated in 1970 would have been looked upon with suspicion. Halfway into the transit of Neptune through Sagittarius, Transcendental Meditation was being taught everywhere imaginable, even in small towns and villages. By the end of the transit, meditation had become respectable; it had gained mainstream acceptance as an excellent method of dealing with stress.

With the influx of different values and religions, new concepts and perspectives, many people came to feel that established churches were no longer relevant; some reacted by drifting away, some worked to make the churches confront realistic issues.

A Libran Example

Now, it is worth commenting that when Neptune changes sign, the work of the previous thirteen or so years is not suddenly abandoned as the entire world turns its focus to some new family of issues symbolized by the newly entered sign. The work begun while Neptune is in a particular sign is, in fact, carried on by those who are born during the period. They will continue to grapple with and bring to the level of personal experience those issues which were the focus of struggle for much of the world at the time of their birth. Thus while Neptune was in the sign Libra (1942-1956/7), the world was dealing with the issues of relationship and tolerance and understanding on a global level. Many astrologers have noted the association of Libra with war and there were major wars during this period, which engaged the efforts of most of the powerful countries of the world.

WAR

Did the transit of Neptune through Libra coincide with a universal readiness to examine the glorification of war? If this was one of the issues, then it should be a major issue for those born with Neptune in Libra, and indeed it soon becomes obvious that this generation has had the illusions of war ripped away— first by events such as the Vietnam War, and then by repeated movies about that war and the hideous, inhuman aspects of it which were so horrifying that for the first time, a war effort became a point of shame rather than glory.

RELATIONSHIPS

The Neptune-in-Libra generation continues to work out the Libran issues, but in more personal ways. They were the group which began by idealizing (Neptune) love and relationships (Libra). The Libran "live and let live" attitude became a cry for "free love." Those in psychology took up the cry and advocated relationships without any strings. Commitment became a dirty word—but soon the generation of free love found it had solved nothing in relationships. It had only idealized one facet of relationships, that of acceptance and tolerance, at the expense of other facets, such as attachment, loyalty and commitment. Still, the need for more tolerance in relationships was successfully highlighted, as was the need for more acceptance of divorce. Allowance is now made for different types of relationship. While casual sexual relationships are no longer upheld as admirable, unmarried partners find a reasonable amount of social tolerance for their chosen state.

The Neptune-in-Libra group is **still** dealing with relationship issues, as the '80s catchword of "networking" demonstrates.

As we take a brief look at Neptune through the signs, keep in mind that the characteristics of that sign, negative and positive, will tend to be first glorified, then gradually some illusions will be exposed as more and more individuals become aware of what is going on underneath the surface. Some people will exemplify the best of the sign, others will be trapped in the worst expressions. The majority will watch from the sidelines, learning slowly as the "public" players act out the struggle on the world stage.

Neptune in Aries 1861/62-1874/75

Issues such as personal effort, self-reliance and adventuresome spirit would gradually work their way into the unconscious value system. There would be widespread glossing over of anger, the use of force, and selfishness. There would be an insidious glorification of the need for personal (Aries) excellence, for each individual to be the best he could be. Traditionally masculine traits such as aggressive and even reckless behavior would be admired. Personal missions would be approved of and encouraged, personal visions would seem wonderfully mystical.

At the same time there would be a gradual exposure of the havoc wreaked by the "rugged individualist" on his mission. Individualism and a "me first" attitude would slowly begin to look less romantically aggressive and more self-absorbed. This generation would repeatedly be confronted by the frailties of the individual, by the inability of a person to function alone and by the need for group support and cooperation.

Spiritual tendencies would center around charismatic individuals or would idealize personal participation in spiritual pursuits. The Christian Mission, which was later reorganized and renamed The Salvation Army, probably exemplifies the better possibilities of Neptune in Aries.

History records that during this period color photography was developed and the first Christmas card was produced. For the first time, a ship was sunk by an attack from a submarine; the concept of an oil pipeline became a reality, wireless radio telegraphy was successfully implemented and the first osteopathic doctor opened his practice. Accident insurance was introduced during this time. The Civil War flared up in the United States as it seemed only military force could settle contentious issues over freedom. Later, the Homestead Act of 1862 encouraged migration to the West and the first transcontinental railway route was completed. In Japan, the supremacy of the military commander, or Shogun, was diminished for the first time in many centuries and the Emperor's power was reinstated.

Neptune in Taurus 1874/75-1887/89

Widespread idealism about resources, wealth, the importance of personal possessions and status would gradually become accepted. There would be a yearning for acquisitions and for solid material security. Land would become valuable. There would be a desire for tranquillity and peace and for not rocking the boat, for security in material affairs, and money. Groups would feel the need to secure possessions, to hold on to territory gained. Nature and her creatures could become idealized, as would creature comforts and pleasures.

Spiritual interests would tend to lean toward the concrete—the established religions which did not demand too much. There would be illusions concerning the stability of money, the security of possessions and the ability of individuals and groups to maintain conditions in an idyllic state. There would be a slow dissolution of peace as attempts to control territory brought resistance. The inability of money and possessions to provide security would repeatedly be shown up. The idealization of nature and sensual pleasures would gradually look like mere hedonism, as people realized that personal gratifications can be taken to excess.

During this period, photography developed remarkably to the point where the first Yearbook of Photography was published. Sound recording was vastly improved year by year. The cash register was invented, as was the concept of third-party insurance. Local anesthesia was tried out successfully. The United States government agreed to buy millions of dollars' worth of silver annually from Western silver miners and to make the supply into silver dollars. In Africa, gold was discovered in the Transvaal, which attracted thousands of British miners. It was an event which caused long-standing British-Boer hostilities in the area to come to a head, leading eventually to the Boer War. Many nations became increasingly worried that their interests were being threatened and began to build large armies.

Neptune in Gemini 1887/89-1901/02

Spiritual leanings would tend toward the factual rather than the mystical. Rationalism, logic, facts, business and commerce would all begin to be highly valued. There would be a recognition of the importance of communication, especially with neighbors. Arts and crafts would be admired, as would those engaged in slick business deals. Learning elementary skills in reading and writing would be seen as vitally important. Common writings of the day would become tinged with mystical ideas, or full of stories about magic and fantasy.

There would be many illusions about commerce, with much glossing over of lying, cheating, stealing and gossip. Gradually all of these would be laid bare as prevalent practices. "Known facts" would become less certain. Fantasy and magic would begin to look tawdry and cheap, and intellectual idealism would begin to look merely escapist and unrealistic.

This was the era which saw the emergence of Esperanto, the first deliberately designed international language. Christian Science spread widely and began to construct its own churches. The first psychoanalysis was conducted by Freud. I.Q. tests were invented and introduced. A motorist was convicted of drunken driving for the first time during this period, while in Europe a revolutionary new instructional use for film was tried out when a surgical operation was recorded and later used for teaching purposes. The more powerful nations continued to maintain large armies and kept a close eye on all their neighbors. In Europe, two large alliances were formed: the Triple Alliance of Germany, Italy and Austria-Hungary and the Triple Entente of Russia and France and, eventually, of Great Britain.

Neptune in Cancer 1901/02-1914/16

There would be much idealization of motherhood, family, home and homestead, country and/or nationality, and food. Qualities such as tenacity, holding firmly onto things, taking care of others, and family loyalty would be greatly admired and upheld. The importance of protection and security, for individuals, families and country, would all become uppermost. There would be little tendency to share outside the accepted family unit, and countries would tend to become strongly nationalistic, disinclined to allow free trade.

Mothers would be glorified as— and expected to act like— saints. When they didn't, it would be glossed over or ignored. Families would feel a double pull— that of the past, as in pride in heritage— and that of the future as in the need to acquire stable property to pass on as an inheritance. The need for a separate home for each family would be seen as vital.

Gradually people would start to recognize that all their efforts toward establishment and preservation of home and country were in fact isolationist, and that this policy is not truly productive either for individual families or for countries.

During this period in history, it is interesting to note that heroin and cocaine were freely available, often in "medicines," and many housewives were quietly but solidly addicted to these substances. It was a widely known "secret." Many expensive sanatoriums thrived on the business provided by rich families who sent their more embarrassingly addicted members for a rest cure for their "nerves."

One of the more interesting historical events of this time includes the establishment of Mother's Day, first celebrated May 10, 1907.

In South Africa, Gandhi came to the fore as he led resident East Indians in a struggle to acquire the rights of citizenship. In many countries, the notion of universal suffrage had taken hold.

Politically, a number of nations, including Japan and the United States, became strongly interested in the benefits of acquiring possessions, and in Europe, the notion of protection for each nation's interests continued to grow, increasing the potential for hostilities and disputes. Germany began to expand her navy; Great Britain soon followed suit. Because the European nations, which had extensive holdings all over the world, had divided themselves into two hostile camps, nearly every military or border dispute which occurred anywhere had implications for Europe and had the potential to cause international incidents.

Neptune in Leo 1914/15-1928/29

There would be great value placed on qualities of loyalty, generosity, splendor, stable if pompous and autocratic government, respect for leadership, financial growth and return, and admiration for individual respect, power and authority.

There would be a powerful yearning for admiration, self-confidence and a tendency to elevate strong personalities to the status of hero. The development of the individual ego would be seen as vitally important. There would be many illusions over power and authority. At first these would be glorified, then revealed as flawed and gradually undermined.

Spiritual interests would be strong but individuals would tend to lean toward a "Divine Right" philosophy, magnificent displays of wealth and power in the church, and would often muddy the lines of separation between church and state power.

Many people would expect to be treated as royalty, or as demigods.

There would be gradual dissolution and cynicism as heroes would be shown to have clay feet and to be ordinary humans after all. Those in power would tend to gradually erode the respect and admiration of their "subjects" through self-important behavior and grandiosity.

Those of this generation who could not resist ruling over their territory or family with a kind of "Divine Right" attitude were, in fact, not able to hold the respect of younger generations.

History records that this period saw the first bathing beauty contest, the first sex-education film, and the development of radio for entertainment purposes. The major event, however, was obviously World War I. The world nations, jostling for power and possessions, jealous and suspicious of each other, had so tied each other up in knots that the assassination of the heir to the throne of Austria-Hungary resulted in escalating declarations of war from all sides until thirty-eight nations were involved. Those who "won" the war and therefore the right to conduct the course of the subsequent peace treaties could not resist the temptation to arrogantly divide up Europe and Africa to their own liking. The treaties were never well-enforced, however, and the seeds of World War II, sown in the resentment of the defeated Central Powers, flourished in the growing militarism and nationalism in Germany and Italy. The League of Nations was formed but was unable to exercise much power because major nations tended to do what they wanted with little regard for the League. It was, however, the important forerunner of the United Nations. The Western powers were preoccupied with the Roaring Twenties and rampant speculation fueled the fantasy of limitless wealth.

Neptune in Virgo 1928/29-1942/43

Neptune in this sign would be associated with an idealization of efficiency, purity, celibacy, quiet focus on work, finding and correcting flaws, idealization of work and duty, of service and labor and a strong feeling against desecration and waste. There would be some glorification of the ordinary worker, the servant, the secretary, and the person who diligently worked behind the scenes to keep things working smoothly. The acceptance of responsibility would seem somehow spiritually correct. There would be an increased concern over purity and cleanliness.

Spiritual interests would tend toward concepts of purification, service for others, looking after the suffering, work as a holy pastime, and spiritual rewards for the long-suffering volunteer, and those who did their duty without complaint.

There would be many illusions over the work ethic, over the "work hard for just reward" concept. Gradually it would become obvious that no matter how hard a person worked, she could not necessarily expect to get ahead, nor even obtain her well-earned reward. Hard work would be seen for what it usually was—dirty, difficult, tiring, and often unrewarding. There would be increased disillusionment with the idea of hard work, with more and more people questioning the purpose behind it all.

During this period, the Stock Market crash and Great Depression affected much of the world. Massive unemployment caused governments to try to correct the flaws in the economic system. New controls and rules were laid down. Improvements did not come soon enough to stave off extensive discontent, however, and both communist and fascist movements fed on this and gained enormously in power. World War II was declared and people were exhorted to do their duty for their country.

In a more mundane vein, health food became more popular than ever before, frozen food became commercially available and grew in popularity and the first crease-proof fabrics were produced. Also during this period, there were major advances in pharmaceutical drugs and antibiotics. While Neptune was in Virgo, these seemed necessary and extremely constructive.

Neptune in Libra 1942/43-1955/57

Interpersonal contact would be highlighted, whether friendly or competitive. Relationships would be valued and glorified. Qualities such as diplomacy, tact, tolerance and negotiation for equal terms would be thought of highly. There would be increased focus on the importance of interpersonal skills and graphic arts.

Spiritual interests would tend to express themselves in

genteel ways, through music and art. The emphasis would be on sharing, kindness and decency, with growing awareness of the value of concepts from other religions.

The people of the world would have to confront their illusions concerning both relationships and the seemingly pretty world of the arts. At first, both issues would be valued and would seem like worthy goals. Gradually, however, there would be a shift in consciousness, an awareness that the tranquillity at the surface only hides the problems underneath.

During this period World War II and the Korean War shattered the world's ability to maintain peaceful relations among her countries. The staggering cost and tragedy of war appeared to hit people more effectively than it had two decades earlier, and no country could afford the arrogance which characterized the peace treaties of World War I. The United Nations was formed, a stronger and more vigorous organization than its predecessor, based on more global agreement than had ever been achieved before.

Drug use became widespread in the music and arts industries, although it was not common knowledge at the time. With Neptune in Libra, it was important to present a tranquil face to the public.

Neptune in Scorpio 1955/57-1970

With Neptune in Scorpio there would be a strong emphasis on the importance of depth and insight, "real" emotions, sexuality and power, especially the power to sway others. All of these issues would become explosively intense. Some people would attempt to keep it all a secret, yet the secrets would keep leaking out. Death, birth, rebirth, and the occult would fascinate many.

Many people would have to confront their illusions over the use of power. Other people would experience intense challenges to their value systems. The struggles could reach explosive proportions as large groups would find their hidden resentments could no longer be contained.

Spirituality would explore intense, deep self-revelation. Secret rituals would attract many, as would the darker side of the occult. Anything simmering at the core of church life would boil over.

During this period, depth psychologies came to the fore and began to exhort people to get in touch with their deeper selves. The movement was particularly strong on university campuses, and many student groups not only got in touch with themselves but with their collective power. Protests became a way of life at universities, and spread to other groups when it was realized that massive marches did have an impact on politicians and on the consciousness of other people. Union corruption was uncovered and widely publicized. The sexual revolution got underway, partly enabled by the increasing availability of birth control pills. There was a rapid expansion of the use of drugs in medicine, and the use of illicit drugs on the street was widely exposed. Few people could avoid the powerful and seemingly inexorable challenges to their value systems. There were many eruptions of violence in previously peaceful areas; racism was no longer tolerated patiently by its victims, for example.

Typical of Scorpio, there was much eruption of anger, frustration and resentment for the duration of this transit, so much so that it seemed at the time that the world was about to erupt from the inside out, that people could not possibly contain all the built-up emotions which were boiling over after years of injustice. Yet with the passing of the transit, people settled down. Much garbage had been exposed, much that was rotten about society's systems had been revealed and some corrections had been made, but only some. We would do well to remember the days of "urban warfare" and that all that anger and resentment continues to fester under the surface

Neptune in Sagittarius 1970-1984

Much of this has been covered in the introductory paragraphs of this chapter. However, to review, the world would have to confront its illusions about issues such as truth, organized religion, higher education, sports, publishing, the practice of law, and so on.

Some people would have glorified these matters, with the special fervor of Sagittarius lending incredible energy to the movements. At the same time others would have seen that one or more of these issues was long overdue for an overhaul. Each side would have experienced a special "rightness" to their position and with their need to expand it, to carry their message into wider and wider circles with evangelical enthusiasm.

Many people would have become interested in foreign religions, philosophies and systems of thought. Others would have done their intellectual expansion (Sagittarius) through fantasy (Neptune): witness the immense success of the *Star Wars* trilogy in movies. Space itself, and its whirling, speeding, ever-expanding mystery, would have seemed like the ultimate adventure.

In the field of athletics, there would have been an increased interest in the artistic sports such as gymnastics, skating, dancing and synchronized swimming. While these were coming to their zenith, however, some voices would have slowly undermined widespread illusions about the "sportsmanship" of professional sports.

During this period, there was a growing disillusionment with scholastic education and degrees as people began to realize that a degree did not necessarily create a useful employee. Young people just out of high school often chose to travel for a year or two before entering a university. Many left with a romanticized view of the countries they intended to visit. Most were disillusioned by what they found in terms of poverty and lack of freedoms, yet at the same time many found a strong sense of basic values from the simple people and lifestyles they encountered. When they returned home, they brought with them a vastly expanded world view, along with a great deal of idealism about how the world **should** be.

The use of drugs in professional sports became common knowledge, as did the use of "recreational" drugs by the very lawyers who prosecuted others for the same activity.

The United States experienced a tremendous disillusionment in politics and politicians with the increasingly unpopular Vietnam War and then the Watergate affair. President Nixon exhibited one side of Neptune in Sagittarius by maintaining that he had done nothing wrong, no matter how badly his position was exposed. President Carter exhibited another side by bringing his religion and ethics into focus during his term in office. He intuitively understood that the public needed a leader they could trust (Sagittarius). His easygoing, simple style ran headlong into yet another expression of Neptune in Sagittarius: the fanatical fundamentalism of the Shiite Moslems under Ayatollah Khomeini in Iran. Perhaps the ultimate negative expression of Neptune in Sagittarius was the arrival of terrorism on the world scene. No longer confined to isolated events in strange areas of the globe, all civilized countries felt the blows delivered by those who were so convinced of their "truth" and "rightness" that even incredible destruction and violence could be sanctioned.

Neptune in Capricorn 1984-1998

With Neptune in Capricorn there will likely be a return to conservative, traditional and Puritan-type values. The state itself could be idealized. Organizations will tend to become more and more unstable as their flaws cannot be successfully hidden any longer or as their authority to do what they have always done disintegrates. There will tend to be many people who try desperately to reestablish values, systems and organizations which seemed to work for their parents. Stability itself, and material security will probably seem valuable and desirable. However the more frantically these are upheld, the more they will reveal their flaws and any underlying corruption. Furthermore, the problems which were tolerated in past decades will not be acceptable with Neptune in Capricorn. The flaws will simply be too self-evident. People have learned too much to be blind to problems which our parents did not notice. There will tend to be a vague but important expectation that governments and establishment organizations should be idealistic and perfect.

There will also probably be a need, vague but having its impact, for authority figures and recognized leaders to be perfect, or idealistic, or charismatic. They will need to appear to be sensitive and responsive. However, it is likely that many leaders and public figures will slowly have their power undermined as they are revealed to be weak, confused or lacking clear direction. More than a few will be living in a dream world of their own, will seduce many into believing in their vision and then will slowly undermine themselves as they are revealed to be out of touch with and unable to deal effectively with reality.

People will be confronted by their illusions regarding security and stability; government structures, systems and organizations; and the role of authority and tradition. The harder these are upheld, the more they will be undermined. Once again common illusions about the use of power will be eroded. Again and again the accepted reality (Capricorn) of issues and situations will shift and seem unreliable. Scientists will repeatedly find new evidence that seriously challenges the basis of their truths and laws. There may be some fascinating, if rather strange-sounding discoveries about the nature of reality, and the nature of time.

Those who seek spiritual security in fundamentalist or other rigid interpretations of their cultural religions will find the ground they stand on increasingly insecure. Despite this, there are likely to be many who seek to reestablish the power of organized religions. Occult groups may find their freedoms threatened and curtailed.

Cultures will need to examine the role they allow their older members, and their concepts of aging. Hopefully, the wisdom and experience of retired and elderly citizens will be recognized and valued, though not to the point of stagnation of new concepts.

On the positive side, there will probably be many who examine the concepts of maturity, responsibility, ambition, governmental power and business leadership with an eye to integrating the best of these into a more compassionate lifestyle and value-system.

While materialism and governmental authority may be glorified to begin with, and then in disfavor as disillusionment starts, as time goes on many people will see that these are legitimate pursuits when kept in perspective and balanced with other aspects of life.

This is a time when occult and spiritual groups could become more grounded. They will have the opportunity to organize themselves into stronger and more lasting bodies which have solid foundations. Perhaps they will find a way to include a practical, business-oriented arm or committee in order to make themselves self-supporting.

Neptune in Aquarius 1998-2011/12

This is a period which in the past (1834 -1847/48) saw the discovery of anesthesia and the first electric telegraph.

With Neptune in Aquarius, it is likely that any illusions regarding technological progress, groups, and human freedoms, particularly the freedom to be different, will have to be confronted. There may be attempts to glorify technology to begin with, attempts to make it look like the supreme goal. There may be those who see rapid progress as the only answer to some of the world's more troublesome and intractable dilemmas. Others will suspect there is something missing in this answer, and will seek solutions through elimination of many old rules and regulations. There may be many times of confusion as to the value and role of spirituality versus the value and role of cold reason.

This will seem like a time when the concept of world government seems closer to reality than ever before. On the positive side, there will probably be many excellent moves in this direction, many innovative and inspired ideas for the peaceful coming together of varied nations. The idea of world peace could make some impressive strides during this period, when nationalistic bonds are likely to be fairly weak. On the negative side is the possibility that Aquarian logic and interest in unique solutions, not to mention its acceptance of anarchy, could seem more important than the human needs such as intimacy, warm relationships and the capacity for fun.

The attempted glorification of technology, reason and relentless progress will slowly be undermined, revealed as incomplete and unable to meet the world's need for emotional, psychological and spiritual stimulation. Favorite political ideologies will come under close scrutiny, as people have a renewed interest in finding a utopian system. The real effects of each system, as opposed to the hopeful dreams of its followers, will slowly be revealed. Out of all this may result a period of chaos, when all systems break down. Anarchy is not out of the question. This does not have to be devastating. The *Bible* speaks of a time when there were no kings, when every man ruled himself according to his own conscience. It was, for a time, very peaceful.

It is a period when spiritual issues could be viewed with the least emotional uproar and the most logic. Occult groups may find their numbers swelling as people's minds open, although the tendency toward individualistic interpretations of any beliefs will grow and may splinter groups into small but relatively tolerant factions. It is also a time when innovation is almost the norm, when the human race has the capacity to look at its problems from totally different perspectives. Perhaps out of this, people will find new solutions to old problems.

Neptune in Pisces 2011/12-2025/26

During this period, the world will, as a whole, need to confront its illusions about spirituality, values, the ideal vision, God, the arts, nature and all things mysterious, magical and make-believe. On the one hand it could be a time of unprecedented inspiration in both spiritual and artistic realms. It could also be a time of great disillusionment and pain as favorite beliefs are slowly eroded and undermined. The whole process and role of illusions themselves is likely to be confronted, with much suffering incurred as people slowly accept the destructive side of this self-protective mechanism.

This could mean that a large mass of people becomes seduced by some fantasy that **looks** real. The fantasy could be a person or an idea, or a person who embodies a concept which seems to hold the ultimate answer for the world's miseries. Such a concept would hold a terrifying appeal for people while Neptune is in Pisces. Pisces often has about it a feeling of weariness, a feeling of spiritual and emotional exhaustion. If enormous numbers of people all feel this way, they will be looking for a way which offers hope for a much better future, and in Pisces, they will tend to be susceptible to anyone who promises them what they want to hear, whether the promises are substantiated or not.

With Neptune in Pisces the world as a whole will need to take a look at the human tendency to deny or evade rather than deal with problems. It will be an excellent time to examine the human tendency to take the easy way out without doing any of the necessary groundwork.

On the positive side, there may be a marked increase in

interest in and development of human psychic potential, probably to a degree we can barely imagine today. There might be a resurgence of interest in spiritual development and its benefits. The legitimate role of spiritual needs would then be accepted and integrated into more lives. The role of cultural value systems could slowly be illuminated and more clearly understood. The role of the arts as an expression of a culture's psychological process will likely be given greater attention.

There may be a period when great visions take hold of people, only to shatter later. People will have to see the tendency to yearn for an ultimate answer for what it is, and learn to direct it into appropriate areas. Every time the answer is sought in the outer world, the vision crumbles. While Neptune is in Pisces, the world will slowly come to understand, on some level, that the answers, after all, lie within.

CHAPTER FIVE

NEPTUNE IN THE HOUSES

The sign occupied by Neptune at the moment of a person's birth is a placement which is shared with millions of people. It indicates that one belongs to a generation of people, all of whom are working with similar illusions and similar inspirations. The house position of Neptune is somewhat more personal, although it is still shared with hundreds of thousands of others. It gives an area of focus to the Neptunian generational pattern. If all people who are born with Neptune in Libra need to work at their tendency to idealize relationships, then all the people born with Neptune in Libra in the third house, for example, will find their tendency to idealize relationships is experienced most obviously in their relationships with brothers, sisters, cousins and neighbors. The house position narrows the area of life, or defines the "stage," on which the Neptune in Libra "script" is to be played out.

Projection

One of the puzzles encountered when an astrologer starts to delineate house positions of Neptune is that some people seem to "do" their own Neptune, that is, they express the traits of that Neptune/house combination personally, while others seem to encounter such traits from other people. People with Neptune in the fourth house commonly have a mother who expresses Neptunian traits, Neptune in the fifth may experience children or lovers with Neptunian traits, and so on. What is going on?

This apparent ability of planets in different houses to describe various people in an individual's life has been known since the early days of astrology, but only recently has it been explained. The concept which answers the puzzle is one called "projection," a term coined to describe the tendency people have to see in others, traits which they themselves possess but have not successfully integrated into conscious use.

Thus a person who is uncomfortable with anger will often deny his own, then see anger in nearly everyone around him. A person who cannot find a way to express his own needs may find himself surrounded by selfish people. Actually, it isn't often **that** simple; the suppressed or unexpressed trait is usually part of a family of traits, a grouping which naturally goes together, but it may not be common knowledge that they are related.

ASSERTION

As an example, take assertiveness. Astrologically it is related to Mars. Mars is also related to anger, aggressiveness, and selfishness as well as physical energy, the head, confrontation and so on. If a female client tells an astrologer that "a lady should not find it necessary to express anger," the astrologer has a hint that this client is probably not comfortable with Mars' energy. The astrologer can start to ask questions about other expressions of Mars energy, about whether this client is able to assert her own needs, face up to unpleasant but necessary confrontations, or has enough physical energy. If the answers to these questions are all "no," the questioning could then begin to explore the nature of the people in this client's life. It will not be too surprising to find she views them as selfish, impulsive, headstrong, bad-tempered and hyperactive. This is projection. The client does not accept Mars energy, will not express it herself— even in a positive way— and then finds the very experiences she wants to avoid coming at her from other people. The problem is, she most likely does not realize that all those nasty traits she detests in others are merely the negative manifestation of an energy which she could express herself, in positive and constructive ways.

LOGIC

In a similar vein, a person who sees himself as deeply and inspiringly poetic may have let his intellectual talents languish, only to find himself surrounded by superficial "airheads." He has rejected his logical, rational side because it seems so cold and shallow, then finds these uncomfortable traits in the people around him. It is as if the rejected part of the personality has found a way to sneak back into the person's life!

NEED FOR WHOLENESS

In actuality what usually happens is that while the person is, on one level, relieved to get rid of the rejected or neglected traits, on another level she misses them. They are, after all, part of herself. She cannot feel whole and complete without them, and when she finds them in another person, she often finds them remarkably attractive, as if they fill a hole in her. At least, at first. If she does not "pick up" some of the traits from her new acquaintance, if she does not learn how to use them herself, they will soon seem irritating and possibly intolerable, because she still will not have come to terms with that family of traits.

The mechanism of projection is not fully understood— perhaps we are unconsciously attracted to people similar to ourselves who will express a part of ourselves which we cannot. Perhaps we simply see in others that which we cannot express ourselves, regardless of whether they really exhibit the trait. It is the author's observation that both dynamics occur, although the frequency of the former greatly outweighs the frequency of the latter.

WAYS TO IDENTIFY PROJECTION

Projection is one possible result of a repressed trait or complex grouping of traits. Astrology gives such a clear picture of possible projections precisely because it groups the traits, both positive and negative, together under the name of a planet, or a sign, and then it is usually possible to distinguish whether you do indeed express those traits yourself or if you meet them from other people. If you meet them a lot from others, if they seem to come at you from out of the blue, if they seem far removed from your control, if they seem to simply "happen" to you, you have identified a projection. Anger is a great "flag" or key to projection. The angrier you get over someone else's behavior, the more likely it is that you do not accept that facet of your own personality. Actually any very strong emotional reaction can be such a "flag," a hint that there is much activity going on beneath the surface, and much energy must be expended to keep it from erupting into consciousness.

Once a projection has been identified, the behavior and/or a related attitude can be traced to one planet or another. Once the planet is known, it is possible to see a wide range of potential expressions for that planetary energy. Naturally some of the expressions will be destructive and some will be constructive. It is up to each individual to foster a comfortable relationship with that planet, or in other words, to find some constructive expressions for that energy, from among the many which are possible. Just as an example, the client who had difficulty with Mars could take an assertiveness training course, tennis lessons or psychotherapy to get in touch with her anger, whichever she was most comfortable with. Any of these would be a positive expression of Mars.

Candidates for Projection

Beyond straightforward question-and-answer detective work, astrology has many hints to help identify potential projections. It is well accepted that men tend to project Moon and Venus qualities on to the women around them— many astrology texts don't know how to interpret these planets any other way for the male reader. Women tend to project Mars, Sun and Saturn traits onto the men around them. Beyond this, most people have some trouble learning to be comfortable with the trans-Saturnian planetary traits, and many cannot successfully integrate them into their conscious vision of themselves. This means they will tend to project them.

Then there are planets in the western half of the chart, which are more prone to projection than those in the eastern half. The western half used to be called the "fated" half, as astrologers could certainly observe the tendency of planets in that area of the chart to describe traits which were not expressed by the client but which "happened" to the client. Fate was the logical explanation when issues were clearly not under the conscious control of the client involved. Ancient astrologers hadn't identified projection, which is responsible for a great deal of what is blamed on "fate."

And, just to make sure that astrologers keep on their toes, any planet whose energy goes against the grain of the majority of the chart is a good candidate for projection. Put aggressive Mars on the Ascendant in a chart dominated by the passive water sign Pisces and this sensitive individual will likely do almost anything to get rid of such an incompatible tendency— anything, that is, except consciously make friends with it and integrate it. For that, people usually need objective support from others, and perhaps guidance from a professional counselor of some sort.

Astrologers are in an excellent position to help people reintegrate planetary energies which have previously been rejected or at least misunderstood. Since Neptune has a history of being misunderstood, under-appreciated and poorly integrated, the study of its house position and likely areas of projection as well as the positive alternatives makes a valuable addition to the astrologer's knowledge. In cultures such as ancient Greece it was accepted that individuals who got into trouble with a particular god or goddess had to take it upon themselves to reestablish a good relationship with that deity. Essentially, today, the astrologer can help clients by revealing the god or goddess— planet— with which clients need to reestablish constructive relationships. The ancient Greeks had to make sacrifices and perform tasks assigned by the offended deity. Modern clients need to learn about the variety of ways to express a planetary energy, to accept that energy as a valid part of life and to choose the expressions of that energy with which they are most comfortable.

Neptune in the First House

Someone with Neptune in the first tends to be a quiet person who would rather wait and see what happens than act too hastily. Other people consider him passive, even lazy, but this is not how the Neptunian sees himself. He **feels** intimately involved, sometimes to the point of suffering, but his outward behavior— geared toward peace and harmony— does not convey what is going on inside.

EXTREME SENSITIVITY

What is going on inside is usually significant to the Neptunian. He feels very connected because he is aware of subtle energies, because he picks up impressions from other people that they are usually entirely unaware of giving. The Neptunian frequently finds himself in the uncomfortable position of knowing— on levels which are beyond the verbal— what others' unconscious motivations are, what they **really** want but usually hide under the veneer of civilized manners. The Neptunian finds it difficult, if not impossible, to confront others with their own truth because he senses their inability to face themselves honestly without great pain. He hates to hurt others, and indeed he may not be able or willing to push his own awareness to the point of words. He will frequently choose to do nothing. This is usually interpreted as passivity or weakness by others, who do not see what pain the Neptunian endures because of his knowledge.

RECEPTIVE

With Neptune in the first house, a person tends to be very idealistic. He is drawn to and prefers to live with harmony: peaceful nondemanding relationships, quiet environments and aesthetically beautiful surroundings. He tends to think kindly of others; his sensitivity to their inner motivations and needs brings out his natural compassion. He tries to treat others kindly. Whether they reciprocate or not, it is part of his value system that he treat others well. He can be most charming, often whimsical, sometimes romantic and usually empathic. He seems approachable and is often receptive to a degree others find startling and deeply gratifying, if a trifle eerie.

He wants life to be perfect for himself and for others. In a chart which indicates the possibility of strength of character, this desire may be translated into volunteer work, social work or some activity devoted to improving the quality of life for others, or into some inspirational activity. In a chart which emphasizes passive tendencies, the desire for a better world may be channeled into artistic creative pursuits, or into mere daydreaming. It is also possible that this degenerates into chronic dissatisfaction with the way things are, with no constructive suggestions or impetus for improvement.

IDENTITY A PROBLEM

The person with Neptune in the first house often struggles with a great deal of confusion about his personal identity. He may be so open to others that he picks up their moods without realizing he is being affected. He tends to mimic, quite unconsciously, the strongest characteristics of the last person he was with. He can be easily misled by others, for he fits himself into their "head space" with such ease that he doesn't always realize he has done so, and may forget— or be unaware of the need— to return to his own thoughts and feelings.

Some Neptunians find they are so open and receptive that they become emotional sponges, incapable of defending themselves from the unconscious messages and energies put out by others. Such people need to learn how to define psychic and emotional boundaries around themselves, but before they can succeed at this they will need to accept that it is necessary. Usually they resist this; they prefer to cling to their illusions of beauty and harmony and in so doing leave themselves defenseless.

The person with Neptune in the first house does not mind suffering. He may protest that of course he does, but in fact he will often accept it when he does not need to do so. He tends to feel that others must always come first, and that it is better to sacrifice his own well-being than be responsible for someone else's suffering. He finds it difficult to refuse requests for help, a trait which other people frequently exploit. He is also easily deceived, not because of any inherent lack of intelligence but because he wants to see the best in people and easily dismisses the worst. When his illusions are revealed he will accept it with a sigh and will often dream up excuses for the one who deluded him.

NEEDS A FIRM IDENTITY

The hardest task for the person with Neptune in the first house is that of establishing a firm identity. He needs it more than anyone and is least likely to accept or honor that need because it seems, to him, egotistical. Yet his beliefs (Neptune) about himself (first house) profoundly influence the decisions he makes and therefore have a major impact on the quality of his life. He needs to realize that his unconscious values and attitudes are the driving force behind his life, and as long as they remain unconscious, they remain out of his control. Therefore, essentially his life will feel out of his control. If he can accept this, and can begin to become aware of what he believes, sort out whether his beliefs make sense and serve him well, and change those that don't, he will build a firm foundation for his Neptunian nature. Quiet times alone are vital for this process, but regular meditation is even better.

With Neptune in the first house, there is almost always a strong awareness of and interest in spiritual energies. The person may actually be psychic, whether or not he is comfortable with or utilizes this ability. He may be deeply religious, although it is likely that he will not be fully satisfied with conventional religions. He feels more at home with belief systems which make room for the currents, promptings and energies which he knows from personal experience do exist.

HEALTH

The person with Neptune in the first house will tend to be physically inactive. He does not usually have the energy to lead a dynamic life unless there are other indications in the chart for this. He prefers quiet, spiritually nourishing pursuits to athletics. His very lack of interest in the mundane world in general and his own physical body in particular can lead him into careless dietary habits and a complete unwillingness to exercise, which can quickly undermine his sensitive health. It is difficult for the Neptunian to accept but he may have to discipline himself to follow a pure diet, to avoid or carefully monitor the use of alcohol and to be especially careful with drugs, medicinal or otherwise. Frequently this Neptunian requires lower doses of medicine than others.

When the Neptunian theme dominates the house motif rather than expressing through it, the person is his own ultimate value. He may simply feel as if he should be perfect, or he may think he already is perfect. Neptune itself is not inclined to arrogance but in combination with fire planets, houses or signs it can certainly produce that effect. A more positive use of the fire/Neptune combination is in the graceful, artistic sports such as skiing, gymnastics, dancing, synchronized swimming and so on.

With Neptune in the first, the person needs to face up to his tendency to harbor illusions or unrealistic expectations about himself and the way he approaches the world, and what he wishes from the world. He may need to confront his tendency to be too sensitive and to take things far too personally. With experience and growth, this Neptunian can develop a most humble and spiritual nature which is still strong enough to withstand the temptations of the world. He can lead others to appreciate the seemingly gentle but very resilient strength of the inner Divine spark.

Neptune in the Second House

The person with Neptune in the second house tends to be idealistic about the use of money and personal resources. Often she is not terribly attached to her personal assets. She tends to look upon her possessions as wards in her care and while she may be saddened when the time comes to part with something, she can let it go where others simply cannot. She has, deep down, an intuitive awareness that "you can't take it with you."

INDIFFERENT WITH RESOURCES
With Neptune in the second house, there may be an indifferent attitude toward personal finances, earning an income and taking care of possessions. Some of these people are very generous and will give away one of their belongings to someone who admires it. They can believe that possessions do not truly belong to anyone but are there for the good of all, and should be with the person who is happiest with them. Such an outlook greatly satisfies the Neptunian idealism. They may be just as easygoing with their money, and can easily be taken advantage of by acquaintances.

Neptune in the second house can signify a fairy-tale attitude toward money— either that it will always be there when needed, or that it is simply another one of the world's idiotic preoccupations and a delusion.

Sometimes this position simply indicates forgetfulness or impracticality with resources. Bills may be overlooked, costing the individual in interest charges. Checkbook balances may be forever incorrect, resulting in N.S.F. checks. Purchases may always cost more than planned because the person is some-what naive and doesn't know to ask about additional charges, or she simply forgets about them. She may not be willing to sit down and figure out which item is the best buy, preferring to simply go on her intuition. Purchasing decisions may be based on the fact that she hasn't eaten yet today rather than what she can afford. She often has no clear idea of what she can afford, and no idea how to work it out. She frequently doesn't care much, either.

She is not inclined to read the small print in a contract, and may easily lose money through trusting the wrong people, through impractical investments which appeal to her altruistic nature and through outright con games. She can often be talked into making loans to people who cannot repay, simply because she yearns to help out. She may leave her finances in an incredible muddle year after year rather than impose effort and discipline on the issue.

MAY OVERVALUE POSSESSIONS

Sometimes, with Neptune (beliefs and ultimate values) in the house of money and possessions, there is a strong tendency to value and perhaps overvalue material possessions. If there is an emphasis on earth in the chart, this person may be inclined to take great care of her things and her money, putting a great deal of time and effort into upkeep. She will usually want her possessions to look attractive and to be aesthetically pleasing. If there is enough drive in the chart to do this upkeep on a continuing basis, it may be possible to turn this into a career.

HIGHLY CREATIVE

Neptune and the second house share a strong creative tendency. It may be expressed as interest and possible talent in pure art, or in music, or in other artistic/creative pursuits, but it will certainly be inherent. This person will need at least periodic access to music and to lovely surroundings, including pastoral outdoor settings where she can soak up the peace and serenity. If there are any other indications of possible artistic ability in the chart, this individual needs to have some background training and some way to express the creativity. Music and/or other creative pursuits as well as visits to parks will all be ways for this individual to relax and let go of built-up tensions.

SEARCH FOR FULFILLMENT

Since the second house also relates to sensual pleasures, it is possible that the person expects these to provide a kind of ultimate ecstasy. She may retreat to these whenever life threatens to get too nasty, looking for reassurance and fulfillment in an area which can only provide temporary pleasure. She may make pursuit of sensual pleasure an ultimate value, something she will cling to in the face of much difficulty.

With Neptune in the second, the person needs to face up to her tendency to create illusions about money, possessions and sensual pleasures, or creative pursuits, to expect more from them than they can provide, or to ignore or deny their importance. With patience and insight, this Neptunian can achieve a truly wholistic perspective on the role of material possessions and sensual pleasures in a balanced life. That is, she can come to understand that possessions and pleasures contribute important experiences, but are not to be clung to as ultimate values for there is nothing truly lasting about either.

Neptune in the Third House

With Neptune in the third house, an individual may be the personification of confusion. The issue is that with the planet of ultimate values in the house of the mind, the mind and mental faculties become an extremely important facet of life. As often occurs with Neptune, however, there can be a strong but unconscious expectation that everything desired, in this case mental processes, will flow with ease, without any effort. Consequently the person may feel it is simply wrong to impose any discipline on his thinking processes, that they are meant to simply flow and shift.

HIGHLY IMAGINATIVE

Such an attitude leads to a double-edged sword. On the positive side there can be a tremendous talent for getting in conscious (third house) touch with unconscious beliefs and attitudes (Neptune). This may happen quite spontaneously through dreams or simply in the course of the continuous flow of thoughts experienced day to day. This individual's imagination is rich and varied, very creative. He may, through his daydreams, get in touch with personal truths and come up with some wonderful insights. He may also, if there are other factors in the chart indicating the ability to apply discipline in at least some area of life, be able to use his active imagination for creative inspiration in books, plays, music, or similar media.

This Neptunian can usually make up wonderful stories on the spur of the moment. He may write them down or simply tell them to others. He has a natural talent for visualization which makes it easy for him to see how something he conceives of would look in reality. He often fails to communicate his conceptions to others, however. Sometimes he feels they lose too much in the translation, but usually he simply assumes that others can pick up on his impressions and there is no need to communicate. This can lead others to seriously underestimate his talent.

Such people often love fairy tales, fantasy stories, myths, television and movies. He may feel overwhelmed by events on the big screen, however, being so open that he becomes profoundly involved in the story. If he doesn't like the ending, he may rewrite the script to his own satisfaction for days afterward!

MENTAL DRIFTING
On the negative side, he may simply drift aimlessly, at the mercy of the prolific spontaneous flow of thoughts, impressions, ideas and feelings. He may find it extremely difficult to concentrate, lacking the conviction that to do so is important. In fact, he may have the conviction that to concentrate is to cut off the very flow which he values so highly. On one level, he is unable or unwilling to cut himself off from outside impressions, yet he may also be an inattentive listener, for anything can distract him, including the latest thought to pop into his head. He may often seem to be, and in fact is, living in his own little world.

His ability to make up fantasy stories may slide into an inability to distinguish between his imagination and reality. Sometimes he knows the difference but cannot seem to help trying to dress the situation up to make it more attractive. Sometimes he simply changes his perceptions around in his own mind to avoid difficulties. Other people may label him a liar for his efforts.

PROJECTION
If Neptune is projected in this house, there is a tendency to see the above qualities in brothers, sisters and close neighbors. These people will seem to be very spiritual, or artistic, or committed to helping other people, or simply vague, unreliable and ineffective, perhaps as outright victims. They may seem confused or unable to see life as it really is, or as gentle and sweet souls.

With Neptune in the third house, the individual needs to make a careful assessment of his tendency to retreat into illusions and delusions. He needs to look at his ability to create fantasy and ask himself if he is hiding out in his make-believe world. He needs to look at the illusions which surround his use of his mental faculties and processes, as well as his brothers, sisters and close neighbors. This Neptunian has the extremely valuable ability to integrate the conscious and unconscious mind. He can make a great psychologist or counselor if he can achieve verbal clarity about the contents of his own unconscious. He can bring to the world a sense of wonder, fantasy and he can fire other people's imaginations with the glorious possibilities he reveals in his stories. He can communicate his inspirations to those in need of illumination, a blessed talent indeed.

Neptune in the Fourth House

This position is a loaded one: an unconscious planet in an unconscious house. Furthermore, it is the house of our most basic and essential emotional security needs. Usually we look to Mother to provide these, so she and the needs all get tangled up with a vague sense of ultimate importance. There may be no easier place to have all our fondest dreams and wishes smashed to smithereens, for with Neptune the needs are vitally important and frequently beyond the ability of a mere human to fulfill.

PERFECT SECURITY
With Neptune in the fourth, the need to feel safe in a secure nest is fundamental. However it is also quite likely unconscious. The person's idea of heaven includes an impregnable home, lots of food and someone around who will take care of her. In the fourth

house we tend to want to feel like a baby and to be taken care of like a baby. With Neptune there, it is all supposed to happen by magic. Furthermore, it can be accepted as our "Divine Right" to have all this.

There can easily be an unexamined assumption that mother, early home life and emotional security needs will all be perfect. That is, all needs will be met with ease, all needs will be in harmony with the general flow of life and there will be no need for upset or disappointment. Mother, or the parent who gives the most emotional care, is supposed to be there when needed, regardless of other commitments.

With Neptune, of course, there are illusions which must be exposed and released. The illusions connected with the fourth house are deeply intimate and any threat to them is profoundly threatening to the individual. She may successfully defend them throughout life because to challenge them is too painful to contemplate. She may go to extraordinary lengths to preserve her images, carefully failing to see any flaws or failures.

Neptune in the fourth generally has to overcome the strong need for the nurturing parent to be not only perfect but to continue to provide the perfect surroundings. This Neptunian has great difficulty separating from the nurturing parent; it may never be fully completed. It makes little difference if the actual parent lived up to her expectations, for this Neptunian can put equal importance on the parent in her head— the parent she wished for or imagined to exist. There is a tendency for the individual to go around with a despondent air because ordinary humans cannot live up to her expectations, so she feels continually disappointed.

Sometimes the Neptunian desire for perfection focuses on the home rather than the parent. In this case, there may have been an idyllic childhood home situation, or it may have been mysterious and elusive. The adult can react by trying to create or re-create the perfect nest. Anyone with Neptune in the fourth house will need to examine her strong need for harmony, beauty and fulfillment in the home. Kept in perspective, it can lead to the creation of a beautiful home with a peaceful, loving atmosphere. An important part of this can be the preparation of one particular room for the Neptunian to use as a retreat. Overemphasized, it can lead to a home where an all-pervasive spirituality and a kind of magical-love are expected, to the exclusion of all else.

IDEALIZED NURTURING

With Neptune in the fourth, nurturing itself may become an ultimate value, a way to find sublime satisfaction. Some individuals will keep this in balance, many will not. Those who do will take care to do their nurturing where it will actually be of benefit. They can make the most sensitive of caretakers, nurses and companions. Those whose need to nurture others is a convoluted expression of their own hunger to be taken care of will often give too much to others; eventually they become resentful because no one appreciates their sacrifices.

Those who repress the need to nurture or be nurtured will tend to project, to see and find strong and perhaps overwhelming Neptunian traits in their nurturing parent. Such a parent could be very spiritual and loving, or vague and confused, or even be absent, so that the individual is left with only a fantasy of what that parent could— and should— have been like, or the parent could be a victim, whom the individual feels obliged to try to save. This can range from the person who wants the parent to take more exercise, more vitamins, to stop smoking and so on, to the person with an alcoholic or otherwise self-destructive parent.

With Neptune in the fourth house, the individual needs to take a long hard look at her tendency to have illusions in regard to her own mother or nurturing parent, to being a parent herself, to children and babies and to the whole issue of nurturance. She will tend to feel that caring somehow involves being swallowed up completely, and this may be something she yearns for or is terrified of. She will also tend to feel that if her emotional security needs, which are often unrealistic, are not met, she cannot survive the disappointment. While it can be frightening beyond belief for this person to confront her assumptions about what she must have in order to feel fulfilled, she will find her life a great deal more satisfying if she can do so, for she will be living according to realistic values rather than mysterious ones.

This Neptunian can make the most patient and loving of parents, one with a strong sense of emotional bonding and yet one who will remain aware of her spiritual responsibilities as a parent. She may do more to create an ideal parent/baby relationship than anyone else, and can serve to remind others of how important it is to strive to do the best for children that we can. She also has the ability to create a spiritually nurturing atmosphere for others, perhaps in her own home, but also in their homes, as well.

Neptune in the Fifth House

Neptune has a depth of receptivity which is quite startling to experience, especially in this modern Western culture where we so often keep others at an emotional distance. The fifth house is also deeply emotional, but this tends to be in an outgoing way. The combination often leads to a definite charisma, an aura of great charm and power and importance. It is one of the stronger indications that a person has acting ability, though this may be used as a teacher or salesperson rather than on the stage.

NEEDS AN AUDIENCE
Neptune and the fifth house share creative abilities, so this is another combination which emphasizes some kind of creative talent. While Neptune in the second is likely to express itself in music, gardening or art, the fifth house tends to indicate a strong need to be noticed and admired for creative abilities and attempts. This Neptunian is more likely to work with video or on stage or in the classroom or in some other area where the applause and respect can be immediate and can also be experienced personally. He needs this; often the unconscious Neptunian focus on the need to transcend this world undermines his self-confidence and self-esteem so that he depends on feedback from others to measure his worth. This can be a deadly dependency because even the highest praise and respect from others can never truly fulfill the yearning he experiences to be loved absolutely. They can only provide a temporary uplift. The individual remains forever vulnerable.

With Neptune in the fifth, a person needs to closely and honestly examine his illusions regarding love, children, creativity and his own self-esteem and ego. This is one of the positions especially susceptible to ego-annihilation, the determination to eradicate the "sinful" ego which was discussed in Chapter Two. Such people tend to become terribly self-absorbed as they watch themselves for any sign of ego, and end up more egotistical and self-important than if they simply accepted their membership in the human race along with the rest of us.

Some of the illusions associated with a fifth house Neptune include the need to have perfect love relationships, perfect children and to always have the perfect artistic creation. Whenever someone expects perfection in the outer world he is doomed to disappointment, although the process of disillusionment may cause him to rethink his outlook. He may need to realize that he needs to let go of some of his more demanding and destructive dreams and expectations.

FULFILLMENT IN LOVE
With Neptune in the fifth, the individual may expect lovers or love relationships to provide a complete sense of fulfillment. The person with this placement can make a very romantic partner, the type who loves candlelight dinners and mood music, who can surround the object of his love with an atmosphere of pervasive love. However he may expect his girlfriend or lover to sense his wishes and to be willing to meet them. Or he may expect himself to be sensitive, caring and receptive at all times, regardless of his own mood and/or needs. He may look for a girlfriend who is completely open to him and willing to give him absolute, perfect and always harmonious love. He may suffer disappointment and disillusionment as lady after lady fails to live up to his image of the perfect lover, or brings out a side of him he can't reconcile with his expectations of love.

Sometimes all this happens with children— the individual might expect his children to be passive, peaceable, serene and patient. He may expect himself to be this way with his children, and it is a distinct likelihood that he will have trouble dealing with issues of anger and discipline with his children. He may value them so highly that he loses his perspective on what they are really like, or he may need them to be perfect so that he feels important and well-regarded.

Since Neptune represents issues which are frequently unconscious, all these attitudes may operate without the individual's awareness.

PROJECTION
If projected, the negative aspects of Neptune tend to become more emphasized. With a lover, the individual might be looking for a lady who is spiritual or magical, inspirational or creative,

or someone "really special"— a princess or goddess he can love, and yet find himself with women who take too many pills, or who can't seem to get their lives together, women who are constantly sick, who are mentally ill or unbalanced, or who dedicate themselves to strange religions. The more the individual denies Neptune expression in his own life, the more likely it is that he will meet it in exaggerated guises outside of himself.

Projected onto children, it is possible to have artistically talented children, children who are more inclined to follow a spiritual path than the parent, or children who have a marked ability to counsel and inspire others. It is also possible to have children who slide into drugs and alcohol, or who are sickly and weak or mentally unbalanced, children who have a great deal of difficulty distinguishing between reality and their imagination, children who use denial as a defense against the world, and so on.

The individual with Neptune in the fifth house really needs to examine closely and honestly his beliefs regarding his creative pursuits and how they reflect on him. He needs to look at his tendency to romanticize girlfriends rather than see them for who they are, and to romanticize love and love affairs in general. He may harbor illusions about all children, or about his own children in particular, illusions which hamper his ability to deal with them realistically and effectively. He may have difficulty developing a strong sense of self-worth, or fancy himself as far more important than others see him. This placement is associated with a great deal of inspired creativity, however, and may, if other chart factors support it, indicate exceptional artistic talent in some field. With humility and self-awareness, an individual with Neptune in the fifth can use his magnetism to uplift those who have lost all confidence. He can balance his tendency to see the best— and perhaps only the best— in others with his natural ability to inspire them to actually develop what he sees, to become the best they can be.

Neptune in the Sixth House

In this house, Neptune is, in a sense, in a place which is its polar opposite. That is, the sixth house relates to Virgo, which is the polar opposite of Pisces, the sign associated with Neptune. The polarity, and the fact that it is not actually an opposite but two different sides of the same coin, shows up clearly with Neptune in the sixth. It is a house of detailed work, of productivity, of nose-to-the-grindstone, of doing a good job for the simple sake of doing a good job. Above all, the sixth house is about the world as it is and how to manage that and work with that on a day-to-day basis.

Neptunian energy seems so totally different: it seeps into the path of least resistance, undermines its opposition, yearns for and hopefully seeks to be united with and absorbed by God, or by some Cosmic Consciousness which transcends this petty world. How can these two ever find a point of cooperation?

Neptune and the sixth house do share some common points, however. Both pertain to health, and to an attitude of service, of somehow doing something to help one's fellow human beings.

INTEGRATION IS POSSIBLE
When Neptune and the sixth house themes are integrated, the individual can dream the dream of Neptune and also use the practical sixth house skills to plan and organize the details which will make the dream a reality someday. Without such plans, the dream is just that: a potential, an inspired idea with no basis in reality. The sixth house can direct and focus the Neptune ability to envision something better, something prettier, something more creative and inspiring. Without the dreams of Neptune, the sixth house is merely a housekeeping unit— a drive to organize and plan and weed out the inefficiencies, but for what purpose? Neptune supplies the purpose and the sixth house supplies the know-how and practical skills.

Neptune in the sixth often relates to some kind of artistic creative work. The sixth house and tenth house both relate to work, but the tenth indicates more ambition and more interest in an important career than the sixth, especially one where some kind of power can be wielded. The sixth is concerned with somewhat more mundane jobs. Neptune in the sixth tends to find expression as commercial artists, hairdressers, beauty make-over consultants, makeup artists, practical nurses and so on. These people are certainly expressing Neptunian themes in their work.

CONFLICT PULLS APART

When Neptune is at odds with the sixth house energies, there can be quite a struggle between the need to dream, to let matters flow and ebb, and the need to be realistic and practical. The individual may feel a strong need to busy herself with details and to make every thing and every process as efficient as possible, including tidying up or at least criticizing people. Coworkers are especially likely targets. The Neptunian need for flowing harmony and ease and grace gets trodden underfoot. Or she may use the Neptune need for perfection in her assessment of her work— does she do it perfectly, with harmony and beauty and ease? She may expect far too much of herself, or never be able to say "no" when more work is piled on her.

Another expression of an out-of-balance Neptune in the sixth is when the individual cannot keep work situations and environments straight. She may forget, be habitually untidy and disorganized, feel tired and drained of energy, get sick a lot or feel vaguely unfulfilled. She may have sought her job for its glamorous aspects, only to get swamped by the details and drudgery. She may have been very unrealistic about what the job was going to provide in terms of wages, attention or emotional satisfaction. She may spend a great deal of her time and energy "rescuing" others: taking on extra work, listening to coworkers and getting behind in her work, shielding a poorly performing coworker because she feels sorry for her and so on.

PROJECTION

Sometimes this is projected, in which case employees or co-workers can display any or all of the range of Neptunian behaviors. If an individual who has Neptune in the sixth constantly ends up with coworkers who have all the artistic talent, or who are "rescuers," who are overly sensitive, who can't focus on the important issues, who are frequently late, or careless, or forgetful, or in poor health, it is definitely time to get in touch with Neptune and to learn to express it personally and positively. Sometimes an out-of-touch Neptune is associated with peculiar events such as floods, which is a physical expression of Neptune and a signal that it is time to come to terms with this aspect of human nature and to integrate it into the personality.

A person with Neptune in the sixth needs to challenge her

beliefs about work, coworkers, service to others, and possibly about the need to straighten and correct everything or everyone she encounters. She needs to check out her illusions regarding all of these issues for she may have some unrealistic expectations which lead to a great deal of dissatisfaction. Or she may be projecting Neptune and find it turns up in her coworkers. This position carries the potential, however, for integration of a polarity, for bringing two seemingly opposite sides of life into cooperative harmony. If the Neptune side can come to value the reliability and productivity of the sixth house, and if the sixth house side can learn to appreciate the visions of Neptune, then both can unite to produce realistic dreams or practical health care, or both.

Neptune in the Seventh House or Eighth House

This is another one of those "loaded" positions, because these are the most likely houses from which to project planetary energies, and Neptune, a transpersonal planet, is not easily welcomed into one's personal repertoire, thus making it an excellent candidate for projection. The result is that Neptune in either the seventh or eighth houses is most often not expressed personally but must be dealt with, at least initially, as if it comes from someone else. The usual and most likely someone else is the spouse, that special person whom we promise to love for better and for worse. The "worse" definitely includes the special agony of projection when we are married to some of our own least comfortable traits.

ARTISTIC EMPHASIS
On the positive side, Neptune in the seventh is another of the artistic combinations. This one may lean particularly toward graphic arts, but any avenue of artistic expression is possible. It is especially positive if spouses can both be artistic, and particularly if they can share this without letting competitiveness spoil it. However, it is most important for the person with Neptune in the seventh to find an artistic outlet for otherwise it is easy to project and expect the spouse to be wonderfully artistic and creative, whether she wishes to be so or not.

WARMLY INTIMATE

Neptune in the seventh or eighth house is an excellent combination for counseling potential. Neptune in the seventh or eighth can be attuned to others on a deep emotional level which may even be psychic. There is an inherent talent for psychological studies and for the ability to share innermost thoughts and feelings.

It is often quite natural for a person with this placement to be at ease with emotional intimacy, with closeness and with a feeling of connectedness. In many cases, Neptune in the seventh or eighth expresses itself as a naturally strong valuation on close, warm relationships, and the individual will feel motivated to create and sustain such relationships. Again, if only one spouse wishes to pursue this, it is most important that it be the one with Neptune in these houses. It is his need; it is up to him to fulfill it. The partner will, however, need to acknowledge that this is a vitally important part of the individual's life, and will need to share at least some part of it with him.

SPIRITUAL NEEDS IMPORTANT

Another positive expression of Neptune in the seventh or eighth is when spouses share a spiritual quest. They may read and study together, meditate together or support each other in exploration of occult concepts or in deep inner seeking. At any time, one may be more heavily involved, but the other is willing to give sincere support and to share and perhaps to contribute to discoveries. This is one case where a single spouse is not likely to be able to do it all. As one learns and grows and changes, the dynamics of the relationship will change. The partner who is not involved in the growth will be terribly threatened by this and usually seeks to stop the changes, which means undermining or blocking the growth. This rarely works, however, since most people, having once seen a richer way to live, cannot go back. Unless both partners have some say in how the dynamics change, or both agree to keep it the same, the relationship usually grinds to a halt.

PROJECTION A SPECIAL DANGER

Being so prone to projection, the negative possibilities for Neptune in the seventh or eighth are legion. Most obvious is the expectation that one will have a perfect mate, or a perfect marriage, or that one is perfect in the marriage. With Neptune in these houses the individual tends to really buy into the Walt Disney stories of the princess and the handsome, rescuing prince, and the way they supposedly lived "happily ever after." Neptune loves a good rescue(r). Neptune also loves a good fantasy. This can simply work out as a very romantic streak, with a deep and abiding trust in the partner, but it may develop into a full-fledged expectation that the mate will fulfill all the individual's deepest needs, will provide unconditional love and support under all circumstances, and will be charming and lovely at all times. This is not exaggerated. One well-known psychologist has written about the shock and utter disappointment he experienced the first time he saw his new bride blow her nose!

Such blind faith in the ability of the partner to be the embodiment of all that is beautiful and delightful is an illusion. It is an invitation to frustration for both partners. The one with the expectations, unwritten of course, will feel betrayed when the mate starts to look distressingly human and capable of obnoxious behavior. The mate will feel the burden of the partner's expectations and feels responsible for letting down the partner. Yet this feels unfair because usually the behavior which has disappointed the partner so much was something minor. The strange truth is that Neptunian partners are often amazingly noble and forgiving over the major incidents which break up many marriages, yet are unable to tolerate day-to-day differences and disappointments with any degree of grace.

CLINGING TO THE ILLUSION

Some Neptunian partners manage to maintain the illusion of the perfect partner, often in the face of an astounding amount of evidence to the contrary. They will overlook ignorant behavior, make excuses for immaturity, protect a weak mate, and generally do whatever is necessary to protect their image of their mate. This may be motivated by a need to have a perfect mate, no matter what the cost, or it may be the result of the Neptunian ability to see the best in others. Often both dynamics are at work. The individual with Neptune in the seventh or eighth who is protecting such an illusion will not give it up until ready to do so on her own. Usually the mate's behavior has to clash violently with some other cherished value before the Neptunian partner begins to see the problem.

A SPECIAL AGONY

It is worth mentioning that the Neptunian who faces the cracking pieces of this illusion suffers a particularly terrible inner pain. It can be survived, **if** the Neptunian can acknowledge that **he** built the illusion personally. Otherwise he is likely to feel forever betrayed and become bitter, hopeless and miserable. If the illusion can be seen as a personally constructed fib-to-the-self, the Neptunian can grieve for the lost dream, can rage at the unfairness of it all and at his own foolishness, and can then let go of it. After a time, peace will settle and the Neptunian can begin to get to know the person he married and to reconstruct a relationship, this time based on honesty.

CHOOSE GOD OPENLY

One constructive choice for the individual who simply cannot give up on the need for a perfect partner, perfect devotion, perfect union and so on, is devotion to the ultimate partner: God. This can be achieved through the ministry, priesthood or sisterhood, or through missionary service. It is a choice which needs to be carefully considered, however, for it is all too easy for Neptune to be overwhelmingly drawn to such a life without consideration for the individual's more worldly needs. On the other hand, some people find that with the devotion to a life of service, pressure is taken off their need for a perfect mate and they can approach relationships with more compassion and acceptance of the human condition. Then again, some simply become more committed to otherworldly perfection and are less able to accept human foibles and differences in needs.

VICTIM/SAVIOR TENDENCIES

With Neptune in the seventh or eighth, there are all sorts of possibilities for the victim/savior game to be played. The Neptunian with a strong chart will usually try the savior role, which means a victim is required. This is a semiconscious procedure; few people deliberately saddle themselves with a frustrating burden. The savior usually simply falls in love with someone who seems so deliciously vulnerable and needy, someone who just needs a little propping up here and there in order to be perfect. Only when the illusion begins to crack does the savior see that the struggling actress wrecks her chances for success with her addiction to drugs; that the talented singer blows his auditions by refusing to cooperate with managers; that the inspired writer won't stick to deadlines; that the sweet, vulnerable creature who is too gentle and loving to hurt anyone is a walking time bomb of repressed anger just waiting to get into another accident; that the charming, childlike waif is determined to remain helpless and actually manages to avoid a great deal of unpleasant responsibility.

Eventually, under the burden of relationships with such victims, the potential savior often becomes a martyr. Many a sickly, bedridden spouse has outlived her caretaker mate!

The Neptunian with a less strong chart will often choose the victim role. Again, the choice is unconscious. Usually the chosen role looks romantic or spiritually worthwhile to the Neptunian, who only wants to create a loving and perfect world. The pitfalls are not apparent ahead of time. The choice which looks like one of sweetness and Christian generosity of spirit may lead to dangerous repression of personal needs and the resultant illnesses, lack of energy, or accidents. The repressed energy is bottled up and the god or goddess is angered— the energy turns inward. The choice which looks like one of loving sacrifice for a troubled partner may well lead to an abusive relationship. The choice which looks like dedication to an ideal may well turn out to be an evasion of worldly responsibilities which is motivated by fear.

HEALTHY POSSIBILITIES
The victim/savior relationship is not always unhealthy. In counseling relationships, hopefully the counselor has enough training, experience and mental stability to gradually empower the client to grow out of the victim role. In marriage, this is extremely difficult to accomplish, although it can be done. It requires that at least one partner be psychologically and spiritually very aware, very patient and very, very strong. Each partner must be willing to take responsibility for his/her own behavior, attitudes and beliefs, be able and willing to grow and to interpret pain as a measure of change which is needed, not a measure of the partner's failure. This very difficult path can only succeed when the roles are alternated to some degree— in other words, each partner takes a turn as savior and a turn as victim, until both can leave these roles behind.

In short it is an extremely difficult path and it is **not** recommended. People who need help usually benefit most from a helping relationship with a professional, or at least with someone with whom they are not in love. The helper inevitably becomes the target of the "victim's" anger and frustration at some point, which is extremely destructive in mate relationships. Few mates, especially Neptunian ones, can understand why they get continually punished, verbally attacked and emotionally blackmailed when all they offered was loving help. They expect loving gratitude but generally end up with a rare fury directed at them, as the "victims" lash out in fear and agony at the people who are "forcing" them to change.

When an individual has Neptune in the seventh or eighth houses, he will need to become conscious of his illusions regarding marriage, his partner, his own role and the satisfactions which are possible from a marriage. He will almost certainly tend to expect too much, and may place unrealistic burdens upon his mate. He will need to be alert for the appearance of savior/victim games in his close relationships, games which can lead to abuse and an unimaginable kind of hell. He will need to take responsibility for his own spiritual and creative needs, and to take steps to express them for himself, rather than wishing the mate would provide the experience. He will also need to take responsibility for the strength and importance of his need to have a mate who can share or at least value and honor his needs for spiritual growth, artistic expression, psychological exploration or all of the above.

EIGHTH HOUSE LESS CONSCIOUS
Neptune in the eighth house is more deeply unconscious than Neptune in the seventh. Again this is a water planet in a water house. With water comes the strong possibility of insecurity; with insecurity comes the strong possibility of strange behaviors designed to help the individual cope with needs so uncomfortable they cannot be permitted to become conscious. In the eighth house, planetary urges often have the feel of being "taboo" in some way which is deeply buried. That is, the individual feels the behavior is forbidden, feels guilty for considering it, usually pushes it away from conscious awareness yet when questioned, cannot say why. It is not that the answers, when uncovered, are really all that dreadful, but that they **feel** dreadful to the individual, and therefore avoidance and evasion seem to be the only safe ways to cope.

CAREFUL EXPLORATION NEEDED

The individual with Neptune in the eighth house will need to carefully explore her attitudes toward sexuality, shared money and shared possessions, and emotional power. Carefully, because in the eighth house issues are nearly always buried in layers, and many of the layers are "red herrings," false hints designed to lead the explorer away from tender areas. It may take professional help to dig into some of the issues, because an objective outsider can often ask important questions which the explorer's mind prefers to hide from. She may discover she expects too much from eighth house issues, or that she gives too much away. She may avoid them due to feeling overwhelmed, an indication that far too much value is placed there. She will need to learn how to continually bring into consciousness her inner values in order to gain freedom from their domination.

The individual with Neptune in the seventh or eighth houses, however, possesses a rare talent for intimacy, perception and insight into others—including the ability to fathom their pain, and the ability to inspire the partner to develop spiritually. With acceptance of personal responsibility for emotional, artistic or spiritual fulfillment, all of these can be shared with a mate to create a truly special relationship with rich rewards for both partners.

Neptune in the Ninth House

Neptune is the planet of ultimate emotional, unconscious values, and the ninth house is one of the keys to our belief systems, and our partly conscious values. Both relate to issues and ideas that we accept as extremely important, perhaps vitally so, in our lives, often without awareness or examination. Sometimes even when we know what is an ultimate value for ourselves, we don't see the implications of that value, the way it affects our perceptions, judgments and decisions. As was discussed in Chapter One, ultimate values can dominate our lives without our ever questioning their veracity. This tendency is doubled when Neptune is in the ninth house, which is associated with a strong tendency to jump to conclusions and to assume that the conclusions are correct.

MANY SIMILARITIES LEAD TO INFLATION

With both Neptune and the ninth house tendencies to need the **right** answer, there is a strong possibility here of an enduring search for Truth. Both planet and house are mutable, leading to restlessness. Both are considered expansive; they tend to enlarge whatever they are associated with. In combination this means there might be no accepted limits— everything can continue to expand (ninth house) into infinity (Neptune). Both are connected to faith, and beliefs. Both are drawn to ever more comprehensive and idealistic viewpoints. Both are drawn to and haunted by the need for perfection, by their often fantastic expectations. Neither is noted for its common sense, nor its ability to do anything by half-measures.

Ninth house issues such as higher education, organized religion, philosophy, and a lifelong search for bigger and better truth could all become ultimate values with Neptune in this position. Often, with a chart otherwise leaning toward physical energy, athletics will become a driving force in the individual's life. The important point is that with Neptune in the ninth, the person will have a strong tendency to greatly overemphasize whatever area or issues that are valued. What is valued is strongly valued, defended and expected to be **right**.

DIFFERENCES CAUSE INNER CONFLICTS

On the natural wheel, Pisces (Neptune) and Sagittarius (ninth house) are square each other, indicating some fundamental differences which must be consciously worked upon in order to integrate these disparate energies. Neptune in the ninth house mixes a water planet with a fire house, a combination that is associated with a particularly high degree of emotional intensity. The receptive, inward-drawing and sensitive, overprotective nature of Neptune can definitely clash with the persuasive, outward-reaching, spirited and adventurous nature of the ninth house.

Neptune operates on emotional and spiritual planes. The person who expresses Neptune wants to follow his instincts, his psychic impulses, the dictates of his heart. He **feels** what is best. The ninth house relates to these but often stays on intellectual, rational-thought levels, at least on the surface. A person who expresses the ninth house may partially bury feelings so that he is free to follow the most logical idea, and in the process he will come up with some convincing rationalizations. He will also frequently react with self-righteous anger if it is pointed out that he has merely found logical reasons for doing what he **feels** is right, but that the feeling came before the logic!

The person who follows the dictates of the ninth house will often tell the truth regardless of who gets hurt. The person who flows with Neptune will prefer to protect others' feelings and may choose to lie out of kindheartedness, misdirected or otherwise. The person who has Neptune in the ninth may be pulled in both directions and will need to find either a middle ground to satisfy the need for truth and the need for mercy, or a place for each. He will need to be alert to situations where he is pulled between what he wants to do— feelings— and between what he ought or should do— thoughts. The dictates of the head and the heart can both be questioned. Out of the challenge may come some clear insights about the best course of action.

EMOTIONAL PRESSURE

When a water/fire combination occurs, there is always the possibility that the water element will dampen or drown the fire. Water represents the unconscious, therefore it also can represent the tendency toward repression. When it is fire that is repressed, there is a buildup of emotional pressure. Unless the pressure is released, sooner or later there will be an explosion. The person can feel shattered by such an occurrence, which often seems "out of character." Yet when seen as the release of energy which has been held in for months or years, the blowup only makes sense. To prevent such events, the individual needs to make all possible efforts to get in touch with inner drives and needs which are being ignored or held in. Then those needs are to be directed into some constructive outlet. Few drives in life are truly "bad;" they usually only look that way because they seem to run counter to the dictates of the dominant value system. Once a person becomes conscious of his dominant values, he can choose when it is appropriate to act according to different values; in other words, he will allow contradictory sides of his nature all to have room for expression.

VALUES TEND TO DOMINATE

Whatever is put on a pedestal, it is likely, in the ninth house, to be overdone, to be allowed to dominate the life, and many other issues will take second or third place. This can be hard on jobs, relationships and other ambitions. With Neptune in the ninth house, the individual will need to take a look at his illusions about the ability of education, knowledge or the endless search to provide the ultimate satisfaction in life.

There will be an important need to examine personal values, to see if too much unquestioning faith has unconsciously been placed in the creation of some sort of perfect ethereal beauty, in service to others without regard to self, in psychic or psychological insights, or in spiritual or mystical growth. There are also the negative possibilities, that abiding and deep trust has been placed in evasion, denial, pretense, confusion, drugs, alcohol or illness to protect the individual from whatever he does not wish to deal with consciously.

BALANCE

Balance is an important lesson for someone who has Neptune in the ninth. The temptation will nearly always be to go overboard on the latest exciting idea. The challenge is to learn to act on those ideas where it is practical and possible without dangerous disruption to other meaningful aspects of life. It is possible to chase one's dreams without immediately resigning from the job that one has worked toward for fifteen years, for example, or without selling all of one's possessions and giving the proceeds to a wonderful new religious organization.

HONESTY

Honesty is another important lesson for someone with this placement. Neptune is the stuff of which dreams are made, and the ninth house is always looking for a better idea, the bigger the better. Both are therefore very susceptible to wild tales and con games. More to the point, both have strong tendencies toward self-delusion over the importance and veracity of the most newly discovered "truth" or viewpoint. Philosophies easily become religions and challenging questions soon become sins, yet even this process can be rationalized and strangely enough, denied. If, however, the person with Neptune in the ninth can exploit his earth planets to keep in touch with what is realistic, and his air planets to keep some objectivity, he can become a genuinely spiritual student, a dedicated and ardent seeker of the truth, with ever more important understandings that he can share with others.

With Neptune in the ninth, it is particularly important for the individual to examine his personal beliefs, conscious and unconscious. He needs to clarify his expectations about truth, philosophy and the meaning of life. He needs to confront his values and his illusions, to be rigorously alert to righteous justification of ideas or feelings and to ensure that he is honest in his musings. With humility, this individual can be the most enthusiastic proponent of positive philosophies, an inspirational force with unflagging energy and a person who always balances the need for truth with the need for compassion.

Neptune in the Tenth House

This connects the issues of father— or conditional love parent— and career with the ultimate values. Both are going to be extremely important in the individual's life, whether positively or negatively.

CAREER FULFILLMENT
Positively, the person with Neptune in the tenth can be drawn into a deeply spiritual or very creative career, or a career having something to do with counseling, or with the sea, or with chemicals, gases, liquids and so on. She would likely be inclined to dedicate a great deal of her time and energy to her chosen career because it would provide such a tremendous sense of fulfillment, something she couldn't match in other areas of life. For this person, the rest of her life would have to revolve around her vocation. As long as she is aware of her choice, and as long as she makes the effort to cultivate some personal relationships and some outside interests, she will stay balanced. She would tend to be happiest when working, and would not even consider it "work," at least not in the sense of "toil." For her work would equal satisfaction of the highest kind, yet there would be other satisfactions available to her.

A PLACE IN THE GRAND SCHEME

It is possible, with Neptune in the tenth, to have a quiet sense of timelessness with regard to one's career. That is, the individual may feel that she has a responsibility to contribute something meaningful to the world, whether that is in terms of helping others or of creativity. This will be important to her yet she will at the same time feel that her contribution is just that, a contribution. She will have a sense that her work is necessary, that it has a place in the grand scheme of things, yet she will not harbor illusions about the special importance of her particular efforts. This individual is most likely to keep her career in balance with the rest of the variety of life experiences.

AMBITION MAY TAKE OVER

For many, Neptune in the tenth is expressed as an unconscious value placed on a life career. A person living at this level will simply be a great deal happier when she has a job, but she will also need to feel she is doing something to create improvements. She will be ambitious, whether or not she is aware of it. She will have an eye open for the possibility of promotion, for the tenth house relates not only to career but to success as defined in worldly terms. That usually means she will have an unconscious need to gain more and more, in position, status and in salary. If this remains unconscious, there is the possibility of career ambition and expectations taking over her life.

ULTIMATE FULFILLMENT EXPECTED

This position holds the danger of illusions surrounding career, and the satisfactions it can provide. Neptune seeks the ultimate satisfaction, the ultimate high, but the tenth house focus is in a limited and limiting area. Few people can find a lifetime of satisfaction in their career unless it is spiritual, educational or artistic/creative. The problem is that with Neptune in the tenth, the individual unconsciously or half-consciously **expects** the tenth house activities to provide this ultimate sense of fulfillment. Heaven is a job. Somehow the job is going to make the individual perfectly happy. This leads her to pour her energy into her job, as she happily assumes her whole life will be rosy and flow smoothly as long as she does so. It is an assumption she may never question.

Naturally her personal relationships suffer, yet she may

simply turn more energy into her career, as it seems to offer the happiness she seeks.

The negative extreme is the person who cannot find any satisfaction or enjoyment in life or in any activity except those directly related to her job. Such a person lives for her job, and expects it to provide for all her needs, physical, mental, emotional and spiritual. She may expect the job itself to be perfect in terms of salary, employees, working conditions or boss, and be miserable when it is not.

UNABLE TO RETIRE

Sooner or later retirement looms, and the person with Neptune in the tenth may be unprepared. She may tend to wish away the idea of eventual retirement, refusing to deal with it realistically. Productivity, so important with Neptune in the tenth, has become a "god." She cannot envision life without a job for her life has been unbalanced for so long. As retirement advances upon her, she faces a choice: rebalance or continue to feed the illusion. She may feed the illusion by switching allegiance—volunteer work may beckon; at least this choice will keep her physically healthy and happy. She may feed the illusion by simple refusal to rebalance, to foster interests in other pursuits, yet be unable to replace one job with another. In this case she is likely to live in misery, either wallowing in memories or retreating into illness and opting out of any life but the one she has vested with such value.

NO ORDINARY WORK WILL DO

Another negative expression is that of continual confusion and indecision regarding a career. The individual may be unable to commit to any direction whatever. She wants to do something big and important, something perfect, something more wonderfully artistic or inspirational or of more help to humanity than anything anyone else has ever come up with. Yet she often wants to accomplish this without any training or effort. While she can't find the way to magically make it happen, she may be unwilling to settle for the ordinary.

With Neptune we tend to either dissolve the trappings of the world or to invest them with imaginary importance. The tenth house relates to the use of worldly power. Neptune in the tenth is a statement that the individual could tend to cloud this issue in unconsciousness or fantasy. It is a statement of the need to get clear about the role and use of power, on a personal level and on worldly levels.

FATHER MODELED NEPTUNIAN BEHAVIOR

Father would have provided an early example of some possible Neptunian behaviors and attitudes. Positively, he could have been a person who was very spiritual, loving and visionary. He could have had artistic or musical talent and been able to discipline it and direct it, he could have been a caring, giving person who had a talent for helping others in practical ways, or he might have been simply gentle and peaceful and sweet-natured, yet able to make a satisfying life for himself. If he provided a positive model of how to express Neptune in the tenth, he would have been able to integrate his values and beliefs with the real world. The individual could think the world of her father, and wish to be like him.

Negatively, she may have expected father to be perfect. If she still thinks he is/was, she may have put him on a pedestal and cannot tolerate any inference that he is less than wonderful. She may copy his attitudes and ideas without question because she has to keep alive the illusion that he is/was everything she needed.

If father disappointed her, she may have felt bitterly hurt and disillusioned. She may have come to terms with reality and forgiven him or she may have clung to her belief that he **should** have been perfect.

Father may be a strange and perhaps mysterious figure. He may be very withdrawn, either through inability to cope with the world or through a desire to simply be left to his own inner workings. He may have gone missing altogether, and the individual is left with only a fantasy figure, a father who exists only in her own mind. The temptation is then to build up this fantasy father, to see him as bigger and better than anyone else. The individual may even have entertained notions about one day being rescued by him.

Father could also have manifested all that is unhappiest about Neptune: alcoholism, drug-addiction, chronic mental or physical illness, fatally weak character, or all of the above.

The flowing nature of Neptune can actually benefit greatly from the discipline and form offered by the tenth house. If the individual can accept these skills, Neptune's gifts are more easily translated into forms the world can understand and appreciate.

With Neptune in the tenth, the individual will profit greatly if she consciously examines her beliefs about the importance of her father in her life and about the nature of the world and reality. She may have fairy-tale attitudes about these, or a tendency to evade or avoid dealing with any of the issues. The same is true of career: she may expect far too much or deny its importance. With acceptance of the benefits of discipline, this individual could bring insight, compassion and inspiration into her chosen career. She will be able to thoughtfully direct Neptunian creativity into productive areas, to accept and meet deadlines, and to channel Neptunian spirituality into practical expression.

Neptune in the Eleventh House

This placement shows a tendency to see other people, in this case those who are not particularly close, through rose-colored glasses. The common man and woman, acquaintances, associates, and members of groups to which the individual belongs will all tend to be viewed with considerable compassion and charity. Their flaws will not be easily noticed nor credited. This individual wants to see others in their best light; he wants to think well of the world in general. This is an attractive trait when not taken too far, and can make him the person everyone wants to go to for a fair hearing. He can be very idealistic and interested in creating a better future for everyone.

Positively expressed, Neptune in the eleventh house successfully combines the need to find absolute perfection and harmony with the need for innovative solutions. The individual may be able to use his artistic/creative abilities or his spiritual/inspirational interests for the benefit of large groups, or for his friends. He will tend to have friends who express creative talent or spiritual curiosity. He may place a high value on independence and freedom.

A MARTYR TO FRIENDS

If he pours too much emotional energy into his friends, groups or causes, he may later feel cheated that he has given so much. Negatively used, he may often feel that he has to rescue his friends or his groups in some major way. It may be difficult for him not to feel personally responsible for the "fate" of the groups to which he belongs. He may repeatedly get involved in groups which demand much sacrifice on his part, or groups which jarringly challenge his value system. They may also confuse him as to what is right or wrong, or convince him that anarchy, chaos or outright revolution are valuable goals.

PROJECTION

If projected, he may attract people who need constant infusions of sympathy, or be attracted to people who let him bend their ears repeatedly. He may expect his friends to be artistic or spiritually awakened or he may have friends who are simply "flaky," or unreliable, or out of touch with reality. They could also be alcoholic, into drugs, illness or make-believe. With Neptune, people often resist growing up and want to live forever in never-never land. Or his friends could be willful, headstrong and determinedly independent or rebellious.

With Neptune in the eleventh, his spiritual pursuits would likely be most rewarding when connected with a group or groups. Naturally there is the danger of becoming too caught up in a group which does not operate for his best interests. With faith and pure motives, however, Neptune often "lucks out" and finds its way to beneficial and very, very special surroundings.

With Neptune in the eleventh, he will need to face his illusions about humanity in general, about the role of groups and causes in his life, and about his friends. He may use the Neptune traits himself, consciously, or he may confront them in his friends. With honesty and integrity, this individual can be a wonderful source of comfort to others, without giving away too much of himself. He can contribute much service to groups and organizations without sacrificing his values or other meaningful parts of his life. He can value humanity and the common human without sentimentality. He can enjoy and value personal freedom for himself and for his friends.

Neptune in the Twelfth House

Neptune is associated with both Pisces and the twelfth house, which means when it is positioned in the twelfth house it can either be a double dose of comfort or dissatisfaction. Both house and planet are water, so there is much here that goes on below conscious awareness. It doesn't have to stay that way, but it certainly tends to, unless deliberate work is done to bring unconscious values, beliefs and faith into consciousness.

The most difficult part of this placement is that very lack of consciousness about itself and how it operates. What works from unconscious levels has far more power— and more freedom— to affect us than those drives of which we are conscious. When we know about particular tendencies, we can make allowances for them, work around them, if we so choose.

CHOICES AVAILABLE

For example, if an individual understands that she has a great deal of ambition in her career, she can realize that perhaps her ambition tends to unbalance her lifestyle. Perhaps her automatic tendency is to put job requirements before her husband's needs. If she realizes this, however, she is in a position to make well-thought-out choices, rather than automatic ones. No longer will she simply assume that her career always has to come first. She will see that sometimes her husband may be more important. It will depend on the circumstances— the important point is, because she is aware of her tendencies, she isn't ruled by them. She is free to respond in different ways, free to make conscious choices which will bring her results she wants and will enjoy.

LACKS AWARENESS

With Neptune in the twelfth house, it is often very difficult to take any notice at all that ultimate, unquestioned values determine how we interpret the world around us in addition to how we interpret our own behavior and attitudes. The values are so unquestioned as to be beyond challenge. The person with Neptune in the twelfth will tend to have a great deal of difficulty just digesting the concept of how values affect perceptions and therefore attitudes and behavior. Her values simply are what they are and they tend to resist categorization or definition. She is so surrounded and absorbed by her values, that she cannot properly separate herself nor her experiences from them. They become absolute in her life, and to challenge them is to challenge her deepest needs.

This Neptunian's deepest need is to discover and live her spiritual heritage. She is closer to it than any, yet less able to translate it into terms the world can understand. This does not especially bother her, but any barrier to her goal can feel terribly painful and unfair, although often she simply comes to view it as part of the unreal world she thinks she can ignore.

With Neptune here the individual is less connected to the world than others, more in tune with the world of spirit, of the healing, harmonizing energy of absolute love which flows through and around all of us, if we are but aware of it. She could well have psychic abilities. She never fully embraces the world and its version of reality because she is aware, if only on a dim level, that the universe encompasses so much more than our minds can handle.

NEEDS A MATURE EGO

The danger is that the person will come fully to this insight before she has developed some ego strength. With ego strength, she will honor herself as well as her vision and can relate positively to the vastness she sees. Without it, she will tend to be overwhelmed and easily terrified. Then she will find Neptune's negative choices are an irresistible temptation. She will think she has found a way out of the nameless terror, and never sees the trap yawning ahead of her.

With Neptune in the twelfth house, the individual will need to take a long look at her tendency to idealize peace, universal love, saintliness, sacrifice and service, art and music, fantasy, and the spiritual path. She will tend to have many illusions about spiritual development and the role it plays in life. She will expect it to be easy, yet she will be willing to suffer rather than give up her dream. There will be a strong need to overlook or deny any flaws in those issues she considers vital in her life.

The positive choices are for those who integrate the yearnings of Neptune into a wholistic lifestyle, or for those few individuals whose whole chart points in a single direction. Neptune in the twelfth is not a problem by itself, if there are no contraindications or clashes. If nothing is repressed or ignored, if all parts and drives and needs are honored and given some attention, all the gods and goddesses will be content. The main problem with Neptune in the twelfth is the aforementioned lack of awareness of what the ultimate values are and how they affect the quality of the person's life.

When the person with Neptune in the twelfth has a deep, underlying faith that everything is already perfect, it amazingly seems to be. This person has not ignored or evaded awareness; rather she has seen through surface appearances to the underlying meaning, to the consequences of whatever is going on at present. She senses a flow to life, a purpose which is usually greater and more important than the temporary setbacks which so upset the average person. She sees events in a different light entirely. Where someone with less awareness might interpret the death of a friend as untimely and unfair, the Neptunian might know on some deep inner level that the friend needed to go on to other experiences in order to take his next step of growth. The Neptunian would grieve for herself and her own sense of loss, but she would feel that everything had occurred for a good reason. From her inner core of steadfast faith would come strength enough to look past the surface for a larger, more encompassing pattern to the flow of life.

This Neptunian can do what every Neptunian yearns to do; she can live in conscious touch with both the world of physical reality and the world of spiritual reality. Each enhances the other.

Meditation

Consider the house position of Neptune in your chart. Onto whom are you most likely to project Neptunian qualities? What can you learn from people who seem very Neptunian to you?

CHAPTER SIX

NEPTUNE IN ASPECT

It is so often an overwhelming temptation to think of aspects between planets as statements of human nature which are essentially static or unchanging. The planets in an individual's chart represent a frozen instant of time. There will not be another instant exactly the same. The chart is a picture. It holds the planets still for us so that we can absorb the meaning of that instant, but as we do so we are living through an ever-changing series of more instants. While we study the still picture that is the chart, the planets themselves continue on their way. The gods do not rest. Neither does the individual represented by the chart.

People Evolve

People change. They grow up, have new experiences, and learn from those experiences. At any point in an individual's life there will be some factors indicated by the chart which the individual will do quite naturally.

Incidentally, "naturally" does not translate to "comfortably." If it did, astrologers would have no clients. The activities in which a person engages are often fraught with discomfort or even outright misery yet it is the way he has always operated and he knows no other. A youngster with Mars square Saturn may quite naturally get into many conflicts with teachers and other authority figures, yet the situations which result from his attitudes and behavior will not make him happy. Only when he sees that he brings about those situations by his attitudes and behavior will he be motivated to change.

"Change" implies a dynamic. It implies that **people are not static** but that they are, in fact, in the process of becoming. Psychologist Abraham Maslow held the opinion that the term "human being" gave too much of an impression that the individual was what she was, as if she were a finished product. He preferred the term "human becoming" to convey his sense of the dynamic process which more truly characterizes a person's life.

Every day in the average life there are many opportunities to learn and, from learning, to change. Not all lessons lead to growth, however. An individual whose faith in his spouse is justifiably shattered may adopt an attitude of mistrust toward her, or he may generalize her nature and decide that all women are untrustworthy; it is his choice. The point is, the experiences of life bring new realizations, new understandings and perceptions, and from these, new attitudes. Hopefully the new attitudes are an improvement but they are not always so.

Age Affects Interpretation

It is vitally important to keep this in mind when interpreting a chart, because the **static messages in the chart are being applied to a dynamic, ever-changing person.** It would be ridiculous to interpret the chart of an infant in the same way as the chart of an adult. The infant will tend to express limited parts of the chart, but she will do so quite spontaneously, without thought. The adult has usually learned that some of her natural, spontaneous tendencies bring her results she does not like, and hopefully she has learned to modify those tendencies. The child with Mars square Saturn, for example, may get embroiled in quarrels and be continually disruptive. She could exude anger and dissatisfaction. The teenager with Mars square Saturn may be suicidal because she cannot seem to get her own way on issues which are important to her, and the frustration is tearing her to pieces. The adult with this aspect, who has not connected her behavior to the situations in which she finds herself, may find she frequently loses her job because she cannot cooperate, or because her temper gets away from her. Later in life, when she has made the connection, she may struggle to be more cooperative and even-tempered. At all of these stages her natal chart looks the same, yet she expresses its potentials quite differently.

Just as it is ridiculous to interpret the chart of an infant the same as the chart of an adult, it is foolish and shortsighted to interpret the chart of a twenty-year-old the same as the chart of a forty-year-old. The experiences of life will bring most people more in touch with themselves on a continuous basis, as well as teaching them more about human nature in general. The forty-year-old will be considerably wiser, at least in some area of life, than he was at twenty. This needs to be credited during a chart interpretation. The aspects depicted in the chart represent areas of differing degrees of skill, ease and comfort. The majority represent problems; the individual may not yet be aware of the problem, he may be aware of it yet not have learned how to manage it, or he may have learned to overcome the problem with conscious direction of new attitudes. More likely, he will have learned how to handle some parts of all that is symbolized by the aspect, but still struggles with other parts and may yet be unaware of or overwhelmed by a few.

Sun Square Neptune: One Manifestation

As an example, look at a woman with Sun square Neptune. At twenty she may have been frequently embarrassed by her occasional lapses into a daydreamlike state. She could have let slip that she knew things which no one had told her, and might have found it not only difficult to explain but somewhat humiliating and threatening. Not only that, but she could have had a streak of whimsy which might not have been appreciated if she came from a family which was strongly intellectual. She could have attempted to cover all this up with a strong facade of bravado, perhaps even putting down other people who were imaginative or creative or gentle or spiritual. Yet when she tried to develop a strong sense of herself, a strong ego, she could not seem to. It was all pretense.

By thirty this woman might have come to terms with her

psychic abilities. She could accept that, but not that she is imaginative and spends a lot of time "daydreaming." She could also be terribly insecure because she has a growing sense of distrust in herself; she is aware on some level that she has no firm inner foundation. She could also be aware that she yearns for something more in life, yet finds this frightening and tends to avoid thinking about it.

By forty, she might have discovered that not only is she psychic but she is also very imaginative and therefore, creative, and that this has value regardless of what her family thought. She could have taken up music in order to express the inner beauty she experiences. At the same time, her sense of self might be more precarious than ever. She might have begun to drink to get away from a heavy sense of something being terribly wrong inside herself.

At forty-five she might have been in contact with a good psychologist, who respected her creative abilities but also saw that psychologically she had no discipline and had never created a strong ego. Through counseling, she might have developed such an ego, and is more comfortable with herself than she has ever been. Yet she still has great difficulty with self-promotion. Logically she knows it is her right and is the way to the success she craves. Emotionally, she feels guilty every time she blows her own horn, no matter how modestly she does so. It is crippling the advancement of her career. She has learned much, she has come far, but she has not learned to handle everything about even this one aspect in her chart. She is still in the process.

Multiple Possibilities

When a chart is interpreted, it is important to **let many possibilities come to mind for each aspect,** so that they can be raised for the client. He can think about them and decide if he needs insight on any of the issues raised. If you ask, he may be able to teach you about yet more ways that a particular aspect can be expressed, ways you had not heard about before.

Harmony Aspects

Whenever there is an aspect between two planets, the energies of those planets interact. They may do so comfortably, or they may clash. The "harmonious" aspects, sextile and trine, generally indicate that the energies and tendencies mesh without inner conflict. The meshing may result in unstable behavior or unrealistic attitudes, but the individual herself is not deeply bothered by these. They represent an area of comfort for her.

Conflict Aspects

The "challenging" aspects, square, opposition and quincunx, generally indicate that the energies seem contradictory to the individual with the aspect, and an inner conflict is set up. For example, a person who has Sun sextile Neptune is usually at home with his psychic impulses and his need for a creative outlet. A person with Sun square Neptune may be embarrassed or threatened by his mystical tendencies, or may feel he has to deny his ego any outlet. The former sees no conflict between ego and spirituality. He can use either, or both. The latter cannot see how to combine them. He thinks they are mutually contradictory.

Even with challenging aspects, however, an individual is not doomed to lifelong unhappiness. The point is **not** that she cannot coordinate two incompatible energies, but that she **thinks** they are incompatible. She can be taught otherwise. She can be shown how the people with harmonious aspects meld the energies without any conflict. She can learn that both energies are perfectly acceptable and valid. She can come to see that each energy needs an outlet— each god has a right to a place at the table. If she cannot combine them, she can alternate them. It is not really possible to turn a square into a trine, because the trine represents an ease with issues over which the square will tend to trip or hesitate. But the individual with a square can learn to apply deliberate, conscious control over these tendencies. She can learn more effective ways to behave. She may never achieve the ease with the issues that the trine person has naturally, but she can certainly learn how to manage them so that she is much more comfortable with the outcomes of her behavior.

It is not uncommon for a person to manage some of the issues highlighted by an aspect quite well, to be entirely unaware of some of the issues and to ignore or have trouble dealing with others. A person with Neptune conjunct the Sun, for example, may be successfully creative, an indication that he has learned to handle the inspiration of this aspect. At the same time, he may be very egotistical, perhaps setting himself up as the spiritual "king of the hill," an indication he has not learned to cope with the Neptunian challenge to the ego in a constructive manner.

Mixed Blessings

The psychological complex represented by Neptune tends to idealize everything it contacts. It romanticizes, makes appear larger than life, glosses over the flaws. The planet which is aspected by Neptune tends to represent something which is seductive to the native because of this very romanticized view. Neptune also, because of the naivete and idealism and faith, is associated with at least a hint of vulnerability. Not only does the aspected planet represent something seductive and extremely attractive, but something which tends to make the person feel vulnerable, weak, passive and if threatened, evasive— often to the point of denial.

Neptune Aspects to the Sun

This represents a connection between the planet of ego and self-esteem and the planet which represents the desire to transcend the ego. The fixed fire Sun symbolizes the urge toward power; the mutable water Neptune is associated with surrender. The Sun is an intensely personal planet; Neptune denotes the totally impersonal, the Cosmic Consciousness. This is not an easy partnership. However, both are associated with creativity and charisma and these are their particular strengths.

EGO EROSION
With the conjunction or the challenging aspects there is a strong tendency for the spiritual drive to erode the ego. The Sun represents our urge to be extroverted and to pour energy out

into the world. The Sun needs to feel recognized, at least, and prefers to feel praised, important and cared about. Neptune sees all these as self-aggrandizement, as false and worthless goals. The individual may feel trapped because each time he tries to meet his ego needs, even wholesome and legitimate ones, guilt can undermine his efforts. Every time he tries to build a strong, healthy ego, he feels as if he has betrayed something important. Self-esteem can be ripped to shreds by constant doubts. The resultant insecurity can run deep, and may well be entirely unconscious. A child cannot deal with such constant internal threat, without help, and will tend to either give up or repress the conflict so that it does not have to be dealt with. When it is unconscious, however, it is actually much more difficult to handle.

The child who gives up can grow to adulthood with no sense of self whatever. She doesn't truly comprehend that she has rights, or needs. She only knows that she "should" be spiritual, as perfectly loving and giving as possible. She may try very hard to never make a mistake, to never hurt anyone else. She is a victim waiting for the right opportunity to perform self-sacrifice. She will often engage in a chronic form of self-sacrifice: she may be utterly unable to credit the extent of her own creative talents.

SUN CONJUNCT NEPTUNE: ONE MANIFESTATION

Delia is a young woman with Sun conjunct Neptune. Her parents recognized that Delia had considerable talent with sketching while she was still young, and they encouraged her efforts. By the time she was ten, however, she simply couldn't be bothered to try any more. She joined various classes but always quit as soon as it became apparent that any work was involved. She joined Brownies but drifted away as soon as they began working toward the various badges. She joined the band in high school where she displayed an impressive natural musical ability, but she wouldn't attend after school practices or practice on her own; this too drifted from her life.

At high school Delia took the easiest courses and graduated without any clear idea of what to do with her life. She only got a job because her parents forced her to. Delia is a lovely girl who can be friendly and charming, and if she thinks of it, quite helpful. She is now, in her early twenties, working at a job as a waitress, earning a little above minimum wages. Her mother says, "If we spend any amount of time around her, we want to poke her to see if she is still alive! She doesn't seem to care deeply enough about anything to put any effort into it, even her own talents!" When asked why she never developed her abilities, Delia shrugs and grins sheepishly and confesses that she could never see anything special about what she did. She simply cannot credit what skilled teachers have told her.

ESCAPISM

The child who gives up may also grow up with a sense of being overwhelmed by the enormity of life. Defeated from the start, he does not do the work of self-development. It looks unnecessary, or too difficult, or both. Without a strong ego, he cannot resist the tides around him and he drifts upon them, helpless and powerless. He never knows what he wants. He simply hurts.

For either of these people, the Neptunian avenues of escape beckon sweetly. Alcohol, drugs, television, fantasy novels, sleep and so on are all ways to avoid a confrontation with the weakness and self-delusion which underlie the surface appearance of victimization.

The child who represses the internal conflict may construct a shaky pseudo-ego. It maintains a weak outward control over Neptune, and turns the Neptunian tendency for expansion to its own purposes. Such an individual seeks to meet the Sun needs, which have been denied at the conscious level, through Neptunian channels. She wants to become more holy, more egoless, more spiritual, more peaceful, more sacrificial than anyone else. The Sun need to feel important becomes an unconscious and often voracious appetite for self-importance. The whole structure is built on fantasy, which cannot support itself; consequently the need for constant reassurance is enormous.

Such a person can soon fall into the trap of self-delusion. His need to be perfectly spiritual, or perfectly loving and giving, or perfectly powerful and successful, becomes so all-important that he can no longer tolerate the risk that he might fail. He simply assumes that he has already made it to his goal. He is really all right already. His arrogance may know no bounds. Whatever occurs around him, he has an answer. He happily takes the credit for anything "good" that occurs in his world, and takes for granted that he cannot be held responsible for anything "bad."

SUN SQUARE NEPTUNE: ONE MANIFESTATION

Carl is a fellow who has Sun square Neptune. Depending on the people he is with, Carl will claim to "be into" health foods or drugs. He appears happy and charming on the surface, and avidly takes each new healing or enlightenment course that he comes across. He loves to expound on his knowledge, yet never follows up on any of the practical or practice sessions that are part of his courses. He is often ill, which he blames on his mother and his unhealthy upbringing. When he is well, he claims he has cured himself with the use of herbs and positive thinking. Whenever he hears of another person making a success of something, he loudly proclaims, "I knew it! I told him he could do that if he just cleared himself of anger and negativity!" If confronted with his own lack of success, he snaps, "Well, that's nothing to do with me. These things just don't work out. I can't be held responsible for everything!" Then he goes on to talk about his latest plan, which will make his life absolutely perfect.

NEVER-NEVER LAND

"Everything is already perfect." Born of genuine acceptance and faith, this is a beautiful, living philosophy. Born of insecurity, it is merely another delusion designed to protect a watery, weak self-image. Everything **has** to be all right because the individual will shatter if it isn't. She has not learned to cope with anything else. In her defensive arrogance, however, she tends to ignore anything that does not support her view of herself as the most spiritual person around, and she may well actively strike out at those who dare to present evidence that her motives and inner state may not be as holy as she thinks they are.

This aspect in a man's chart is one of the indications of a possible "Peter Pan" complex. The individual may have an unrealistic view of the male role, or he may romanticize it. It is an aspect which can indicate a real unwillingness to accept responsibility, with the result that the individual simply refuses to really grow up. He prefers to live forever in his never-never land. It is such a fitting name— a label of denial for the fantasy world so seductive to the Neptunian. He wants a Wendy to come into his world and look after him, while he offers little but illusions in return. Thus he needs a psychologically weak, emotionally vulnerable partner who will accept his fantasies and self-delusions and boost his ego by admiring him. Strong women who are aware of themselves will see right through him and he will detest this, and them. Carl, mentioned above, attracts any number of passive women, and boasts about his ability in this area. Forced to deal with mature women who are not fooled by his superficial charm, however, he complains that they treat him badly. In truth, he does everything he can to discredit and undermine them, including telling outright lies.

INTEGRATION
The positive expressions of Sun/Neptune contacts come from mutual tolerance and acceptance of these two very different sides of life. The ego needs to be respected as a vitally important human psychological structure. It also needs to be respected as an important prerequisite to genuine spiritual growth. Genuine spiritual growth needs to be respected as a vitally important human pursuit. It also needs to be respected as the true reason behind the importance of a strong ego. The spiritual path is strewn with obstacles, most of which relate to self-delusion in one form or another. It takes a sturdy ego to tread this path; it takes courage and determination and perseverance, all of which are under the rulership of the Sun. Thus it can be seen that these two energies can work together most positively, if both are honored and given room to be expressed.

On other levels, Neptune and the Sun can combine to indicate an **exceptional level of creative talent**. This person can tune in to levels beyond the ordinary, can sense experiences and feelings that are not of the everyday world. This may well be an area of focus for her, to the detriment of worldly affairs. She will need to make a conscious effort to ensure that the rent is paid and other necessary chores are done before she indulges too deeply in her visions.

Neptune can provide a channel for extraordinary inspiration in the Sun's creative work. Solar themes can represent energy and stamina for Neptune's mystical, psychic channeling. Neptune themes can bring compassion, sensitivity and insight to the Sun's romances. The Sun can denote flair and charisma for Neptune's insights, so that others will listen attentively when Neptune is ready to teach. The combination often represents an ability to envision wonderful possibilities, and to inspire others to believe in those possibilities. The individual will, however, need to be careful not to let his awareness of the best in life blind him to the worst. This is a position which indicates potential gullibility.

Physically, Neptune's focus on otherworldly concerns, or repression of its needs, may result in low energy, poor physical vitality and the possibility of mysterious, debilitating health problems, for which no cause can be found. Conscious acceptance of the implications of Sun/Neptune combinations and deliberate expression of at least some of the aspect's potentials will usually result in improved energy levels and greatly improved general health. That is, the individual will need to find some interest to pursue from among the choices represented by Neptune: art, music, handicrafts, gardening, psychology, counseling, design, spiritual studies, psychic development and so on.

When Neptune and the Sun cooperate, the individual usually possesses a **special, whimsical charm** which comes across well on the stage or in the classroom. The Sun lends flair and magnetism, while Neptune offers a hint of vulnerability which others find irresistible. This aspect represents the ability to tap into sources of inspiration which can be especially uplifting and healing for the individual and for others, as long as the watery Neptune does not dampen too much the fire of the Sun.

Moon Aspects to Neptune

This combines two water planets. Since water relates to the unconscious, many of the manifestations of these aspects will be at least slightly beyond the awareness of the individual. They are not completely out of touch, but do require conscious effort to bring into awareness, particularly with the conjunction.

EMPATHY
This tends to be a combination which indicates great empathy and, frequently, psychic sensitivity. With the harsh aspects or the conjunction, the person may feel buffeted by her impressions and unable to control them, while with the harmonious aspects there tends to be less of a sense that the impressions are unwelcome intrusions. There can be a deep inner awareness of

strange forces and energies, without any sense of detachment or ability to turn it off. There can be great moodiness, perhaps brought on by the exquisite sensitivity both to the spirit world and the often unruly emotions of those nearby. There may be a great deal of unconscious value placed on the importance of feelings and subliminal impressions.

ROMANTICIZED MOTHERING

Neptune tends to idealize whatever it touches. In this case there is a strong tendency to put motherhood and nurturance on a pedestal. With Neptune, the expectation is not just for ordinary sustenance, but for an all-enveloping, all-encompassing kind of love which is supposed to be magically provided. The Moon/Neptune person is usually sure he provides this unceasingly and unquestioningly for others, and equally sure that he never gets enough for himself. He can be a bottomless pit of emotional need, ever hungry for an endless supply of the kind of enchanted, mystical and all-absorbing love which mere humans are not very good at providing.

The Moon/Neptune person on such a trip will usually experience a level of dissatisfaction in exact proportion to the degree to which she expects someone to provide this love for her. She will also tend to suffer from repeated delusions as she thinks she has found someone to provide what she so desperately needs, only to find after a while that this new person cannot live up to her expectations, either.

In order to escape from this pattern of delusion and painful disappointment, he will have to be willing to admit that what he wants cannot be provided for by ordinary humans. He really wants complete Cosmic love, but cannot experience that until he gives up his demand to be loved perfectly on the Earth plane. It isn't so much that what he wants is wrong, or impossible, it is that he insists on looking for it in the wrong place. Once he accepts that, he can take a look at how much he quietly expects a mother to be a saint, children to be little angels, and how much he is a sucker for anyone who needs to be nurtured. He will also need to take a look at his own mother, and to forgive her for having been human, after all.

UNREALISTIC FEMININE ROLE

Frequently this aspect indicates a general **attitude that all women should be passive, supportive and self-sacrificing**, sometimes to a ridiculously unhealthy degree. If it is in a woman's chart and there are other factors which indicate a need for self-expression, there are problems brewing. Such a person has a lot of trouble achieving clarity over the feminine role. If her values concerning womanly behavior clash with a strong need for independence, she has the potential for a very devastating internal conflict. She cannot express one without betraying the other. If she tries to always be unassuming, loving and quiet-natured, her independent side will be repressed. If she tries to assert her independence, she will feel guilty. Such an individual needs to examine the contradictory nature of her beliefs and see where they can be modified to achieve peace.

In a man's chart, such an attitude may lead him to expect the women in his life to express Neptunian characteristics, whether that is their nature or not. He will tend to feel disappointed and badly let down when they do not meet his expectations. He will need to look at his one-sided view of femininity, and to learn to appreciate the real characteristics of the individual women he meets, rather than projecting his Neptune onto them. He will also need to learn to "do" his own Neptune, to get in touch with and express his own mystical, sensitive and creative side, rather than waiting for a woman in his life to provide that for him.

MOON OPPOSITE NEPTUNE: ONE MANIFESTATION

Sometimes, with the harsh aspects, the Moon/Neptune connection indicates a mother who had unrealistic expectations, either of herself or of the child. Mother might have been a victim, or an especially unreliable person. With Neptune, she might even have been missing all together. Or her whole way of being might have clashed markedly with the individual's values. For example, Maria is a woman with Moon opposite Neptune. Her mother has Neptune conjunct the IC—an interesting family pattern.

Maria grew up under a seemingly constant hail of perfectionistic demands. When Maria became an adult herself, she intuitively felt there was more to raising a child than she had experienced and she began to study parenting skills and developmental psychology. She soon discovered that her mother had been unrealistic, had failed to make any allowances for age or to lower her standards to levels appropriate for a growing child. At this point Maria began a twelve-year struggle with her "internal" mother; her own mother was constantly ill (!) and Maria felt it was not right to confront her directly. She chose instead to fight the battle inside herself.

She admits that when she held her first baby in her arms, her fondest dream was to be able to take the child away to a beautiful garden, away from the noisy, ugly, demanding world. She wanted to give the baby a perfect, idyllic and loving childhood. She experienced many moments of despair over the following years as it became obvious she could provide no such environment, and indeed the arrival of another baby meant less time was available for the first child. Maria was, during this time, dredging up memories of how her mother had behaved with her, and while she found many of these memories painful, it made her very sensitive to her own children and she vowed not to repeat her mother's mistakes. She learned more parenting skills. Ultimately Maria came to accept that her mother had done the best she could, and "said three Hail Marys over my childhood and let it go."

Once she came to terms with her own childhood, accepting that it had been pretty miserable but she could do well for herself as an adult, Maria became more comfortable with her own role as mother. She no longer reacted with guilt if she left her children to pursue personal interests, and she learned how to set realistic standards for herself. She developed rather good relationships with both her children and feels she has made the best of what might have been a poor start in life. She has learned, too, that her mother has markedly different values than herself, values with which she was never comfortable, and she has now learned to honor her own way and her own beliefs.

POSITIVE OPTIONS

With the harmonious aspects come the possibility that mother provided a wholesome role model for spirituality and/or for artistic/creative expression. She might have simply had a solid sense of right and wrong, which she passed successfully to the individual. She might have been very religious, in an unconventional but positive and growth-enhancing way. She might have been psychic, and at home with it. There is always the possibility, too, that mother was none of these things, but the individual has such a positive regard for mother and motherhood that all was readily forgiven.

The person herself, with the harmonious aspects, likely has a high regard for motherhood and the whole domestic lifestyle. She tends to romanticize it and dismiss the drudgery, but this is not overdone. The individual may be psychic, but the experiences are more likely to be pleasant and nonintrusive than they are with the difficult aspects. Still, it is the people with the challenging aspects who tend to do the work necessary to develop their psychic abilities, or those with a strongly placed or aspected Saturn, which can also provide a prod.

The "easy" aspects tend to create an easy compatibility of urges between these two planets, but not much energy. With two passive planets connected by a flowing aspect, there is no challenge, no conflict and no reason to do anything except what comes naturally. However, what comes naturally may be considerable psychic openness and empathy. These people can be very loving and sympathetic but not overly practical unless other chart factors indicate it.

There can be great vulnerability to other women, with either type of aspect. The tendency will be to expect great things from other women, to place great faith in them. This can be inspiring or a terrible burden for the object(s) of that faith. Women with this aspect also tend to look for satisfaction within the role of mother, nurturer or baby. If taken too far, they may expect one of these roles to provide complete satisfaction. Women in general tend to be a source of inspiration and great emotional support, or of disillusionment.

Generally speaking, this is a warm, caring and instinctively empathic combination. People with this combination will tend to look after other people's feelings, which makes them deeply receptive, a talent which is greatly appreciated by those who need to talk over their inner experiences.

Mercury Aspects to Neptune

Both of these planets are capable of whimsy, and there may be no more delightful combination of Neptune. There may also be no more exasperating combination, for Mercury is a Peter Pan type of energy—the eternal youth—and Neptune tends to expand and romanticize whatever it touches, thus making the problems look charming. Neither planet is especially determined to deal with reality. Mercury is certainly associated with information, but it is not particular about the veracity of the information. This planet of rational thought is also the planet of businessmen and thieves. (Ancient astrologers obviously had a sense of humor along with a touch of cynicism!) The myths about Mercury tell us that he was less than a day old when he stole Apollo's herd of cows. He had questionable ethics right from the start!

When the planet of deception contacts the planet of delusion, there is bound to be some potential for mental confusion. This could work out as outright lack of mental focus, inability to concentrate or to apply discipline to intellectual processes. The individual may have trouble communicating with others, because his ideas are so complex and mysterious, and his language so vague that others cannot understand him. Furthermore, his "logic" may well serve his imaginative longings much more than it serves practical reality. This can be great for creativity, but only if the individual can let go of the tendency to be vague and instead learn to deal with the world on the world's terms when that is necessary.

The **imagination will tend to be excellent** with any aspect between Mercury and Neptune, but with the hard aspects there would be somewhat more tendency for flights of fancy to lead into trouble rather than inspiration, particularly early in life. This person usually experiences great difficulty in being candid because she hates arguments. She is very vulnerable to the strong emotions which emanate from others and she usually seeks to avoid these. She may develop a tendency to tell lies whenever it is more convenient to do so than to tell the truth, whenever the "truth" seems to need prettying up or whenever she simply does not wish to admit to reality and invents a more satisfying version. She doesn't always perceive these as lies, however, but as expedient "stories" which keep her in a "peaceful" space, at least for the moment. She can turn avoidance into an art form.

When Neptune aspects Mercury, it may indicate that the rational mind is, for the individual, an ultimate value. The world of facts and information can be made to take precedence over everything else. Business, commerce, transactions and contracts may seem like the most important activity in life. These people can turn everything into a bargaining issue, and may, with the harsh aspects, ignore the need for compassion. More likely, however, is that they will feel pulled between the need for logic and the need for compassion.

It is also possible with this combination to turn very intellectual over the subject of values, to try to deal with spiritual promptings by being coldly logical, or to undermine values with rationalizations. There may still be plenty of creativity, but it is directed into inventive excuses, imaginative and admirable reasons why one behaved as one did, all as a way to avoid examining the real motives.

There will likely be an ability to move freely back and forth between the world of the intellect and the world of the unconscious. With the harmonious aspects this is likely to be under the individual's own control. Consequently he will be able to use the talent for his own and others' growth. He will have the ability to listen to others, to give them words to describe their experiences. In a way he is a catalyst, a transformer, for he intuitively comprehends the symbols of the unconscious mind and can translate those into words for himself and for others. He would, therefore, make an excellent counselor and an expressive writer. With the harmonious aspects, however, this ability may be taken for granted and never developed into a true skill, unless other chart aspects indicate self-discipline.

With the hard aspects, the ability to move between the conscious mind and the unconscious may not be under the individual's control, or she may not be able to discipline herself to hone the skill. She may daydream when she needs to employ logic, and be cold and rational when intuition and insight would serve her better. She may often misunderstand others, and others can take advantage of her at the verbal level. She frequently weaves castles in the air when she should be alert and on guard. She can walk away from an encounter feeling that she got treated badly, but it may take her hours to figure out

why, and exactly what happened, and what she **should** have said. She will get caught repeatedly, and others are often tempted to think of her as stupid or slow-witted. She is anything but. She does, however, often have her head in the clouds when it would be in her best interests to be mentally disciplined and sharp. She may be secretive when she ought to be open, and inadvertently pass on secrets which would have been better kept to herself. She is not deliberately malicious, unless other aspects in the chart indicate this, but she does not often focus on the important points of an issue, instead she deals with everything as a hodgepodge, a soup of details which she absorbs as a whole.

LOGIC AND INTUITION
It is also a distinct possibility, with the hard aspects, that the rational mind will be at war with the intuitive mind. On one level this can be experienced as constant switching back and forth between what the individual **thinks** is right and what he **feels** is right. He cannot seem to reconcile rational thought with compassion; one seems contradictory to the other. This can tie him up in knots because no matter which course of action he chooses, he will feel uncomfortable. He needs to learn to accept that both urges have their place and have intrinsic value, but it is up to him to choose which one is most appropriate for each situation.

This individual will be sensitive to **all** the messages which are passed on in the course of a conversation. She will be receptive to body language and the very subtle nuances of tone which betray a person's true inner feelings. This may confuse her if she is not fully aware of this ability and doubts the subtle messages which she picks up. Or it may make her wish to retreat into herself because she cannot cope with the conflicting messages which other people often deliver. At the same time she has an ability to anticipate what others will think or do that borders on the precognitive. She may use this for manipulation or for self-defense, depending on her strength of character and other factors in the chart.

A person with a Mercury aspect to Neptune will be very sensitive on a physical level as well as the psychic and emotional. He will tend to have highly strung nerves, a delicate nervous system and a body which rejects drugs or requires only minimal doses. He will also probably be highly susceptible to psychosomatic ailments, to physical problems which are essentially caused by psychological discomfort or unresolved conflicts. Because this part of his nature prefers to deal only with lighthearted issues and with the flowing, lovely aspects of life, this individual tends to ignore his problems until they find expression in physical illness, at which time he almost **has** to deal with the issue.

The person with an aspect between Mercury and Neptune has a great imagination and loves fantasy in any form— written, verbal or visual. This aspect tends to erode any limits on the imagination, so she is free to range over wide possibilities and may come up with visions no one else has considered. She is a wonderful storyteller, for she can create images with her words. She will generally get along well with children, as long as they are essentially well-mannered, for she appreciates their perceptions of the world as much as they appreciate hers.

PETER PAN
This is another of the Peter Pan aspects, a strong indication of the unwillingness to give up the fantasies and unrealistic expectations of childhood. This type of individual is often remarkably charming, capable of great fancifulness and generally appealing foolishness, yet he is also adept at dodging any responsibility. He is more interested in playing games and talking endlessly than in doing anything productive. He is often absentminded, and unreliable. He loves to talk, to play word games, to seduce others into his never-never land but will kick them out quickly if they drag a little reality in with them. He wants to be helpful, when it occurs to him, but does not wish to be confronted with his failure to keep promises nor his unwillingness to take responsibility for his behavior. If his chart indicates a generally passive nature he will simply avoid people who confront him. If, however, there are indications of temper, his sweet charm may suddenly change into a vicious defensiveness.

INFINITY AND SPECIFICS
There may be much confusion and being "spaced out" due to Mercury's limited and essentially orderly perceptions which tend to be at odds with and have difficulty trying to organize

Neptune's multidimensional insights and perceptions and understandings. Mercury works best with words, Neptune with symbols and pictures. Mercury can find Neptune's world bewilderingly complex and disorderly.

Only when Mercury surrenders a place to Neptune can they work well in tandem. Mercury needs to accept the Neptunian experiences and input without imposing Mercurian logic patterns, which don't fit Neptune, on the impressions. Neptune will inspire, and Mercury will translate, perhaps losing much, just as an energy step-down transformer greatly modifies the amount of power which can come in. But the translation is still useful; it still brings the contents of the unconscious into consciousness, where it can be dealt with by and contribute to the growth of the mind and the ego. One by one, issues which are raised by the unconscious can be "realized," transmuted into a state which can be recognized by the individual as a problem which needs to be worked on. Each problem which is confronted becomes another step on the path to maturity— psychological and spiritual.

This is much like the process of a person learning to master a team of horses. He starts with one, and works with one until he has mastered it. Then he can begin to work with two, then three and so on. Maturity or spiritual growth demands the same process: first you take one item out of your unconscious, and you learn to deal with that. It may take a long time; you may not recognize it or know **how** to deal with it. After you learn to master it, however, you may dig into the pool for another. Each time you master an issue, it is yours; you add it to your cache of talents and abilities. It becomes a tool which you can use to help deal with the next issue you face.

Mercury/Neptune aspects carry the ability to retain a sense of play, a sense of lightness about life and development which can create a lovely balance in life between the need to learn and the need for simple, fulfilling joy. When this ability to play is directed so that it can be called upon when the appropriate occasion arises, it becomes an important part of a healthy, creative personality.

Venus Aspects to Neptune

Neptune has often been referred to as the "higher octave of Venus." These planets are associated with artistic ability, the emotions and passivity. Both are expressed most easily by those who are comfortable with the feminine side of their nature. Venus and Neptune represent the principle of attraction. Other planets such as Mars and Jupiter represent the principle of action: whatever is desired is pursued actively. A person who expresses Mars or Jupiter will reach out for whatever it is that she wants. A person who expresses Venus or Neptune, however, will wait for what she wants to come to her. She will do whatever she can to attract it to herself, but once she has done that, she feels she can do, or wishes to do, no more.

RECEPTIVITY
It is this quality of attraction which allows Venus and Neptune energies to seem so changeable. They symbolize the urge to become whatever seems most likely to successfully attract whatever is needed or desired or yearned for. Someone on the receiving end of this attempt to attract will find the Venus or Neptune person remarkably receptive, open, interested, inviting and encouraging. The Venus or Neptune person can make others feel incredibly important, fascinating, exciting and desirable. In combination, this ability is considerably heightened. The individual with an aspect from Venus to Neptune has the ability to let down her own emotional defenses. She is able to welcome someone else into her own world.

Not everyone reacts favorably to Venus/Neptune's seductive "Come hither." People with a predominance of air or an air/earth mixture may not respond; they are literally on a different wavelength and may not make much room in their lives for the emotional fulfillment most people yearn for. There is also that rare individual who is aware enough and centered enough to not be dangerously emotionally needy. Most people are, however, easily bewitched. The Venus/Neptune person seems to be, and in fact usually is, ready and willing to offer a **rare emotional intimacy**. It is too tempting for most people to resist.

The emotional intimacy yearned for and offered by Venus/Neptune in combination actually seduces the individual with the aspect as much as anyone on whom he sets his sights. When he lets down his emotional defenses, as he must in order to invite others in, he also leaves himself very vulnerable. He does this willingly in order to attract what he wants and needs: a companion with whom to share on the deep emotional level he craves. In fact, he searches for the ultimate satisfaction within a relationship, and the lure of that satisfaction makes any emotional risk seem worthwhile. Even if he sees how open he leaves himself, he will continue to do so because he chases an ultimate dream. He too is seduced by the aspect.

She is also seduced by the expectation that someone else besides herself will provide the ultimate fulfillment for her. She is looking for that incredible sense of at-one-ment which can only be found when one is connected somehow to that Consciousness which is Cosmic. She is searching for perfect, complete and unconditional love from a very imperfect source: another human being. When Neptune aspects Venus, the tendency is to assume that the path to the ultimate sense of connection is through Venus, through earthly relationships and love. She is overwhelmed by her need for an experience of God. She **must** have it, but looks for it from the wrong source. Her need is so strong that her ability to judge is often suspended. When she sees a likely candidate, all qualities which clash with her expectation are dismissed and ignored. It is not unusual to find that a person with a Venus/Neptune aspect, especially one of the hard aspects, has no common sense at all when it comes to love. She will attract and relate to others with an alarming lack of discrimination. She literally cannot see that which she does not wish to see.

One such girl, with Venus square Neptune, fell into a relationship with a man more than thirty years her senior. He did not, as might be expected from a psychological point of view, provide a father figure for her; she was attracted to and fascinated by his variety of spiritual experiences and pursuits.

The depth of yearning for deep emotional intimacy also can easily overwhelm the chosen partner. It is wonderful for one night, or perhaps a week, but the Venus/Neptune is not only absorbed by the lover but tends to absorb him as well. Sooner or later he will feel the need to breathe a little fresh air or to reestablish a sense of himself as an individual and he will pull away. This is usually interpreted as rejection by the Venus/Neptune individual, who, having given her all, feels taken advantage of. She is willing to give everything to her lover, but when he doesn't want or cannot take a steady diet of her absorbing kind of relationship, she feels martyred.

For his part, he will often feel guilty because she did, after all, give him more warmth and surround him with more love than he ever has experienced before. He will also feel torn between his need for her warmth, which requires him to immerse himself, and his need to be himself, at least some of the time. She will not be able to understand why he now apparently rejects the very things which drew him to her in the first place. Since he reacted well to them originally, she usually tries to intensify her efforts, which naturally only makes the situation worse. He may feel totally suffocated, and leave, or he may strike out at her in frustration. If they cannot resolve the situation, they may attempt to live together in frustration, the perfect breeding ground for an abusive relationship. If, however, the Venus/Neptune partner's vision "clears," so that she sees her lover's failings, she will feel badly disillusioned and usually will leave him. He isn't perfect enough, after all.

Occasionally, the Venus/Neptune person actually comes to see the partner in a realistic light. He must give up his attachment to his own image of the "perfect lover," which is very painful to him. But if he does this, he will see her as she really is, an ordinary human being with particular strengths and particular weaknesses. Not God, nor even a magical princess, but a frail person with a Divine spark within. This relationship stands a chance of success because he is now prepared to make the best of what he has, rather than trying to force it to be ever more unrealistically perfect.

"RESCUE ME"
People with Venus/Neptune aspects are strongly attracted to Neptunian types— the starving artist, the creative but crippled genius, the inspiring guru who can't get his own act together, the wounded underdog, the chronically ill semi-invalid in need of tender, loving care, the noble or holy priest or minister, the unfairly treated actor, the seemingly gentle lover who only partly hides a host of insecurities, and so on.

People with Venus/Neptune aspects need special awareness of their particular vulnerability to those who offer a path to "Heaven" or seem to need help. There is a strong tendency to get involved in relationships which quickly degenerate into victim/savior/martyr merry-go-rounds, with the result of incredible damage to both partners. In this type of relationship, someone has to be the strong savior, and the other partner gets to be the weak victim. The victim then leans on the savior, often to such an extent that the "savior" soon turns into a martyr, going to enormous lengths to satisfy the demands of the partner. It is an unhealthy situation at best, extremely destructive at worst. The one who was originally the victim can maintain a strong hold with guilt, and it soon becomes difficult to tell who is the real "victim" and who is in control.

The way out of such a situation is to stop playing whichever role one has been locked into. The apparent victim needs to stop leaning on and expecting things from the "savior" and also she needs to see how she drains him. The apparent savior needs to stop rescuing the victim and also to see how he prevents her from developing her own strengths. The sections in Chapter Seven discussing "Helpless" (or "Anything I Can Do You Can Do Better") and "My Very Own Cross" shed more light on this.

Venus is looking for intimacy; Neptune may turn it into an ultimate value. Venus goes looking for someone to lift her out of herself. Neptune wants the experience to be transcendent, more incredibly wonderful and special than any ordinary relationship can sustain. Venus/Neptune may want the relationship to be perfectly harmonious, inspiring and fulfilling. There will be a tendency to avoid confrontations and quarrels. Issues and problems will be denied, avoided or covered up rather than confronted and solved. Anything which looks less than perfect can easily be denied.

NOT QUITE PERFECT

There are other ways these aspects can be expressed. In a chart with other indications of potential artistic talent, this could set up expectations that what is created will always be mystical, spiritual, whimsical, or somehow exactly "right" or perfect for the situation. The individual could sense or actually "hear" celestial music and go half-mad attempting to translate it into our limited musical patterns. On other levels, she could have a sense that she ought to be able to create something just a little more delicate, a little more ethereal, something a tiny bit more beautiful. No matter how lovely her creation, or how strange, she may be haunted by a feeling that more is possible. Once again she is looking outside herself, this time to her own creations, for something which will bring her that ultimate sense of fulfillment.

Neptune tends to bring an exquisite sensitivity to those issues related to any planet it aspects. People with Venus/ Neptune aspects therefore often are so sensitive on an emotional level that they feel raw, unprotected, easily damaged. They need to learn to close some of their doors, to be less deeply involved with other people all the time, and to simply be less touchy. On a physical level they tend to be strongly attracted to sugar and sweet foods, and easily unbalance their health with their sweet tooth.

INNER WISDOM

Naturally there are those who learn to manage this aspect successfully. The person who comes to understand that what he seeks can only be found inside himself will be able to lessen his demands on the world and on other people. He will always yearn for a sense of ultimate fulfillment, but he will learn to look for it inside himself rather than from another person. He will learn that it is an impossible burden to place his expectations on a partner, and that every time he does so, he sows the seeds for the destruction of the relationship. He will learn to reach for harmony and to express his delightful romantic nature, but also to face with courage those conflicts which do arise.

He will learn that the expectation of complete perfection and fulfillment is an impossible demand to place on his artistic creations, that every time he does so, he sows the seeds for his own pervasive dissatisfaction. He will learn to strive for that perfection without totally expecting it, so that his creations are wondrous and inspiring, but they are not a substitute for Heaven.

Ideally, Neptune will uplift and transmute Venus's understanding of love. Venus tends to be self-oriented, physical and emotional. Neptune can bring a new dimension to Venus, that of selfless love, the kind of love which is truly healing. Neptune and Venus in combination can grow together to express and receive the kind of love about which we all dream: love based on unconditional— not blind— faith and belief in the best in each of us.

Mars Aspects to Neptune

Here there is a flow of energy, a connection, between a cardinal fire planet and a mutable water planet. Mars energy shoots out into the world; Neptune seeps gently. Mars represents the urge to exist, to be active, to be first. Mars is self-oriented and often self-centered. It is impulsive; flashes of desire flare into action then quickly subside. Neptune represents the urge to transcend worldly problems, to be passive and receptive, to connect with and unite with other souls or with the Cosmic Consciousness. Neptune has little concept of self. It flows around, under and over obstacles and it has a sense of timelessness which is completely foreign to Mars and its stress on "right now!"

BEAUTY IN MOTION
These two can cooperate. With the sextile and trine, there tends to be an easy flow of energy. Mars can bring initiative and energy to the artistic and spiritual dreams of Neptune. At the artistic level, there could be great interest in those sports which incorporate rhythm, grace, creativity and beauty, such as dancing, gymnastics, synchronized swimming and ice-skating. On the spiritual level, there could be much desire to seek out ever deeper levels of understanding and insight. This individual is usually comfortable with his psychic tendencies, or his need for a spiritual or at least an inspiring aspect to his life. He tends to accept the little inner promptings he experiences, with few doubts. He is comfortable with his faith in the universe and with its faith in him.

HIGHER SELF
At its finest expression, Neptune/Mars aspects denote the ability to use Neptune's energy to enhance the growth and maturity of the sense of identity. Neptune accepts Mars' assertiveness as a valuable trait for an individual rather than as a "sin," and permits it expression. There will also be the ability to use Mars to provide the drive to actualize some of Neptune's dreams. Neptune does not look like a threat to the identity, but a way to connect the personal identity to a much larger, more complex, complete and satisfying impersonal identity. The former is not lost to but incorporated into the latter because it

is not undermined but gently transcended. There is a sense of a little self which is included in but surpassed by the sense of a Higher Self, a sense of and acceptance of the Divine spark within each of us. This becomes "I (Mars) am a spiritual being (Neptune)." With this understanding and sense of connection may come the ability to channel spirits, or to channel healing energy, to see auras or use psychic abilities.

Neptune/Mars aspects, used constructively, can also represent a wholesome and healthy balance between assertiveness, the ability to stand up for oneself when necessary, and compassion, the ability to consider another person's needs on a par with personal needs. Neither takes precedence; each is used in the appropriate circumstances.

These two planets do, however, represent vastly different needs and ways of dealing with needs. There is far more tendency for these divergent energies to clash than there is to cooperate.

LOSS OF SELF

Neptune, with its tendency to erode barriers and expand endlessly, can undermine the sense of personal identity or the ability to assert personal needs. People may find it easy to believe that it is wrong to think of oneself, ever. Mars/Neptune can, particularly in difficult aspect, in the most literal terms, represent self- (Mars) sacrifice (Neptune).

The individual might unconsciously choose to repress Mars traits altogether, a situation which leads to immense frustration. All personal desires may be seen as "bad," as undesirable and intolerable. A host of unpleasant results await the long-term exercise of this choice, from chronic headaches and/or depression to repeated accidents, illnesses and surgeries to sexual dysfunction to complete mental breakdown. Projection is another possibility— having to face Mars energy in the outer world because there is no allowance made for it in the inner world.

MARS SEXTILE NEPTUNE: ONE MANIFESTATION

A woman who had Mars sextile Neptune was, as a child, very willful and never easily cowed— she also had Pluto conjunct the Ascendant. From an early age she saw spirits and more than once she frightened her family with her precognitive visions.

Periodically she would try to repress the images which came to her. During her teenage years, when she was, by her own admission, out of control, the family home was troubled repeatedly by poltergeist activity. As an adult, she was aware that strange— and fortunately minor— explosions might occur around her but she was well into her thirties before she realized this happened whenever she was in an incredible fury over something.

Shortly before coming to have her chart read, a bottle of pop had exploded in a supermarket, not far from her, while she was thinking angrily about difficulties with her husband. She had been vaguely aware, just moments before the bottle exploded, of a need to "throw off" some energy and then she spotted a large pyramid display of pop bottles. The display really "caught" her attention, as she described it, and then she "knew" something was going to happen. When it did, she hurried from the store and tried to forget the whole incident. Only when she was introduced to the many positive possibilities for psychic ability was she able to come to terms with her psychic power.

Neptune/Mars aspects, particularly the hard aspects, can leave the individual feeling terribly vulnerable. If Neptune erodes enough defenses, enough self-awareness, there is little barrier between the individual and the universal consciousness. But this time, the former gets lost in the latter. Psychic experiences can be powerful, yet very strange and disturbing. Dreams may be vaguely frightening. The individual may frequently feel that he lives on ever-shifting quicksand, that nothing is as it seems and nothing is to be trusted, not even his own feelings and perceptions. The resulting insecurity can be miserably uncomfortable and may lead to withdrawal, to anti-social behavior or outright loss of conscious control.

"ME FIRST!"

When Neptune erodes defenses, it often erodes inhibitions as well. Sometimes the identity can become expanded to include God. It can be "I (Mars) am God (Neptune)"; the sense of the Divine spark within overwhelms the helpless and immature identity which seeks a fraudulent, too-early association without doing any of the developmental work. Or not enough of it. The individual, aware that she is a part of the Divine, simply concludes she is also already spiritually developed, with all attendant privileges. Her Martian need to be out in front may be inflated by Neptune to the point where she takes for granted that whatever she has to do to be first is perfectly all right.

This combination may indicate a tendency to inflate other Martian traits— being first becomes a vital necessity, or assertion becomes an unquestioned way to live. The person may expand the adventurous, risk-taking nature of Mars, or the selfish, arrogant, obnoxious side of it. It may be experienced as a tendency to romanticize temper or aggression or selfish and self-serving behavior. Rugged individualism may seem appealing; sports or constant action may look like the ultimate challenge.

When Mars and Neptune clash, Neptune may erode the Martian energy and initiative, may create crippling self-doubts and constant start-stop behavior, or inflate the value of assertion to such a degree that the individual believes, or acts as if he believes, "I have the right to whatever I want."

Ideally, the Neptune energy will use compassion to guide the Mars energy during the early years of life, until the identity is well formed and sturdy enough to withstand challenges. Artistic talent and spiritual inclinations would exist peacefully alongside healthy exuberance and self-assertiveness. With maturity, the individual will seek to follow the inner promptings of Neptune, will seek to know more about herself, and then about the nature of the universe of which she is a part.

Jupiter Aspects to Neptune

This represents a double dose of idealism and is the most expansive and least sensible of all the aspect combinations. It can be a helpful aspect in a chart where a large dose of optimism is required to offset depressive or excessively earthy or materialistic tendencies. In a chart already full of fire and/or fantasy, it may glorify the passion and the magic until they are completely out of balance and control. Its importance, since neither planet is a personal planet, will be measured by the closeness of its involvement with other personal planets or the angles of the chart. If, for example, the Jupiter/Neptune aspect occurs around the same degree as the Sun, then there is a direct connection to the individual's personality. If the aspect occurs well away from the degrees occupied by all the personal factors in a chart, it is not going to be felt very strongly by the individual, or it may only operate sporadically as, for example, it is activated by transits or progressions.

THOUGHTS VERSUS FEELINGS

In the conjunction and hard aspects, this combination can represent a tendency to ricochet between what "should" be done (intellectual values) and what "feels" best (emotional values). Jupiter represents a part of human nature which wants to be "right," to be justified. It has all sorts of logical reasons and precedents for its opinion. It has made a judgment and come up with the "right" answer. Neptune symbolizes a part of human nature which wants to be compassionate; it senses that there is more to life than what is intellectually correct. Jupiter is not much inclined to consider people's feelings, but Neptune usually cannot stand the idea of hurting someone. Thus there is a clash between perfectionism and compassion.

EXCESSIVE FAITH

Since neither planetary theme is noted for its discrimination and both are vitally interested in "truth," there can be a tendency to be very vulnerable to and gullible over religious or spiritual issues. Both may be in a big rush to place faith in something huge. People with this aspect tend to be inherent "True Believers;" that is, they will believe what they want to believe without deeply challenging their assumptions, without even realizing they made those assumptions in the first place. Ideally, they will find a transpersonal philosophy to adopt, as both planets are inclined toward the transpersonal— larger than the individual or interpersonal. The spiritual philosophy adopted should be comprehensive and expansive, optimistic and growth-enhancing if it is to be constructive and healthy. However, people with this combination are easily attracted to intensely emotional faiths unless there is the strength of will to resist as shown in other chart factors.

It is a **profoundly emotional combination**. Jupiter may idealize Neptunian traits, so that deep emotional sensitivity, psychic abilities and compassion— as well as weakness, evasion and denial— become ultimate values. The strong need for connection to Universal Love which is associated with Neptune can become the most vital issue in life. The Neptunian tendency to save others can become infused with Jupiterian zeal. The result may be a charismatic evangelist or missionary, the true zealot. The person with a Jupiter/Neptune aspect of any kind may be subject to occasional bouts of overwhelming emotional intensity. He may swing from ecstasy to agony.

On the positive side, there will often be an ability to uplift and inspire others. There may be incredible sensitivity to others' feelings and the resultant empathy and compassion can be very strong. It may be so strong that the individual will need to withdraw periodically to clear herself and her aura of the feelings so easily picked up from others.

MAKE IT BETTER
On the negative side, any tendencies toward victim/savior/rescuer behavior may be expanded out of control. Savior tendencies particularly will be glorified and justified and may be pursued with particular zeal. But in a chart lacking strength, victim tendencies may be idealized and played to the hilt. Jupiter can support these "games" with a self-righteousness which knows no bounds and a complete lack of inclination to double-check beliefs and attitudes.

This combination can also indicate that any talents represented by Neptune may be glorified to the point where they seem almost holy, or Divinely ordained. Such an individual may feel anything he wants is justified if it contributes to his creativity or his ability to be inspired or inspiring.

It is also possible for the Neptune side to dominate the aspect. In this case the person may idealize higher learning, intellectualism, philosophy and/or books. Foreign travel and people may be romanticized and infused with great value. All of these issues may also be undermined with doubts; Neptune's insecurity could hamper Jupiter's optimism. Jupiter might even be repressed if it seems to present too much of a threat to Neptune, in which case Jupiterian traits will have to be experienced as if they come from the outer world.

Teachers in this person's life could be either inspirational and uplifting, providing a model for the spiritual aspect of life, or they could be overly sentimental, have unrealistic and/or unattainable expectations, be unreliable, impractical, ill or frequently out of touch with reality. There would be a tendency for them to like to talk and to disseminate information, but not necessarily to teach well. That is, they could have many brilliant and exciting ideas and concepts, but they would not have organized their ideas into a cohesive system, and they might not teach them properly. There would be a tendency for them to be disorganized and vague in their explanations, and perhaps they expect the individual to simply absorb the concepts by osmosis.

Neptune and Jupiter are both **vitally interested in faith and beliefs**, but the latter can feel quite comfortable— at least for a time— with conventional religions, while Neptune generally cannot. There may be, therefore, some clash between the religion in which the individual was raised, and the spiritual direction in which Neptune points. With the hard aspects, this conflict may take a long time to resolve, and the individual may suffer a great deal in the resolution, because she thinks she must give up one to have the other. As usual, true resolution comes when she gives value to both sides of the conflict and allows each of them an important place of expression in her life. She may, for example, take the best lessons from her conventional religion and continue to live those, while opening her mind to wider possibilities.

At its best, this combination is inspiring due to the **boundless faith** it represents. It is never, however, a practical aspect, so its tendency toward expansion and total trust will always need to be tempered, whether the aspect is "harmonious" or not. That very expansionism may be a blessing to— and work well in tandem with— an otherwise "heavy" chart, for example, one with a lot of earth and water placements. With discipline, it can become **the** inclination toward spiritual development.

Saturn Aspects to Neptune

In this combination, the complete pragmatist meets the ultimate mystic. It may be a particularly difficult aspect to express comfortably and constructively. There are such differences between Saturn, which is the planet of hard, cold reality, and Neptune, which is the planet of fantasy, that it takes a large measure of maturity and ego-strength to handle and express both energies. Moreover, neither planet is personal, in the way of the Sun, Moon, Mercury, Venus and Mars. Those planets seem to represent strongly personal traits, idiosyncrasies of which we are usually aware, and which set us somewhat apart from others. When a personal planet aspects an impersonal planet, the connection to the individual's nature is still quite strong; it represents a tendency with which the person can identify. If an aspect between two impersonal planets happens to aspect a personal planet, or a personal point such as the Ascendant or Midheaven, there is still a connection with the personality.

If, however, an aspect between two impersonal planets stands on its own or connects only to other impersonal planets, the individual has a difficult time integrating that part of his nature with the rest, and often is not aware that it exists. It tends to become part of his experience only when activated by transit or progression, at which time it seems like a very strange and foreign experience to him. Sometimes it describes conditions or traits which he encounters only in particular areas of life, such as the individual who is usually congenial and tolerant even over issues such as religion and politics. Let money enter the picture, however, and he may experience a sudden urgent need to control with a resultant loss of perspective.

INSPIRATION AND PERSPIRATION

When Saturn and Neptune do find constructive expression together, there is a wonderful balance between vision and responsibility. The Saturn talent for organization and discipline can provide a stable environment within which Neptune can create and successfully meet deadlines, free from outside distractions. Saturn might provide determination to see a project through, which Neptune is inspired to design and dream about, but not always able to actually create. Saturn can provide the business sense which Neptune needs in order to promote spiritual concepts and ideas. Saturn can take Neptune's vague promptings and expanded insights and organize them into a cohesive system of spiritual growth. Saturn can provide the practical know-how required to turn a dream, whether an artistic or spiritual one, into reality. Neptune might dream up a wonderful play; Saturn will organize the financing and production!

Neptune brings faith, optimism and inspiration to Saturn's

demands that everything be useful and **real**. Neptune provides a less harsh view of reality, a view with promise and hope and a dash of magic, to Saturn's world of demanding responsibilities. Neptune softens and expands Saturn's certainty that everything in life has a practical scientific explanation. It brings an uplifting measure of hope and an awareness that there is much more to life than the material. Neptune brings compassion to Saturn's tendency to be cut-and-dried about issues.

When Saturn and Neptune clash, there can be a conflict between the convictions of scientific truth and mystical, spiritual needs. Neptune tends to erode Saturn's concepts of reality, which can be very threatening if the individual has accepted Saturn's way for most of his life. Neptune is gullible while Saturn is cynical, optimistic where Saturn is pessimistic, and full of faith and hope where Saturn is beset by fears and perhaps feelings of hopelessness.

Saturn is bewildered and threatened by Neptune's ability to accept things on faith. Saturn represents that part of nature which wants proof, signed contracts in triplicate and money in the bank. Neptune is bewildered by Saturn's hard-nosed refusal to see beyond the materialistic possibilities of the world. Neptune symbolizes that part of nature which knows that life is much richer and there are far wider possibilities available to those with eyes to see. It's just not very good at explaining it!

Neptune can be threatened by Saturn's demands for proof. Neptune wants to indulge in flights of fancy or faith without the burden of always being practical. Neptune wants to believe in her best friend's ability to finish and sell her new painting, even though Saturn knows that the woman has never completed a project. The Neptunian part of a person wants to daydream or learn more about a new spiritual leader; the Saturnian part is worried about the drop in sales at her office. Saturn wants to know exactly what happens to each penny she spends; Neptune can't remember what she spent it on, let alone how much!

BLOCKED DREAMS

Needless to say, these two in combination can lead to a particularly distressing stop-and-start syndrome. When feeling Neptunian, the individual could start some promising mystical pursuit, only to reprimand herself for sheer impracticality later when she is in a Saturn mood. Saturn could begin a new project certain to improve his salary, only to end up distracted by a fascinating new television series on magic. Neptune could yearn to find an outlet for artistic leanings, but finds that some part of herself insists that such pursuits are frivolous. Saturn could organize a tight schedule and make up lists of things to do, but "accidentally" sleeps in late so that the whole day is thrown off. Whatever one starts, the other can sabotage.

Worse, whatever one planetary motif inclines toward, the other can judge as useless so that whatever the individual does, there is some part of himself which is unhappy and may feel guilty. In this case, the aspect is indicative of the potential for chronic depression which is particularly intractable. No matter which conventional approach is used to treat the depression, one or the other planetary theme feels left out and tends to undermine the other.

This kind of continuous discomfort is tolerated by some, but many are driven to remove it in some way. They may, of course, take counseling and learn to accept both needs in such a way that they learn to prevent the sabotage and use each drive to support the other, or learn to express each in appropriate situations.

PROJECTION
Usually, however, the individual attempts to solve the quarrel by evicting one of the quarrelers. She chooses one planetary theme as more valuable and expresses it, while condemning the other as undesirable. Typically, in the square, opposition or quincunx, one planet and all that it symbolizes is repressed while the other is expressed. The individual with the aspect takes on one planet and "gives" the expression of the other away to someone else.

If she expresses Neptune, for example, she will tend to give the Saturn qualities to her father or the parent who taught her about responsibility and the realities of life, as well as to authority figures and superiors. They will express Saturn, with demands that she get her feet on the ground, make something of herself, finish what she starts, stick to deadlines and schedules, plan for her future and save money. She, on the other hand, will express Neptune, with consistent daydreaming, inability to focus on a job, and lack of concern about the mundane affairs of the world. Because she has chosen Neptune, she will feel very vulnerable to those people who express Saturn, and she may become particularly evasive or denial-oriented around them.

Because Neptune tends to make an ultimate value out of anything it contacts, the individual who has a Saturn/Neptune aspect but expresses only Neptune may find himself in the uncomfortable and guilt-producing position of denying the very thing Neptune endows with value.

If he expresses only Saturn traits, on the other hand, he will "give" Neptune to someone else, perhaps described by the house placement of Neptune. For example, Neptune in the third house could be ascribed to a brother or sister, in the sixth house to a coworker, in the ninth to a minister, and so on. While the individual acts responsibly, is ambitious, cautious, respectful and reliable, there will be at least one person in his life who believes in fairy tales, or tells them, who spends his time drinking or watching too much TV, who is frequently ill or who simply cannot cope with life at all and opts out, at least as long as Neptune is projected.

The individual who has attempted to split off the offending planet in this way needs to learn that both Saturn and Neptune represent positive, beneficial qualities, and that those qualities can actually enhance each other if used consciously and wisely.

The individual who tolerates the push-pull between these two planets also needs to learn to appreciate the constructive capabilities of each, and that there are appropriate times and situations for each to be expressed. The individual can learn that one planetary theme naturally tends to make the other look like something which is better dismissed, but that this natural lack of respect can be overcome with insight. Then each group of qualities can be used in situations where they are most helpful. Saturn can be drawn out during work, or when discipline is required, and Neptune can be drawn out when creativity or a sense of hope and faith is needed.

For the individual whose Saturn/Neptune aspect is not connected to personal planets or points, the experience of this aspect will tend to be sporadic, triggered by transits or progressions. That means the person will have little chance to develop the skills necessary to express this combination. At the same time, she probably won't have built up resistance between the two planetary motifs either. This individual may need only a short explanation of the significance of each planet and how to use each of them most constructively, rather than repeated counseling sessions.

INTEGRATION
Saturn and Neptune in combination are certainly capable of indicating that the individual generates a great deal of pain when he attempts to express either grouping of traits, but when he has learned to utilize each one in its appropriate situation, there are wonderful and greatly satisfying rewards. Neptune may have difficulty confronting the issue, but Saturn is always willing to work at problems, and this provides hope that the individual can, with maturity and patience, learn to handle this aspect.

Uranus Aspects to Neptune

This is an air/water combination, which heralds the possibility of conflict between thoughts and feelings. However, as another aspect between transpersonal planets, it may not be felt especially strong in the personality unless it ties in to more personal planets or points in the chart.

FUTURIST
At their best, Uranus and Neptune combine to indicate an extraordinarily farsighted individual with both the ability to visualize innovations and the compassion to make those innovations benefit humankind. There could also be a great deal of psychic sensitivity and awareness of energies and forces not normally dealt with by people. The individual would tend to be a strong utopian, with real appreciation for developing a society where science and technology held equal value with psychology and spirituality. He would have a vivid sense of the possibilities of which humanity is capable, and the feeling that society should be structured in such a way as to encourage the development of all that is best in each individual.

These two planets represent themes which are not easily combined, however. Uranus represents a tendency to be detached, aloof, highly intellectual, logical, independent and individualistic. Neptune represents a tendency to be loving, warm, highly emotional, and arational and it hints at the need for surrender of the individuality to reconnection with the Universal Spirit of which we all are part.

HEART VERSUS HEAD

When they clash, Uranus can devalue Neptune's compassion and empathy, while Neptune can undermine Uranus' technological pursuits. Uranus may lend its erratic quality to Neptune's traits, indicating that the person is warm and loving one minute, cold and aloof and unreachable the next. Neptune may glorify Uranian traits only to find they are not the source of ultimate happiness after all.

IN LEFT FIELD

Transpersonal planets which are not handled well can also bring out the worst in each other. Uranus and Neptune share a tendency to be attracted to the unusual. With Uranus the attraction is for the innovative, the new and different. With Neptune it is for the otherworldly. These two can combine to produce a taste for the very strange and the downright weird. If Neptune romanticizes Uranus' need to be shocking, the bizarre can seem very appealing indeed. This can particularly affect the belief systems and thought processes, if the individual is inclined to give rein to this tendency. However it may be associated with a taste for chaotic electronic music, "pop" art, fashions which range from innovative and eclectic to startling, or really "way out" science fiction.

This aspect, like several between the outer planets, lasts for many years and exists for many individuals. It therefore tends to describe in some way important circumstances into which a large number of people are born, and issues with which the world will be grappling as they grow up. Those members of the group who have the aspect connected to their personal planets or chart points will be most affected by or most influential in those circumstances.

Pluto Aspects to Neptune

In this era, we are dealing with only one Neptune/Pluto aspect: the continuing sextile. It seems to signify a time when the world as a whole will experience a significant openness to unconscious and spiritual issues. Indeed, there will be a tremendous flow of emotional energy, of energy and material from the collective unconscious and of powerful spiritual forces which are normally very subtle.

OPENING UP THE DEPTHS

The fact that the aspect is a sextile is a real boon. With the sextile, there is much opportunity for the world community to deal with "occult" knowledge in an open and tolerant way, rather than with fear. Much that has been hidden, taboo or cloaked with ignorance and misunderstanding can now be accepted with some degree of comfort. Furthermore, this aspect provides a welcome component of feeling and compassion to a world gone slightly crazy with technology. Since both are water planets, much of the work goes on beneath the level of awareness at which people commonly live, but it does go on. Issues which concern people often arise from a sense, a feeling that something is not quite right. People pay more attention to their so-called "instincts," and more and more respect is given to intuition and "gut" feelings.

This aspect may indicate that the world community has the opportunity to develop a very strong sense of the power of the unconscious and an awareness, vague but meaningful, of the need to pay attention to issues which have traditionally been swept under the collective carpet. It may be symbolic of increased power on the spiritual levels, and it may mean that many individuals will have the ability to tap into these levels to an amazing degree. Certainly it is indicative of the increased consciousness of our spiritual heritage, although individuals react to that consciousness in different degrees and in a variety of ways.

OBSOLETE IDEALS

The spiritual nature of human beings could be in for some major renovation as ideas generated for the last two centuries or so are brought up for some in-depth examination and either upheld as valid or eliminated. The unconscious part of human nature and the power of its drives could be granted considerable value and may be overvalued by some. Generally speaking there will be a willingness to look at the painful parts of our spiritual tendencies and needs.

Unquestioned values will also come up for review. There will be some tendency to place too much importance on Plutonian issues of sexuality, power, the unconscious, intimacy and so on. If these get far out of balance, people will have to face their illusions over the issues and try to become more clear about their role in a wholesome life.

Since everyone born within the last few decades has this aspect, the importance of it in an individual's life will be determined by its connection to other important personal points in her chart.

CHAPTER SEVEN

SHORT CUTS TO THE PROMISED LAND

By this time, you will probably see just how many ways there are to misdirect Neptunian drives, not to mention how easy it is to be confused about the planet of confusion. The big question is, are there any ways to help those who have trouble with Neptunian themes to create a better relationship to, and use of, the Neptune in their lives? The answer is yes.

Clarify Constructive Options

The first step is to clarify the truth and the reality of the constructive, healthy expressions of Neptune to those who find this energy anything but clear. However, it is important to keep in mind that many people who have chosen the "suffer" part of the "serve or suffer" theme with Neptune will not be willing to change. This group includes those who **think** and **say** they want to be different, but who are unwilling to give up their present attitudes and habit patterns, for whatever reason. Usually the reason is that they are unwilling to give up something else which goes along with the "suffer" scene, such as the maintenance of an image of themselves as very special. Without a change in beliefs and attitudes, outward change is at best temporary.

Savior/Victim Interchanges

It is also important to recognize that the very attitude of wanting to change others puts us into a "missionary" frame of mind, which ties right in to the potentially negative expression of Neptune as savior. Saviors have a nasty habit of ending up as martyrs. So many times, what begins as one friend or lover offering a helping hand turns into a contest between monsters.

The very act of offering a helping hand implies that the other person is somehow helpless. The not-so-subtle message is that she cannot help herself. This is a significant put-down if not handled very carefully. The person being helped is nudged into the role of victim, while the helper takes the role of savior. The victim may well resent her role, and may unconsciously seek to punish the savior by becoming **more** dependent rather than less. In other words, it is as if she says to herself, "He wants to play savior, does he? Well, then, he can darned well play savior and he can carry the whole load, all by himself!"

Such a shift of power may cure a would-be savior, if the shift is deliberate, conscious and obvious. For example, a woman struggling to learn how to handle an electric drill may ask for some hints from her spouse. If he insists on taking over the job, however, she has several options. She can feel useless, or foolish or put-down or patronized, all of which are ways to accept the victim role. She can tell him off for his lack of sensitivity, which makes him the victim. Or she can realize that he— unconsciously— has initiated a victim/savior game and she can choose to play along or not.

If she chooses not to play along, she can deliberately, consciously and obviously shift the power he thinks he wants over to him, with a sense of humor. She could tease him about coming to her rescue, playing up her supposed helplessness. Done without malice, this usually results in a slightly sheepish would-be savior who will relinquish his game fairly quickly. If the prospective savior is enormously insecure, however, a straightforward and gentle but firm explanation of what is desired will yield happier results. Teasing such a person only results in hurt feelings, which he will usually feel justified in displaying so that the other person feels guilty.

To return to the main point here, we cannot help or save those who aren't willing. They will only intensify their own role or game. Furthermore, it is questionable whether we have any right to impose our own timetable on them. To do so is arrogant and disrespectful of their own abilities and process.

Furthermore, if we encounter Neptunians in our life, it will also be the case that it is our own Neptune which is not being expressed well. If you find yourself having to engage with a Neptunian, you also have a Neptunian lesson to learn, you also will be very susceptible to Neptune games and mistakes and confusion. You also will easily drift down the wrong path. That person you want to rescue so badly could well represent a test which measures how well you handle your Neptune. Have you learned enough to resist getting dragged into a victim/savior game?

Clarify Worldly Rules

If you have, you may be ready for the second step in dealing with Neptunian problems. The first was clarification of the constructive possibilities. The second is clarification of the rules of the world, or those facts and laws within which we have to work until we can transcend them, such as the limits of time and physical energy, and the limits agreed upon by most people as to what is acceptable behavior in relationships. The Neptunian may have great difficulty with these, knowing as he does that these laws are not of the spirit. They feel so limiting and so burdensome, yet he needs to appreciate that they also provide a framework within which he can grow and learn some extremely important concepts. Those concepts will only become real to him and for him when learned through actual experience. Without acceptance of the worldly laws, both physical and social, the Neptunian may easily spend his efforts in meaningless pursuit of unattainable dreams.

Accept Personal Responsibility

The third step in dealing with Neptunian problems, after acceptance of the constructive possibilities and the limits imposed by the physical and social world, is that of acceptance of responsibility for personal behavior, attitudes and values. Only when this step is taken will the roles and games cease. They will, in fact, no longer be necessary because they were defense mechanisms designed to protect a vulnerable self. With acceptance of personal responsibility usually comes a sense of personal power, and with this usually comes the implementation of healthy coping behaviors rather than unhealthy defense mechanisms.

The actual process of change generally takes some time. Even if the individual suddenly sees in a revelatory flash that she has had a "victim" mentality which has contributed to much of her unhappiness, she cannot change her habit patterns overnight. She requires some time to become familiar with all the little self-defeating behaviors and to turn them into self-promoting behaviors. In actual practice, she may need to be taught about exactly how she backs herself into an uncomfortable situation, and what options there are. Even those who desperately want to change often cannot begin to imagine how to be different. Given some insight and some ideas, however, they often rework their attitudes and then their behavior.

The following sections are all about insight and ideas. Take what is appropriate to yourself and use it. It can serve no higher purpose.

The following "roles" are rarely found in solitude in a Neptunian. Rather, they are all aspects of the negative Neptunian path. The Neptunian will often draw on all of them, switching back and forth as it suits his purpose. They are isolated here for the purposes of identification and learning how to handle these behaviors in an effective manner.

Pretend with Me

"Pretend with Me" is a perennial temptation with Neptune, which is the planet associated with God, Heaven, Nirvana, the ultimate spiritual ecstasy, the ultimate fulfillment and so on. Neptune represents the energy which reminds us of our spiritual heritage and the Divine spark within each of us. It operates on emotional, psychological, and spiritual levels. At the highest levels, energy flows without effort, without resistance or pain, and this is part of the expectation of Neptune.

AN EASY LIFE

Effort, on the other hand, is part of the experience and expectation of the physical world, in which Neptune may be truly as uncomfortable as a fish out of water. Neptune energy yearns for fulfillment, but never expects to have to work for it. Somehow it is all **supposed to happen by magic**; it will simply flow and be perfect.

At some level, that is true. The energy which is Neptunian really does flow without any effort. If seen from the perspective of the physical world, such a flow may seem magical, mysterious, beyond understanding. At the level at which Neptunian energy works, however, the rules are simply different. At its own level, Neptunian energy and its flow makes perfect sense. Neptune is the planet which symbolizes **surrender**— the abandonment of resistance, the removal of barriers and demands. Somehow we humans— even we enlightened ones(!)— need to accept and understand that until we are able to transcend this world and our own resistance, fears, barriers and demands, we have to live by its rules. And one rule of this physical world is that work gets done by the application of effort.

ATTACHMENTS

Mind you, the effort spoken of here is not necessarily physical work. It is more like the effort of change. As long as we perceive ourselves to be creatures of flesh and blood, we tie ourselves down with attachments. Some attachments are to images we hold about ourselves, about others, about the nature of reality. Every time we wish to change, we have to let go of one or more of these attachments. We have to make a new definition to suit our new understanding. This involves a challenge to our established basic perception of the world and that process is very threatening. It is the effort involved in overcoming fear and allowing the challenge to occur that is part of our earthly experience. Neptunian energy can only flow without effort when there is no fear, no resistance, no regret, no dishonesty. There has to be perfect openness and receptivity.

Many people do not understand this. They expect the ease and harmony without realizing that it only comes when we transcend our very human habits. They may be so caught up in the wonderful vision of Neptune that they cannot live comfortably with the reality of the world. Unwilling to live in the world as we know it, unaware that they have to change themselves to make their world better, they block it out of their minds and create one that is more to their liking. There is a strong element of **self-protection** involved in this process. Many Neptunians subtly ask those around them to join in their pretend world, or at least to leave them with their illusions.

For instance, take a father who cannot cope with his daughter growing up to be a sexual being. Perhaps he has not come to terms with sexuality in general, or perhaps he is somewhat jealous of this youngster who has all the excitement and wonder of discovery ahead of her. Perhaps the overt signs of sexual awakening in his daughter makes the father aware that he is no longer the most important male in her life. Often, he has to cope with what he knows is an entirely inappropriate attraction to her. This can easily occur because many men in Western society view all reasonably attractive females as potential sexual objects. When his own daughter begins to fit into this category, he is attracted, but he may also be appalled by this feeling and be unable to account for it. Whatever the reason, if he denies the reality of his daughter's maturity, he will also ask her to deny it.

He may do this overtly; he may come right out and set rules which are more appropriate for a much younger child. He may forbid her to dress in tight clothes or wear makeup, even though it is common and acceptable for teenagers her age to do so. He may be verbally critical whenever she attempts to behave like other kids.

He may also do this covertly. He may withdraw from her so that she feels abandoned and somehow unaccepted. He may ignore her when she dresses up, be preoccupied when she is jittery about an important date, and look walleyed or bored when she mentions boys to whom she is attracted. She will soon get the message that he does not wish to be a part of her new experiences, that he is uncomfortable with them and that he would prefer that she did not talk about them around him. He is subtly asking her to protect him from her own growing-up process! He refuses to deal with her new maturity, he pretends to himself that it is not real, and he plays on her love of him to get her to protect his pretense.

IGNORING TRUTH

There are many different forms of "Pretend with Me." People who are prone to sudden bouts of destructive behavior often tell themselves that they don't really do any harm and they try to charm those on the receiving end of the destructiveness into a quick and easy forgiveness which supports their lie. Anyone who won't look honestly at the effects of her behavior, whether those effects are constructive or destructive, is playing "Pretend." If she also asks others to participate or to keep silent, she is playing "Pretend with Me."

Wherever a person has illusions, romantic notions, big dreams or is unrealistic, and asks others to support his images rather than their own sense of reality, he is playing the game. Everyone has such areas; there are always some issues which people push away or about which they tell themselves only part of the truth. Often these are minor and do not threaten in any major way the quality of life, but some people play with more dedication and on more intense levels than others. Those who push the role beyond the level of everyday foibles get into prolonged daydreaming, impossible idealism, gullibility, artificial glamour, chronic dissatisfaction, deceit and so on. The next level includes hallucinations, mental illness, drug and alcohol problems, and ongoing and debilitating illnesses.

GETTING OTHERS TO SUPPORT PRETENSIONS

What distinguishes "Pretend with Me" from plain old "I'll Pretend" is that the former involves other people and asks them to protect the Neptunian from the reality with which he does not wish to deal. In so doing, the Neptunian asks them to value his pretensions more than their own perceptions. It is an excellent way to make other people feel confused, used and abused, which sounds like a victim/savior/martyr scene. It is also virtually guaranteed to drive close relatives and friends into insanity.

It is a basic human need to feel that life is orderly and predictable and that the rules are known, understood and within our ability to carry out. Some sturdy individuals are able to play along with a Neptunian pretender with amused detachment. Many people, however, find their own sense of reality badly damaged. A child particularly may suffer and feel that what he sees is obviously not real. Such beliefs lead quickly to a sense of hopelessness and defeat, if not outright schizophrenia.

DEALING WITH IT IN SELF

If you recognize yourself in these pages, understand that your **overdone strength is creativity and idealism.** However, every time you pretend rather than deal with an issue, you build on a weakness. You reinforce it. You pamper it and give it a warm and welcoming environment. You feed it and give it power. It may already be big enough to overwhelm you! You reinforce your belief that you cannot deal with that issue. The next time you are faced with it, you will carry that much larger a burden of belief in your inability to deal with it, and it will become a self-fulfilling prophecy— eventually you will be completely convinced that you cannot cope and you will see no possible way to do so.

In many ways you won't allow yourself to see other options. The problem with taking charge of an issue is that it might make you see what a lot of time and energy you have wasted perpetrating the old belief that you couldn't cope. It can be very humiliating to admit that you were defeating yourself all by yourself for ten years or forty years or more. It can really hurt to admit that you did so to protect a weak and vulnerable part of yourself, rather than because the issue was too big to handle. It can be so painful to see that you could have changed years ago and didn't, out of lack of confidence or lack of strength or unwillingness to give up some benefit of playing on your weakness. There is another side to realization, however, which is that from this moment on, you can take charge of your life rather than running from it.

A change of attitude is vital. You will make the outer changes you desire much easier to achieve and maintain if you make the inner change as well. Look at the beliefs which enchain you. Think about the last time you felt threatened or uncomfortable and shut someone up or dismissed them or changed the subject because you didn't want to have to deal with it. Think about all the times you squirm and look for a pattern. Do you always shut people off when quarrels are about to erupt? Then ask yourself how you feel about anger. Perhaps you hate bad manners and gloss over them when others display them. Possibly power makes you uncomfortable, or maybe you don't want to talk about your feelings. Ask yourself how you feel about the issues you have tried to avoid. **Write down your answers** so that you won't forget (Neptune) them. Ask yourself if there is any other way to handle these issues. What do other people do? Is there anyone you know who handles these issues, or one of them, with grace and effectiveness? How?

Look at the effects of your behavior on yourself. See how the evasive tactic of pretense reinforces your sense of weakness, not your sense of strength. See how it affects others— look at how you ask them to deny their reality in favor of yours. Doesn't this seem disrespectful and in fact tyrannical? Does this attitude lead to behavior which makes you feel genuinely good about yourself or only temporarily secure? Do you feel stronger and more able to cope, or more insecure so that you overreact to a challenge in this area? If you feel you **must** defend yourself in a particular area, ask yourself if everyone feels that way. Not everyone does. This must mean it is an issue which you personally find threatening but it is not intrinsically evil or everyone would be scared of it.

It takes courage to admit that fear is the basis of the attitude and therefore of the behavior. Ask yourself if you want to change. Are you willing to settle for the fraudulent luxury of pretense? Are you willing to face the pain of knowing you are wasting years on a defense mechanism rather than growing in skill and strength? Are you willing to see that you make this issue increasingly difficult for yourself? Are you willing to face the initial pain of self-confrontation, of knowing and accepting yourself as you are, as others see you, rather than pampering yourself with comforting images?

This pain, incidentally, will not last long; it will only be experienced while your carefully cultivated images are in their death throes. When it is all over, you will feel very clear and clean and strong. **With self-honesty and focus comes a remarkable flow of inner power** which more than compensates for any loss of "safe" concepts. In fact, when you have truly made the necessary changes, you do not mourn the loss of anything for you see clearly what a terrible price you paid in the past for your illusions and you experience immense relief to be free of their thrall.

Learn to use discomfort as a warning signal for ruthless honesty and clarity rather than for evasion and pretense. The usual process is: the experience of discomfort or threat, which leads to the fastest defense— the one which you've practiced the most. If you've practiced evasion, that is your fastest method, and if you want to become good at another method which you think will give you better results, you will need to practice that one as much as possible.

Step by Step

Take one issue at a time. Begin with one that is not too threatening, but from which you habitually turn away. It could be something such as deciding what programs your children will watch on TV, and putting up with their vehement protests, quarrels and sulky retaliations because you have come to accept the parental responsibility to monitor what your children are exposed to.

It could be a decision to tell the truth next time a person who habitually tries to impose on you asks for something you don't wish to give. Decide to say, "No, I don't think I will do that this time," with no apologies or explanations. If you have changed the inner belief about what you owe to other people, you will remain firm because you will be clear about what you wish to give and what is an unfair imposition on you, considering your time, energy and circumstances.

The point is, to conquer this habit of "Pretend with Me" in yourself, you must first admit that you do it, then look to see what effects it has on others. If you do this a great deal you will find that few people communicate with you on any meaningful level because you have carefully taught them that you don't like the truth. At the same time you will probably find that other people ask you to protect them from reality, ask you to protect their favorite little pretense. We tend to get back what we put out. All of life is a mirror, albeit a maddening and frustrating one when we don't wish to take an honest look at our behavior.

If others do not communicate with you in depth, or certain subjects are not brought up around you, then you can be sure that you cut people off on those issues. So stay alert to the next time you feel that someone asks you to pretend for their sake. Ask yourself how you feel. You probably lose some respect for them. When you play the game, others feel the same way. They too lose respect and withdraw.

Loss of Intimacy

The next step is the examination of how this behavior rewards you and how it harms you. The reward is comfort, although it is a fraudulent comfort bought at the price of losing intimacy in your relationships. Still, it has been an important reward. It has served to protect something vulnerable in you. It harms you by nibbling pieces and hunks out of your self-respect, self-esteem and self-image. It harms you by reinforcing a sense of weakness and inability to cope. It harms you by perpetrating a self-fulfilling prophecy.

Then you need to look at exactly what belief or beliefs are being protected by this mechanism. What is it in you that needs such pampering and cannot withstand any challenge or even a close look? Be thorough and determined in this question, for Neptunian issues are often covered in layers of fog, confusion and false clues.

Neptune Tools

You may wish to use the many available Neptunian tools to get at the inner issue. Dreams, the myths behind the planets aspected by Neptune in your chart, or any planet in a water sign or house, tarot cards, Astro-Dice, analysis of your favorite verbal expressions and regular meditations all allow the answer to filter through from the unconscious to the conscious mind.

Now, do you need or wish to continue to reinforce this particular belief? If so, it is your decision. If not, you will have to challenge it: ask yourself "Who says I have to...." and "Where did this attitude come from?" "Is it true?" "Is there something more true with which I can replace this?"

You may find that inside you is a wholesome belief about your self-worth but a habit of feeling too weak to defend yourself against certain kinds of attacks. In this case the belief about your self-worth is healthy, but the belief about your right to assert your worth is not healthy. Question it. Look at where it came from and see if it was formed under circumstances where you genuinely were in a weak position. As an example, perhaps you could not defend yourself against your parents without risking their wrath or withdrawal of their support. As an adult, do you still favor acquiescence rather than assertiveness? Do you pay a price for this? If so, what is that price? Is it one you think is worth paying? Do you want to go on paying it? If not, reread this whole section again.

When you find a better truth, one that is more appropriate for your life as it is now, reinforce that with affirmations, always keeping in mind that they may, in turn, need to be replaced one day.

Next, begin to **plan how you will handle yourself the next time** you feel uncomfortable over this situation. Use the Neptunian ability to be creative and imaginative to think of ways to behave. Try to remember if you have ever seen anyone else handle this situation successfully, and if so, analyze what s/he did. Could you do the same thing? It might be appropriate for you but it might not be. His/her behavior might clash with a value you hold dear. If you have a strong value that says it is wrong to hurt other people, honor that value as far as it goes, but do not try to protect other people from yourself or from the consequences of their own behavior. If you assert your own rights and they feel hurt, often it is just a manipulation on their part to make you feel guilty. You do not have to participate in this game, either.

With this type of issue, belief in your right to assert yourself and to assert your worth, your sense of reality, and your beliefs is vital to success. With a strong belief comes the ability to be "up front," to face issues which formerly made you run for cover emotionally or psychologically. Practice makes perfect. It will probably be difficult to believe that you can handle a situation which has always baffled or intimidated you in the past, but the more you actually do it, the more that strength becomes yours.

DEALING WITH IT IN OTHERS

Often, the reason you find many people in your life are evasive or deceptive or destructive but charm you out of your anger, or simply "space out," is that this is an issue for you. You may do the same things or you may condemn them, but either way you are out of balance in your relationship to this side of life. You have declared that you do not need the god Neptune in your life and have refused to honor at least this aspect of all that Neptune represents. The gods will never stand for this. It is hubris, and the god so offended will demand a place in your life one way or the other. His role will make you miserable unless you realign yourself with him, accept his importance and plan to use his energy.

Collusion

When other people in your life play "Pretend with Me," you can walk away from the encounter feeling dismissed, used or negated. You may feel that the person will only love you or respect you or be nice to you if you do support her pretensions. You may feel that she is too fragile to face reality, so you will voluntarily protect her. You may think and accept that the person has some other kind of power over you and will use that power against you unless you support her particular illusion. Whatever reasons there are, genuine love is not one of them. Love includes respect, and there is nothing respectful about collusion in a fabrication.

We often do collude out of politeness, which may be acceptable to us on a social level. There is no need to go around pulling the psychological supports out from every individual we meet. The intimacy of the relationship and the importance of the issue will tend to determine whether it is necessary to "get real" about it. In other words, if you feel someone is using your affections to gain your cooperation in their illusion, you will feel used. It is time to stop playing along. If the issue is an important one to you and a casual acquaintance asks you to support his fantasy, it is time to refuse, for the sake of your own sense of self-worth.

Kind, but Firm

The first step in dealing with this problem in others is to question yourself quite rigorously about why it is important to you to do so. If you are doing it for one-upmanship or for revenge, out of resentment or outrage, you will turn the problem into a power struggle. You will be focused on winning rather than on living according to your values. You may well win, at least on the surface, but no one ever really wins a power struggle. The apparently vanquished individual always has a route for revenge, even if all she can do is talk about you behind your back and weaken your reputation.

If however, you can approach the issue from the perspective of standing up for your view of the world, because you no longer wish to play a role which leaves you feeling weak and a little soiled, you will be firm in your resolve and very strong in the face of temptations to join in new Neptunian games. You will see clearly where you contribute to undermining your self-esteem and you will accept responsibility for that part and be determined not to continue in that behavior.

You may wish to confront the individual outright, a situation which can arise when the person concerned is close and/or is encountered frequently.

In this case you could initiate the conversation and invite the other to sit down and listen to a problem you have. Gently but firmly you would lay out your case. You can listen with compassion to his side of the issue, for he frequently has a complaint against you, too. If he gets into name-calling or blaming, it is time to interrupt and bring him back to the main issue. If he tries to use guilt, it is time to bring him back to the main issue. You can question him to find out what he really wants, and in this way bring clarity to what is usually an incredible Neptunian muddle in his mind, as it once was in yours. In the end you can, if you have it in you, express support and confidence in him, an example of Neptunian acceptance, but at the very least you make clear, in a kind way, that you will no longer play "Pretend with Me" for him.

Rephrasing

In a less intense relationship, confrontation will likely be more comfortable on an as-it-happens basis. You can plan ahead how you will handle yourself the next time you encounter this person and his particular favorite role. What works best is usually a blunt but not rude rephrasing of his remarks and requests. If, for example, a person who promised to meet you at a particular time shows up an hour late with a grin and a charming, "Well, you know me," you can answer "You want me to know that you are always late," or "You want me to know that I am not supposed to rely on you," or "You want me to accept that you won't show up when say you will."

Needless to say, the person so confronted will receive a nasty shock. Up until now you have played along and allowed her to gloss over her behavior and the effects it has on others. Furthermore, you have even allowed her to subtly ask you to play along without having to actually ask out loud. Everything has been handled on a very civilized basis.

Some recipients of this type of confrontation can be expected to get rather vicious. You will need to be prepared for this— especially since you are probably struggling with Neptunian issues yourself and tend to have a horror of fights. The other person may be aware of this and may attempt to hit you in your weak spot by creating the very situation you detest.

Others crumble right in front of your eyes, playing into your easily activated Neptunian guilt and protective instincts. They are stronger than they look. You are stronger than you feel. They will never grow themselves if you protect them from the results of their own behavior.

Some will mumble whatever comes into their heads and retreat. If the relationship is not particularly important to you, this may be enough. All you wanted was to assert your own position and you have done this. You may have to do it again next time you encounter this individual but soon you will teach him to relate to you honestly and without roles or games. If the relationship is important to you, you may need to do what you can to assure the person that you care for him, but you reassert your refusal to play a role for his sake, until he learns to relate to you openly.

Anything I Can Do You Can Do Better

People who play "Pretend with Me" want to stay in some control of their lives, unless they play on the very intense level of mental illness. People who fall into the attitude of "Anything I can do you can do better," however, are in a rush to relinquish apparent control. That is, they want someone else to take control, at least on the surface. They cultivate helplessness. They actively refuse responsibility, ignore opportunities to grow and learn, and panic when anyone tries to force them to stand on their own two feet. They are dedicated to the principle that responsibility equals guilt, and guilt is to be avoided at all costs.

This particular Neptunian problem overlaps not only "Pretend with Me" but also "Victim/Savior." "Helpless" is a specialized sort of victim who more or less lives according to the dictum "Let George do it." "George" is, in this case, any nearby would-be rescuer who is willing to do whatever "Helpless" is not willing to do.

"IT'S YOUR FAULT"

"Helpless" knows that whenever he can make someone else responsible for his life, he can always turn around and blame them if things go wrong. He doesn't want to worry about it. Since he prefers to float and dream and wish, he hasn't developed the ability to analyze the details of his life so he isn't sure what might go wrong, or why it might, but he is convinced that if it does he must not be blamed. A quick way to get rid of the guilt and any pressure to work effectively or take responsibility for himself is to be vague, confused, out of focus and therefore helpless.

"Helpless" may have to scramble once in a while when some determined person tries to shift the power back into her hands, and occasionally she wishes she had it back herself, but this yearning usually disappears quickly. She is in too much of a self-imposed fog to notice the price she pays for her role.

POWERLESS

In the first place, he is at the mercy of whoever is willing to take responsibility for his life, or for aspects of it. Teachers may direct him into boring, nondemanding courses which have nothing to do with his interests and don't teach him how to cope with life but he won't know what he does want to do so he goes along with their choices. Parents will tell him what to think about politics and religion, but since these subjects bore him he will agree with them, at least in public. Employers will tell him when to be at work, exactly what to do and how long to do it for. They will also pay him poorly, which he resents, but since he doesn't know how to stand up for himself— and cannot do so without taking back responsibility for his own life— he will accept this treatment. Medical doctors may recommend pills and surgery which may be in their own interests rather than his, but he won't know how to stop it. Mates may bully him into working at a job he detests, but since he can't remember what he needs, he will do as they say. His children know they can demand anything from him and get it because he is easily worn down. They will be rude and obnoxious long before they reach their teens, or they will take over the role of his helpers and protectors, having learned early in life not to expect too much from him.

UNCONSCIOUS SELF-DISGUST
In the second place, it won't be long before chronic boredom and unconscious self-disgust eat away at "Helpless" to a painful degree. She can't concentrate long enough to find out where the pain is coming from, so she will blame others. If she can't make any impact on them, which she might not be able to do since she has handed them all the power along with all the responsibility, she may turn to fantasy novels, television, alcohol or drugs to dull the pain. Or she might be particularly good at ignoring it so that she can function in life in spite of it. Then she will tend to find herself suffering from mysterious ailments, allergies, and perhaps, if her unconscious frustration is profound enough, chronic illness.

The "Helpless" role is every bit as destructive, if not more so, as the "Pretend" role. In fact, the helpless person has to play "Pretend" in order to support his helplessness. He cannot admit to having any strengths lest someone expect him to act on them. He has to pretend that everyone is more competent, more intelligent, more healthy, has more initiative and more drive than he does so that they will all carry out the roles he is unwilling to do.

ISOLATED INCIDENTS GENERALLY HARMLESS
As an aside, often individuals slip into a mini-helpless role around another person who is known to be much better at a particular job. Women commonly do this to get a man to change a tire for example, or a child with a difficult piece of homework might do it around a parent with a special ability in that type of work. Spouses often do this: a man will play helpless in the kitchen just as much as a woman will pretend she is not patient enough to cope with the inner workings of an electrical toaster.

In such instances, although the behavior is designed to convey a covert message, the helplessness does not blight a person's whole life. Ideally people would be able to turn to each other respectfully and say, "I could do this if I had to but I know you can do it properly and more easily than I. In this case I would appreciate it if you would do it." But when they don't, and the incidents of helplessness are isolated, little harm is done. There is a big difference between these socially acceptable modes of communication and the full-fledged dedicated life role of help-lessness.

The role of "Helpless" does carry the benefit of feeling taken care of by others; however this only partly compensates for the growing sense of self-disgust which usually hides just below the surface. Many people who engage in this particular role find themselves more and more helpless, and less and less secure. They may need constant reassurance that they will be looked after, or they may suffer incredible boredom because they do so little, build few strengths in themselves and accomplish so little. Eventually their inner emptiness may yawn like a beckoning chasm in front of them, impossible to fill.

DEALING WITH IT IN SELF

If you recognize these traits in yourself, know that your over-done strength is psychological insight into others. If you have really, honestly had it with being pushed around by everyone, with finding you cannot even have fun without someone else dictating what you can do, of suffering from an inner feeling of emptiness and dissatisfaction, you are ready to think about the possibility of change.

Find the Motivating Belief

First of all, you will need to examine the belief behind the behavior. Where did you learn that getting out of things was preferable to coping with them? How old were you at that time? Where did you learn that you were too weak or stupid or incompetent to handle various jobs and situations? Who said you had to live your whole life that way, never accomplishing anything of which you could be proud?

Then you will need to look at all the things you tell yourself which undermine your ability to be competent and to cope successfully. In many ways you will unconsciously reinforce your position of helplessness. You need to become aware of these ways and seek to reprogram them into positive messages. Every time you tell yourself you can't do something or ask another person to help when you could do it for yourself, you are undermining your own sense of self-worth, you prevent yourself from developing any inner strength and confidence, and you hand over control of your life to your rescuer. You may even heap praise on your rescuer in an attempt to make it clear to them that you need them. In the process, however, you also convince yourself.

You need to decide whether you want the rewards of self-sufficiency and are willing to do all the seemingly difficult things which you have previously avoided. There is no need to take it all on at once; it is too much when you have not built on your strengths. It is no different than any other skill; you need time to practice in order to become good at it. Build your strength and your skills on one thing at a time, and your self-confidence will rise. With a rise in self-confidence will come increased ability to cope with situations which currently look far too complicated or threatening.

Start Small

Decide now to begin taking care of one problem which you have habitually let others look after. Begin with an easy-to-handle issue with which you feel relatively comfortable. Plan now how you will handle it the next time it arises. Take your cue from the people who normally handle this for you. Do you like the way they manage the problem, or would you prefer to try a different approach? If so, what approach would you use?

A special feature of the "Helpless" role is the mental confusion or lack of focus which contributes to the feeling of an inability to cope. If this is your problem, you know that every time you think you have made up your mind to change, you either promptly "forget"— so quickly that even you get suspicious— or you grow tired and cannot concentrate enough to think a problem through.

Keep Working At It

Perseverance really is the only answer here. Unconsciously there is a lot of resistance, and this can only be handled by continuous, long-term insistence on doing what you set out to do. Usually this means writing down thoughts and especially decisions. When you try to think something through, every time your mind wanders, gently pull it back on task. If you feel enormously sleepy, get up and do some deep breathing and a little exercise. Or you can go to sleep, and literally sleep yourself out until your body cannot sleep any more, and then go back to the problem or issue. Sooner or later the resistance will lessen and you can begin to explore that in itself. Do not ignore it for it does not go away unless resolved.

Once you have had some successes at handling minor issues, take on something a little tougher. (You will have had some "failures" too, but you will have survived those and learned from your mistakes.) Do you need to learn a skill in order to take care of this problem? Then give yourself permission to be not too skillful at first. Learn what you need to in the most appropriate way for yourself. It may be that a friend or neighbor can teach you, or perhaps a book or a class is in order. Promise yourself that you will honestly do as much as you possibly can on this problem, even though it might be scary or tiresome. **The more you can solve problems and handle issues on your own, the better you will feel about yourself.** It is, incidentally, permissible and even advisable to talk many issues over with others, who can provide different perspectives and may be able to offer important advice based on personal experiences.

Bear in mind that while it often **looks** easier to let someone else handle problems, the price is a poor sense of self-esteem and an ever-increasing sense of inability to cope. Dependency on others also carries a price: they will expect to "mother" or "father" you and consequently you will be treated somewhat like a child.

A certain degree of self-sufficiency, however, brings increased feelings of self-worth, self-liking, self-confidence and inner contentment. Build on your strengths and you will **have** strengths. They will be yours, but you need to take care of yourself to a large degree in order to develop those strengths, and the inner peace that comes with them.

DEALING WITH IT IN OTHERS
This can be frustrating beyond belief. To begin with, it bears repeating that we do not have the right to try to force another being into change or growth.

Then we need to realize that even a person who says she wants to be less helpless may have so undermined her self-esteem that she now may unconsciously believe she cannot be anything but helpless. Also, having been pampered and protected by others for a long period of time, she may not be entirely willing to give up this fraudulent security. Many people want the freedom to make their own choices but wish to avoid all traces of responsibility for themselves. They do not realize that their attachment to lack of responsibility—which feels to them like lack of guilt—stands in the way of their independence.

However, if you are determined to deal with the problem, helplessness in someone close to you can be confronted with simple nonaction on your part. Helpless people get away with their behavior because they attract helpers who can't wait to do something for someone else. They feed into each other's role, meshing nicely.

If you have been a chronic helper, simply stop. Ignore all silent indications that help is expected. You are too sensitive to these and "Helpless" usually doesn't even need to ask out loud. When he does begin to seduce you with protestations that he simply cannot be expected to do something for himself, or that you've always done it in the past, calmly adhere to your new position while reassuring him that you are confident he can manage.

It is important not to push too far too fast. Left to do too much for herself too quickly, she may well get ill, or have a horrible accident to make it doubly clear that she cannot survive without you. She truly believes on some levels that she has to have your help. She may also believe that she is entitled to it. She can, however, be gradually weaned from the helpless position if **you** are willing to give up the strong and superior role. Give up one helping behavior at a time, and start with the little things.

A Healthier Perspective

It will help your resolve considerably if you can resist seeing your new role as mean and nasty. See instead that you have chosen to step back from the "helpless/rescuer" game in favor of a more equal relationship. See that he will be a far more interesting person if he develops some strength of character. Give him the opportunity to discover for himself the joy of independence and the joy of accomplishment, no matter how much he resents you for abandoning him. In time he will gain confidence in his strengths, and in so doing will release you from a terrible burden and himself from a terrible prison.

If you don't succeed at this, it is time to question what you really want in the relationship. Perhaps you need a lot of control in the relationship, and being helpful feeds your own sense of control and, therefore, of security. Until you are ready to give this up, the other person will have a real uphill battle to give up his role.

In relationships which are not intimate, but where you get trapped by someone who is committed to the helpless game, you may wish to think ahead to your next encounter. Recall as clearly as you can all the little phrases this person uses to hook you into the helper role. She may say, "You're so much better at this," or "I'm useless at this," or "You always do such a great job," or something similar. She may also imply that she has too much to do and she has to have your help, that **only** you can help her, she can only trust you and your work, and so on. Pretty hooks, but hooks nonetheless. You will need to plan how to resist these.

One of the best forms of resistance is outright silence. Often a helpless person will drop little hints which are usually eagerly picked up by any nearby helper person. If you become nonreactive to these hints, you almost force the other to either give up the role or escalate it. A helpless person who is on the verge of giving up the game as a life-role may quickly drop the hints and the game, and relate to you respectfully.

Escalation is the more typical response to a lack of reaction, however. The helpless person, convinced he needs you, panics. The demands become more obvious. At this point you can simply state that you do not want to do what is being asked, without apologies or explanations. The helpless person will then frequently try to make you feel guilty. As with all other roles, you do not need to cooperate, even when the other person plays dirty and hits at your weaknesses. After all, you are certainly exposing one of his.

If the "hints" the helpless person drops are fairly blatant, you can feed back the hints, rephrased bluntly, but never unkindly. "You think you are busier than I am, and that I have time to do this," or "You think I do this better therefore I should do it," and so on. This will work well if "Helpless" does not want to face the role she habitually plays. In other cases it is not particularly effective because "Helpless" doesn't see anything wrong with asking for or even expecting help. In these cases, you will have to repeat your message of noncompliance every time you are imposed upon. Eventually "Helpless" will get the message that you no longer will play the old role. She may be forced to cope for herself, or she may simply turn elsewhere for a new rescuer. Either way you are free, and hopefully you have learned something about helping too much.

When the person who plays helpless is in a position of power over you, you may have to resort to simple silence and noncompliance, which forces "Helpless" to ask outright for whatever he wants. At this point you may be able to refuse the request in a respectful and straightforward manner; if it is not really part of your job it may be best to simply say so.

A useful strategy is to learn that when you are trying to communicate something to someone else, **stick to your own feelings or thoughts**. Say what you can or cannot do, simply. Do not make excuses, which may get you what you want but you will diminish your self-respect in the process. If you don't have time, say so. If you simply feel put upon, you may wish to say that; "No, not this time. I already take on more than I can handle comfortably and I resent feeling put upon." Most of the time, when you respect yourself, others will respect you and your position. When they don't, you have to be doubly sure of your feelings and motivations and you need to be very clear about how far you are willing to stand your ground. "I" messages help you get your position across clearly.

The word "you" shouldn't be allowed to slip in to the message at all, because it is almost inevitably followed by a blaming remark, which is guaranteed to provoke hostility and probably retaliation. "I" messages give you an effective way to communicate the real essence of what you feel without hurting the other person.

My Very Own Cross

People in the Armed Services usually have some blunt expressions to describe certain types of behaviors. While designed to shock people's sensibilities, the expressions also frequently have the effect of startling them into a whole new perspective on a situation.

"Easter Kit" is one such expression. Originally designed as a mildly derogatory slap at conventional Christians, the "Easter Kit" supposedly refers to a hammer, some nails, and a large wooden cross. To the earthy minds of servicemen, anybody who volunteered for crucifixion would get exactly what he deserved.

SELF-SACRIFICE

It may be difficult to accept, but every Neptunian comes into this world with her very own "Easter Kit." It is standard equipment, along with emotional sensitivity, creative ability and other-worldliness. The area of life in which she will most likely erect her cross— and will sooner or later get crucified— may be clearly described by Neptune's house position and close aspects, if Neptune is truly a highlighted planet. A stellium in Pisces can also indicate a likely area, by its house position.

Impossible as it may seem, every Neptunian who ends up a victim or a martyr has worked himself into that position. Usually he saw it as the only option; not infrequently, when confronted with the fact that he actively contributed to his own unhappy situation he will say, "Well, what else could I have done?" He genuinely believes he had no choice. A more honest Neptunian will perhaps be able to admit that, in truth, he didn't like the other choices.

How do Neptunians volunteer for self-sacrifice? It starts out as exactly that: sacrifice. They are often quite conscious that they are somehow making a sacrifice. A husband sees that his alcoholic wife has no one else to take care of her, so he accepts responsibility for her, unaware that he may not be capable of the unstinting unconditional love he thinks will heal her.

A wife sees that her husband cannot free himself from his tyrannical father's clutch, so she decides to place herself in the role of loving, supportive wife. She is unaware that her husband cannot break free because he hasn't the will, and that she is in fact encouraging him to depend on her, rather than helping him break free of his tendency to depend on a strong person around him.

A compassionate psychiatrist takes on a particularly diffi-cult psychotic patient, convinced that the patient only needs a more disciplined and caring counselor than any who have worked on her case before. He may cheerfully ignore the fact that other very caring and talented workers have been unable to make any headway with this particular patient. He is determined to do more. He will soon have to.

The Neptunian who is a would-be savior actually sets

herself up to expect to offer more to the supposed victim than anyone else has. This is supposed to result in victory. How much will be given? Where will she draw the line? She may not, for she has dedicated herself to her cause and in her mind, no sacrifice is too great to bring the cause to success.

Every time the Neptunian extends himself for someone else's sake, he is in severe danger of erecting his cross and handing out the hammer and nails. It is not wrong to help others. It is, however, unhealthy to think that this kind of self-sacrifice is necessary in order to help others. It almost never is, at least not to the extent that Neptunians take for granted. Furthermore, even when the Neptunian does give everything, it rarely helps the one it is supposed to.

NEED TO BE NEEDED

For example, someone with a pretty good sense of self-worth may get into a relationship with a partner who is very needy. Perhaps she is emotionally unstable. As a result of her instability or insecurity, she may be in the habit of self-destructive behavior whenever she is upset. The Neptunian can hardly resist such a person; her need is too obvious and the compassionate Neptunian cannot turn his back. He will see what he can do to make her feel better about herself. The Neptunian who has some self-respect will be able to tell whether his efforts are having a constructive effect. He will see improvement if there is any, and he will also see it if there is none, or if the situation is worsening. He will agonize over the right thing to do if he can see that he is not, in fact, helping her, but he will try to do the best thing for her, including get her professional help. He will also know, though he will grieve, if she is really beyond help.

The Neptunian without enough self-respect will also knock himself out to help, but he will not necessarily see it if he is not having a beneficial effect. He will tend to get too caught up in her particular role, too involved to be truly helpful. When he is faced with overwhelming evidence that she is no better, or is actually worse, he will redouble his efforts rather than relinquish his role. In so doing, he sacrifices himself in many ways. Perhaps she makes excessive and long, drawn-out calls to him at work, which lower his productivity and endanger his job. Perhaps she is too insecure to endure his relationship with his parents, so she becomes miserable every time he sees them, until he feels guilty and begins to cut back on his visits. Maybe she spends money to make herself feel better, running up large bills which he has to figure out how to pay.

IMPOSSIBLE TASKS

The point is, the Neptunian has a built-in blind spot when it comes to how far to go when helping or caring for others. She starts out by extending herself; usually she is willing to offer more than others. In this sense she starts out as a savior. If she hasn't learned to rein in her savior tendencies, she will believe she only has to try harder, and she will save or help where no one else has been able to. In a sense she volunteers for crucifixion, not because she extends herself more than others, but because she doesn't know when to quit. Frequently she will take on impossible tasks, then beat herself unmercifully when she does not succeed. In such a way, saviors often end up as martyrs, burned-out, bitter and resentful. If they are lucky, in time they will come to see how they contributed to their own downfall. If not, they may have to go through the whole exercise again with a new partner, until they learn that the savior role is as fraught with dangers as the victim role.

This type of Neptunian has a strong earth emphasis in her chart, or a strong drive for power. She has a certain amount of strength of character. She wants the Neptune experience, but she cannot easily live with the idea of giving up control. Consequently she takes the "savior" option, the role where she can give to others and take care of others. Underneath it all, however, is still that Neptunian consciousness which believes that self-sacrifice is necessary to avoid guilt.

LEARNING YOUNG

A different type of Neptunian victim starts out in his role very early in life. As a child, he may have been quite literally set into the victim role by his parents or other children. This Neptunian tends to have a lot of air or water in his chart, and little drive for power. The fire planets tend to be repressed; this may be shown by the placement of fire planets in water signs or houses, or in close aspect to water planets. He doesn't have the will to resist the stronger people in his life, so he becomes submissive to their needs. He gets right to the self-sacrifice part without going through all the complications of the savior role.

Not only does this Neptunian get right into her role, but she hones it to a fine art. When her parents abandon her, by death or some other way, she will feel temporarily free. Certain that her misery is at an end, she will wait for the world to bring her something— and someone— better. She is attracted to strong people; this could be constructive if she learns from them. Usually however, she encourages their strengths and cultivates her own weaknesses. Like the person who plays "helpless," she heaps praise on her partner's head, admires him and compliments him and puts herself down. If he is emotionally healthy and stable, he won't play the game. She must either give it up and grow herself, or leave and find someone else who will act out the role she expects.

SETTING UP THE GAME

If the Neptunian finds a partner who can be hooked into the expected role, the partner is quickly turned into a strange combination of savior/monster. The victim cannot resist recreating his victim role, because he wants to be rescued. This equals love to him. It was the only expression of "love" or attention he could win as a youngster; it is now the only role he feels secure in. He may not like it, but he knows it and he knows how to get attention this way. But in order to be a victim there must be a victimizer, and who is handier than the strong partner? The would-be victim will praise her strengths: "You are so clever. I could never do that." In so doing, the victim hands over power to the partner. The victim actively creates an unequal relationship. The partner feels increasingly powerful, but it is a fraudulent power; it is borrowed from and nurtured by the victim. If the partner can be addicted to the sense of power, the game is complete. The victim can threaten to yank back the power; the partner is enraged and can be relied upon to punish the victim.

Following are two examples, with different results.

JEAN AND RICHARD

In the first case, the participants are Jean and Richard. Jean is a classically recognizable Neptunian. She was abused by an alcoholic father, got into drugs and alcohol at an early age and while she now stays away from those downfalls, she strikes those who meet her as fragile and "not quite all there." Richard fell in love with Jean on first sight. Dismayed to find out that she was a well-known drug-user and drunk, he thought long and hard about following up his attraction. He knew he could be taking on a lot of trouble; he had only been divorced from his alcoholic ex-wife for two years. In the end, Jean's soulful expression and apparently strong admiration for Richard won over his doubts. He decided she could be reformed, given the right atmosphere and enough love.

To his delight Jean did indeed clean up her act. They moved in together and everything seemed wonderful. She got a job and could be relied upon to turn up at work and to come home at night. Richard couldn't believe his good fortune. Jean was rather helpless at a lot of things, but this didn't seem to matter because she was so encouraging when he took care of them. Richard proposed. They were married. Jean became pregnant and had a baby.

Only when the baby arrived did Richard notice that Jean had very little common sense. She seemed unaware that the laundry had to be done frequently, so Richard had to remind her. She seemed content to watch TV all day, so Richard had to tell her to walk the baby, although Jean was a warm and loving mother. Then Richard realized that Jean was not careful with money. The grocery allowance he gave her was often used up before the week was out. She forgot to pay bills. Richard nagged her for a while, then took over the finances completely. Jean seemed relieved by this, telling him he was better at it anyway. Somehow the praise grated on Richard's nerves; he expected Jean to share the responsibilities more. She was pregnant again, however, so he let it go.

By the time Jean and Richard had been married a few years, Jean did little except tend their two children, which she did very lovingly, and tend their house, which she did carelessly. Richard was increasingly exasperated to find his laundry not quite done on time, his meals improperly cooked and that Jean was a crashing bore; all she talked about were the children. He contemplated taking over the laundry and cooking, but became furious when he realized the position she had put him in.

He decided to make sure she shared the load. He began to criticize her, at first quietly, but increasingly sarcasm and belittlement became commonplace. Jean withdrew. Richard doubled his efforts to make her a responsible adult. Jean barely talked to him. She focused all her efforts on the children. After a few months of this, Richard was wildly bitter and resentful; Jean said she didn't care about anything except her children. Strangely enough, neither made any move to leave. In spite of the fact that he resented Jean's helplessness, Richard derived a sense of power from being around her that he was unwilling to give up. Jean was utterly dependent on Richard for the quality of her life; she would not give that up. Both resent the inequality; Jean flaunts her ability to withdraw, Richard abuses her verbally. Occasionally they go to counseling, straighten themselves out for a few weeks, but soon one of them backslides and hooks the other into the roles again.

BARB AND STEVEN

In the second case, Barb and Steven met at a mutual friend's house. It was not love at first sight but Barb was strongly attracted to Steven, who was a commercial artist. When they met again later, she decided to be a little more assertive and asked him out for coffee. From there, the relationship developed quickly. Barb was thrilled that she had finally met a man who could be respectful. Not until they moved in together did Barb notice that Steven had a number of issues he couldn't or wouldn't cope with. He quit his job because his employer "picked on him." He quit his next job because the pressure was too much and he couldn't handle the stress. Barb tried to show Steven how she handled stressful situations, hoping that he would learn from her. Instead he turned around and told her that she was much stronger than he was. That surprised her, and she began to think about it. After a while, Steven had convinced her that she expected too much of him; he simply wasn't capable of it.

Barb was disappointed, but since Steven was still loving and considerate, she worked to lower her expectations. When he couldn't keep a job, she told him to take some time off and think about what he wanted, her salary would support them both. He began to call her "mom," teasingly at first. She thought it was an affectionate name, but something began to niggle at her.

Steven could not seem to find a career which pleased him. Months passed and Barb began to get frustrated. When Steven continued to call her "mom," she began to think long and hard. She quickly realized that Steven called her "mom" every time he wanted to be looked after in some way. He was quite literally setting her up to **be** "mom," the responsible, loving one, for then he got to be the irresponsible one. Barb was horrified. The next time Steven called her "mom," she confronted him with his pattern. He denied it, but she insisted that he not call her "mom" any more, and she made up her mind not to respond if he did. He did. Many times over the next few days he called her "mom." Barb would not respond at all. Eventually Steven gave up that tactic.

Next Barb realized that Steven had systematically cultivated her strengths by praising them, and his own weaknesses by harping on them. She could see how that behavior also was designed to make her be responsible for both of them. The next time Steven made a too-strong case for her strengths, Barb lost her temper and shouted at him, abusing him for his weakness for the first time. He withdrew. Barb withdrew too, to do some more thinking.

Soon Barb had it all straight in her own mind. She realized that she had felt powerful when Steven repeatedly praised her strengths. She also realized that with the sense of power he gave her, he also all but invited her to kick him verbally, because he put himself down so much. Again she confronted him, explained how she felt and insisted that he stop. He couldn't seem to help himself; he started to admire her mental clarity and praised her psychological insight. Barb almost fell for it; she hadn't expected it to start up so quickly, but this time she held her temper and simply told him to stop it. To her shock, Steven burst into tears and wanted to know what impossible expectations she had of him. Barb felt sorry for him but was wise enough to see that it was really just one more ploy. She could see that if she comforted him, Steven would have simply put her in the "mom" role again. She would be one-up, he would be the underdog.

Barb realized that Steven needed counseling. She had done quite a bit of reading in psychological literature, which was possibly what helped her see the roles being set up. She insisted that Steven get the counseling, adding that she would also go because she understood that it was something between the two of them that needed to be healed. They made appointments as soon as possible, each going to a different counselor for a while, then eventually they worked together as a couple with a single counselor.

Steven still has a tendency to play victim. He sometimes retreats into "I can't handle this," or "What do you expect of me?" whenever he is under a lot of pressure, but if Barb points out what he is doing, he now understands and pulls himself out of that behavior. Barb has come to terms with her tendency to come to the rescue too quickly. She has learned that it is somewhat arrogant to assume that she is stronger and more capable; she has learned to have more faith in other people's strengths. She has learned to let Steven own his own struggles. She encourages him and supports him, but she does not try to solve his problems for him. As a result of being forced to solve his own problems, Steven has become a stronger person, a man Barb can admire. For the most part, Steven's "Easter Kit" remains packed away.

DEALING WITH IT IN SELF

If you should discover within these pages tendencies which you recognize in yourself, understand that your overdone strength is compassion.

If you commonly take the savior role, you know how quickly it can turn into a nightmare for you, and how often you are left feeling bitter and used. In this case, you can restudy Barb's lessons— they are the lessons every would-be savior has to learn. The big, and most painful, lesson for habitual saviors is the confrontation with a **possible addiction to power.** The more you have repeated the savior pattern, the more likely it is that you have to have a power "fix" from time to time. The problem is that such a "fix" is only possible in an unequal, unhealthy relationship which cannot provide other, meaningful satisfactions. Is this the way you want to live your life? If not, find some other way to help people.

Saving other people is commendable and admirable when practiced as a job, with formal training on how far to go and when to back off. Consider changing careers to get yourself into a counseling role or do it on a volunteer basis. If you see that your friends or spouse need help, ask yourself if you are helping in order to serve their needs or if you are helping because you **need** to help. Learn about the psychological concept of "problem ownership" and cultivate respect for other people's right to make mistakes.

Problem ownership means that you can care, you can listen

to people's problems and commiserate but you **do not take over their problem**. You don't even give advice unless it is specifically asked for. This is not because you are cold-hearted or uninvolved, but because you truly appreciate that to take over someone else's problem denies them the opportunity to solve it for themselves and in so doing, to grow in strength, competence and self respect. You can support and root from the sidelines all you want, but ultimately you allow them to fight their own battles and to have the joy and satisfaction of eventual success.

If you have been engaged in a milder form of the savior role, all of the above still applies. Put your natural and very practical skills to use in a job or a volunteer organization rather than with your friends and family.

If you have been a chronic victim, ask yourself if you can **see how you behave in ways which keep you a victim**. Think about it as often as you need to in order to identify those behaviors, then take them as they occur to you and resolve to change them into more constructive behaviors. It may make you feel mildly important to be miserable, but if you give up misery and dare to struggle for something better, you will gain so much in self-esteem, inner strength and inner peace that you will feel you have gained something far more precious than anything you have lost.

DEALING WITH IT IN OTHERS

If you are one of the Neptunians with victim tendencies, who is about to reform, doubtless you are surrounded with saviors and/or victimizers who will make your changes very difficult. If you have been giving them power "fixes" for a long time, they may well be addicted and loathe to give them up. In this case you may need professional help to overcome old patterns— not only those you wish to give up in yourself but those by which others hook you into the role.

Would-be saviors offer to help long before you ask for help. You can tell the difference between a kind and loving friend who is offering to help and a savior, by their intensity. The friend will ask if you want help and will abide by your decision. The savior will insist that you need help and may snatch your problem out from under your nose before you know what has happened. It will be up to you to practice keeping your own problems! You may have to jealously protect them and hoard them until the nearby saviors get the message that you are learning to stand on your own two feet! Most saviors, being basically good-hearted, will applaud your efforts, even if they do slip up and can't resist telling you how to handle your problems **better**.

If you have been an intensely dedicated victim, you may find yourself in a close relationship with a monster, who has no intention of letting you or your power "fix" go. Such a person usually needs professional help, and you would benefit from it also, if only to teach you how to back gracefully out of this role. It is strongly recommended that you seek help from an experienced counselor to handle this situation. If you decide to go it on your own, cultivate a group of friends who can be turned to as a refuge when the going gets tough. You will need trusted people to talk to, to bounce ideas off of, to offer helpful insights and with whom to share triumphs. Take out a library card and read every book you can which seems to have something to teach you. Use and adapt what you learn to your own situation.

If you have been a chronic savior and now have a victim on your hands, restudy the material on saviors under **Dealing with It in Self**, as well as the story of Barb and Steven. Like Barb, you will have to learn how your victim hooks you into the savior role, and how to disentangle yourself from your own need to rescue. If you are easily brought to your knees when your victim manipulates you with vaguely implied guilt, learn to ask the question, "What is your point here?" It forces the would-be victim to either come right out with the implied accusation or to retreat.

If you have been repeatedly hurt while being a savior, you can keep that in mind as incentive to learn new ways to behave. If you have had a lot of success at the savior role, and have won great praise and gratitude, it will be harder for you to give this up unless you make sure you can still achieve this success in some healthy way. Perhaps you can make it your job or a part-time volunteer activity— if you are naturally good at it, it is a shame to waste a very valuable and badly needed skill. In your intimate relationships, however, savior behavior betrays a one-up attitude which is an implied put-down for your partner. If you don't want to have to deal with a victim, stop putting that person down, even in subtle, perhaps inadvertent ways.

The Focus on Avoidance

There are many defense mechanisms available to the Neptunian who prefers his own pretty dreams to reality. Most of them overlap; that is, most people engage in more than one of them at once and most of the "games" are closely related.

A person who is habitually or frequently out of focus mentally plays a form of "Pretend." Such a person can **selectively ignore** whatever he wants simply by losing his ability to concentrate the moment an issue arises with which he does not wish to deal. He will change the subject, look blank or bored, ease out of the room or drift off to sleep. If confronted with the issue, he will usually retreat with a remark such as "Well, I'm just no good at that!" or "I can't handle that right now," or "This isn't a good time for me." He will either go out of focus altogether or focus on something else which promises to be less stressful. Needless to say, he will never, on his own, find a "good" time to handle the issue.

Being out of focus carries a reward many people find hard to resist. It occurs when an individual has a **basic inner conflict** which is a real dilemma. That is, she has two very important values which are in mortal conflict with each other. Perhaps as a result of childhood experiences she detests powerful people and, by association, does not wish to use power herself. Yet she may have a natural, and very strong, need for power, which she denies because it clashes with her acquired value against the use of power. Here she has a real dilemma because she cannot satisfy one value without betraying the other. Whatever she does, she will feel uncomfortable; this is a situation many people try to solve by deliberate— but rarely conscious— burial of awareness of one side of the dilemma. This can easily be achieved by lack of focus. Let us say that this particular woman chooses to be out of focus whenever she uses power, and to retain awareness of her value on equality and fairness. Every time the need to use power becomes too strong to resist, she will slip out of focus in order to do whatever is required to satisfy the now-unconscious need.

It looks like a beautiful arrangement, and if the logic is followed, it does make sense: each requirement gets satisfied but in such a way that the feeling of betrayal of a value is not experienced on a conscious level. The only trouble with this arrangement is that the person is basically out of control of his behavior in some area(s) of life and will often do things which seem either out of character or downright self-destructive.

As an example, a mature woman who had only a part-time job after years of going to school defaulted on several payments on her student loans. She confessed to a long-standing outright hatred of handling money. Not long after she received notice that she would have to pay off the loans in full, she went out shopping and, as luck would have it, found a table on sale at a price she couldn't resist. She put a substantial deposit on the table, but within an hour was truly upset as she realized that she couldn't afford the table, and didn't even particularly **like** it. She already knew she should let it go. Her question was, "Why do I do these things?"

It was obvious that she had slipped out of focus right after receiving notice that she would have to pay off her loans, which she could not do. She had felt out of control and sought, therefore, to do something which made her feel in control again. When asked if she equated money with power, she readily confirmed that she did. She volunteered the information that she hated the idea of power and felt it was very wrong to use it. Herein lay her dilemma: one part of her condemned the use of power, another part of her needed it.

The obvious way out was that she slipped out of focus whenever she used power, or money, which equaled power in her mind. She quickly realized that she had actually managed to satisfy both sides of her dilemma, for spending the money made her feel temporarily powerful and in control again, yet she had not been truly conscious of her use of power so she had not consciously offended her other value. The trouble was, this solution left her feeling more out of control afterward when she realized what she had done.

TAKING CHARGE

Being out of focus leads inevitably to feeling out of control, for in this case the individual is yielding control, not to someone else, but to his unconscious drives. Naturally, when doing something to satisfy an unconscious drive, the person will turn around later and wail, "Why do I do these things?" He will be utterly bewildered because he truly does not know that he has these drives; consequently he cannot make sense of his behavior when he tries to satisfy them. As long as he is unwilling to re-own the drives and needs that he has pushed into unconsciousness, he will feel out of control and bewildered by himself. When he looks honestly at the evidence of his behavior, however, he will be able to see what need it satisfies and how that might conflict with another value he holds dear.

It takes courage to re-own an unconscious drive. It was pushed out of awareness in the first place because it brought discomfort and often guilt. If both values were particularly strong, satisfaction of one at the other's expense could have brought a vicious form of psychological agony. The conflict could have been too strident; one of the values had to go. To bring it back is to bring back all the fears and discomfort and possibly even agony right along with the conflict. It is difficult to remember in such a case that the original repression occurred because no other solution seemed possible, usually because the individual was a child and didn't know any other way to cope. As an adult, she has more experience and may be able to devise a healthier resolution. If she cannot do it on her own, which is common due to getting in a rut mentally, friends or a counselor will often be able to see options which can be immensely helpful.

DEALING WITH IT IN SELF

If you realize that you frequently engage in this type of behavior, understand that your overdone strength is the ability to slip into the unconscious mind and bring its contents back into consciousness. You are using it backwards.

Loss of focus begins so quickly that it usually occurs without any awareness whatsoever. It is often only **after** the unconscious need has been satisfied that awareness returns, along with a strong sense of bewilderment. A person who knows that sugar-laden foods eaten late at night make her sleep restlessly, for example, may happily forget that fact until after she has finished a hot-fudge sundae. This is particularly likely if she has learned to equate food with comfort and is unhappy or feels slightly unsatisfied about something.

Step One

Because of the nature of this problem, it will take some perseverance to teach yourself more constructive behavior. The first step is to identify those situations which provoke your slide into unconsciousness. To do this, think back to the last few times you did something you later wished you hadn't. Then think about the circumstances in your life at that time. Was there a particular stress?

You might have to think hard about this for two reasons. The first is that you probably slipped out of awareness before you were aware that you were uncomfortable, because the whole purpose of this defense mechanism is to avoid discomfort. It may, therefore, be difficult to identify what situation or event was the provocation. The second reason it can be frustrating to try to find the event is because you will tend to automatically employ this very same defense if you get too close to recalling the situation which threatened to bother you in the first place. That is, suppose you have written down a list of all the events you can remember from the last time you went out of focus. If you have actually recalled, but not yet identified, the event or situation which was the one your unconscious wanted to avoid, it still wants to avoid it. You are still "programmed" to push away awareness of this situation or event. You will only know this is happening by watching your reaction to the list of events.

Frequently you will simply make excuses to avoid making the list in the first place. It doesn't seem exciting, or even effective. In this case you will have to tell yourself to make the list anyway, on faith, if you will. You may then find that when you try to recall the situations from the time you have picked, you suddenly feel enormously tired, or burdened. You may want to cry, for no reason that you can think of. You may also find your mind wanders away and seems to refuse to concentrate. A few people will feel explosively angry. Meet all of these reactions with patience. Sleep if you have to— until your body cannot sleep any more. Cry if you need to— there is an element of grief involved when you confront a habitual defense mechanism. If you find it nearly impossible to concentrate, keep bringing your mind back to the problem at hand. If you feel anger, try to hold on to the anger and to explore it, find out **why** you feel angry. The answers are bound to be illuminating.

This first step in dealing with the "out of focus" game is a great deal easier, albeit not less frustrating, when taken with a trusted friend or counselor. S/he will be able to catch you at the moment you begin to slip out of awareness, and while this can be embarrassing or maddening, it will quickly teach you two important clues to your behavior. Because you will be "caught in the act" as it were, you will learn to identify the way you feel just as you start to engage in this behavior. Then you can learn to use that feeling as a warning flag to hold on to your awareness. The second clue will be that you will see just what kind of situations make you want to engage in this defense mechanism, and you can learn to identify those situations for future reference.

Step Two

The second step is to try to think out more constructive ways to cope with the stressful or threatening situations which you have avoided in the past. You will probably find that you have some inner prohibition against dealing directly with these situations. The prohibition may be outright fear, a belief that you cannot win— powerlessness— or a belief that you **should** not win in these situations; a value dictates your behavior. It will take some time to think through whichever of these prohibitions arises, and they may all arise, layered over each other. You need to challenge and rethink whatever prohibition(s) you expose. Sometimes you can remove its fetters simply by exposing it to yourself. Sometimes you need to constantly remind yourself that you don't think that way anymore before you can behave in more constructive ways. Sometimes the prohibition covers up much deeper memories which can be painful to look at. In this case, a trusted counselor can be a great support and friend when you are in need.

Step Three

The third step is to decide upon new, constructive ways to deal with those situations which formerly provoked "out of focus" behavior. You have to have a certain amount of belief in yourself and your abilities to be able to think you can learn healthier behaviors but this belief tends to reassert itself when you expose the old prohibitions which held you back. The very act of being honest with yourself seems to build self-esteem. You will build more each time you successfully employ constructive rather than evasive/defensive behavior. Start with a situation which is not too strongly threatening, and make your decision now that next time you will deal with that situation with one of your new behaviors. Plan ahead, imagine yourself employing this new behavior. Deal with the feelings that arise. As always, review every time you can make an opportunity to think in peace.

Build on your strengths, no matter how small those strengths look in the beginning. Remind yourself about the gains in self-esteem that you will earn, and the fact that your frustratingly self-defeating behavior will now slow down and eventually stop. After some time of practice, of dealing with issues rather than evading them, you will feel much stronger and more capable and you will find that you respect yourself. Amazingly, others will respect you, too.

DEALING WITH IT IN OTHERS

Unless someone specifically asks for help with this, it is a problem best handled by a professional. A reasonably sensitive person with a background in counseling or psychology may be able to identify the situations which induce the slide out of consciousness. However, unless the individual with the problem is determined to work on it, he will simply employ this defense more and more when confronted with the fact that he does it. This can be overwhelmingly frustrating, a condition which professionals have been trained to handle. Most people eventually react to the frustration with judgmental condemnation, which only drives the evader deeper into his unconscious conviction that loss of focus is the only way to survive.

If you are in contact with a chronic evader who slides into lack of focus, check out your own relationship to Neptune. It is quite possible and even likely that for you, consciousness and awareness and focus are issues. You may expect yourself and others to always be rigorously aware, or you may unwittingly employ lack of awareness yourself when certain situations arise. If you get in touch with your own problem, and solve it, the other person may change her behavior. Even if she doesn't, it will no longer be such an issue for you and you won't find yourself so exasperated by her behavior.

Perfect or Not at All

Most people have dreams and goals. Some goals may be well-defined and have clear steps which lead to attainment. Other goals might be vague, with no obvious route to follow. One of the most insidious traps into which a Neptunian can fall is that of indiscriminately applied perfectionism. That is, everything which the Neptunian tries has to measure up to some incredibly high standard of perfection or is judged to be a miserable failure. Against such harsh dictates, the gentle Neptunian nature can soon feel overwhelmed and doomed to defeat before he even begins. This can manifest as a complete unwillingness to try anything at all, or as a constant sense of frustration when the very first attempt fails to meet impossibly high standards.

Neptunians with a strong creative drive may live with the frustration and repeated sense of defeat, yet continue to create. But many drift from one form of expression to another, disappointed to discover their dreams and visions resist easy translation. Although very talented, without persistence such people simply give up. They often settle for fantasies, in which they can experience, with little effort, the perfection of which they dream. They fail to see that this choice leaves them with only make-believe successes and fantasy self-esteem, for their inner self knows perfectly well that they are wasting their talents and are settling for yet another Neptunian delusion. Like Tigger in *Winnie the Pooh* they are sure they could do anything they wanted if they wanted to— they just don't want to, somehow. In reality, they shun the ego-risk involved in turning a dream into something concrete. They refuse to take the chance.

DEALING WITH IT IN SELF

Your overdone gift is creative imagination and inspiration. The images you see in your head are wonderful, so wonderful that you may despair of ever being able to translate them into reality, or you may have already given up and do not even try any more.

Neptune and its images are not of this world, however. It might help to remember that your task is **not** to translate Neptunian inspirations exactly as you see them, but only to bring to life the essence or impression of what you see, to the best of your ability. Furthermore, while your initial efforts may be painfully inadequate in your own eyes, it is unlikely that anyone else will be as hard on your creations as you are, and they may receive them with delight. A poem which you feel is weak and ineffectual may uplift someone else; an article which seems to not make the point you wanted as cleverly as you think necessary may still ring lots of bells for another person, and teach her something valuable. A piece of music with which you are exasperated may totally enchant someone else. The rest of the world doesn't **know** about that ethereal or perfect standard which you are trying to reach, and they may find your creation enjoyable or even terrific.

Another point to consider is that only a few prodigies are born every century and the spaces may already have been filled by the time you came along. The rest of us get to **practice** our skills until we get reasonably good at them. Then the people around us, blissfully ignoring all the hard work we put in, pat us on the back for our good luck in being born with such a great talent! If you make the mistake of buying into this attitude, that great talents are born, you will not see the point of developing whatever natural abilities you do have. The truth is, most great talents start out latent and rudimentary. The individual who becomes marvelous at what he does usually has put in years of study and practice.

The prevailing attitude that great talents are born is only perpetrated by those who are unwilling to develop their own abilities, so they delude themselves that those who gain recognition do so out of sheer luck. It is easier to accept that one missed out or failed out of bad luck than it is to admit that one simply didn't wish to do the plain hard work needed to bring success. Neptunians, always open to beliefs in magic and her close cousin luck, are most susceptible to this mistaken attitude.

Partly this is because the Neptunian tends to see the **possible** perfection. That is, she envisions something so inspired and grand, and is so moved by the perfection of her visions, she does not wish to settle for anything less exalted. Partly it is because Neptunians often believe or wish that work and effort should not be necessary and that everything should flow with ease, just like in the dream or vision. And partly it is because Neptunians tend to have a difficult time dealing with the mediums presented by the real world. There simply is not the range or speed of flexibility in the written word, musical notes or painting tools that exist within the imagination. What can be conjured up in seconds in the head may take weeks, months or even years to painstakingly translate into a concrete work of creation.

Finally, **Neptunians are by nature wholistic**; that is, they create a whole impression, or a mostly whole impression which needs only a few refinements. The actual creation, however, usually develops through some sort of step-by-step process which seems quite foreign to one who started out with the whole image intact.

Neptunians who wish to satisfy their creative drive have to come to terms with the tedium of learning to develop their skill(s) which is in fact a lifelong process anyway. The process itself presents endless opportunities for discovery and new challenge and can bring tremendous joy if approached with an attitude that learning is, or can be, exciting and rewarding. Then the budding creator has to come to terms with the fact that first efforts are often little but "skeleton" sketches. That is, the writer needs to accept that a first draft is just a hodgepodge of ideas; it is necessary to get them out of his head and onto paper in order to organize them. The artist has to learn to start with a rough sketch which is nothing but a preliminary. The musician also starts with a basic tune, which will be built upon and elaborated upon bit by bit as each instrument repeats the tune.

If you find you are constantly defeated by your inability to do what you want as perfectly as you want, you may find solace in the fact that all the rest of us Neptunians are equally frustrated. I can personally guarantee that the last piece of music you listened to and loved was written by someone who wished he could have done it better. The last book you read and got so much out of was written by someone who finally had to stop trying to make it match what he started out envisioning, and the last picture you saw that really caught your attention and moved something in you was only reluctantly released by the artist who couldn't get it exactly the way he wanted it!

You have to start somewhere. Be nice to yourself and revise your expectations to include some time to develop your skill. The world won't collapse in shock if you make mistakes along the way. Learn to **break your projects down into manageable steps**: first there has to be an outline, then a few major themes, then the important details, and finally the refinements. Then you have to bless your creation and let it go. Have faith that someone somewhere will be inspired by it, because no matter how awful it looks to your eyes, others are judging it by their needs, not by your standards. You are not trying to and cannot express your entire soul in one project—that is your ego chattering in your ear. You are only doing the best you can with your abilities, and if you accept that you have a place in this world and a reason for existing, you will understand that no creation of yours will go to waste. The worst that can happen is that you will learn more clearly how you want to do it better next time.

DEALING WITH IT IN OTHERS
This is a particularly intractable issue because it is one which really has to be given up by the individual herself. You cannot force her to change, and you may be threatening an especially touchy defense mechanism. You can, however, periodically discuss how unrealistic the world is when successful people are labeled "lucky." You can even get disgusted with this attitude— as long as you don't accuse her of having it— and point out that the supposedly lucky person has usually worked long and hard to develop her talents.

You can make note of the fact that people who produce wonderful creations start with rough drafts or sketches and spend long hours building on and elaborating on the initial effort. You can express sympathy for the frustration every creator must experience with the difficulty of reworking her first attempt until it more closely matches what she envisions. In other words, you can slowly and repeatedly expose the "perfect or not at all" individual to the idea that there is a process to be followed, and that it doesn't all happen by magic and that great talents are developed, not bestowed by fate. It is a process of reeducation which has to be done indirectly, because the defense mechanism itself is usually too painful to bear open challenge from outside. The Neptunian within will be listening intently, however, especially if no pressure is put on to **do** something immediately with her God-given talents. This one needs to be weaned away from her comforting fantasies.

Summary

There are many ways to misdirect Neptunian energy, but all of them are reversible from the level of conscious decision except unreachable mental illness and permanent damage from drugs or alcohol. These can only be turned around, if at all, when the appropriate unconscious changes occur, by whatever means. All other Neptunian pitfalls, no matter how enthralling, can be left behind for more healthy and genuinely satisfying behavior.

Behaviors which misdirect Neptunian— or any other— energy all stem from attitudes which are unhealthy. The attitudes must be ferreted out, challenged and changed before behavioral changes which are permanent will result. In many cases, however, behavioral changes can be consciously practiced while attitudes are found and explored. Changed behavior **can** lead to changed attitudes. Acting "as if" you already had the new attitude can actually help develop and cement the desired change. When the attitudes have changed, automatic patterns of coping behavior will change. All **unhealthy Neptunian behaviors attempt to bring the individual heaven on earth**. That is, she is aware of the harmony, peace and beauty possible at exalted levels of existence, and wishes to have at least some of that immediately. The healthy Neptunian works consciously to purify herself and to transcend negativity in herself in order to participate in the glory that is Neptune. The unhealthy Neptunian engages in various behaviors designed to let her pretend that the glory, or part of it, is already within her grasp.

Because of the element of pretense, or fantasy, involved in Neptunian problems, **the antidote is clarity**. Neptunian problems need to be confronted with a clear picture of what the behavior actually achieves, its effect on others, and its negative psycho/spiritual cost to the individual himself. The Neptunian needs to learn the constructive and satisfying ways to express the planetary energy, such as meditation, the pursuit of spiritual growth, psychic development, artistic development, psycho/spiritual studies, the study of dreams, positive occult studies, and so on.

While the chart cannot reveal the particular trouble an individual might have with Neptunian energy, it does point out the possibility and general area when Neptune is harshly aspected by a particular planet, or placed in a house where it is associated with especially troubling difficulties. For example, Neptune square the Sun alerts the astrologer to the possibility that the person has conflicts between the Sun ego and self-esteem and the Neptunian need to transcend the self. Neptune in the seventh house is a warning of the tendency of that individual to muddle up the search for God and ultimate satisfaction with the search for a mate.

When the message is repeated in various ways in the chart, it becomes a definite possibility. For example, a client who has Neptune in the seventh house, Venus in Pisces and the ruler of the seventh house placed in the twelfth has three indicators that ultimate fulfillment and the mate are all tangled up together. The likelihood is that this client has had at least some trouble with unrealistic expectations in relationships.

The good news is that people can, if they wish, learn to experience their own natural tendencies and impulses with a sense of tolerance, a sense of recognition that, yes, this is certainly the way they naturally wish to act but that they no longer wish to suffer the results of acting that particular way. Then they make a conscious decision to modify their own behavior.

To carry on with the Neptune in the seventh house example, a woman with this placement can come to understand that her natural tendency is to throw herself so deeply into a relationship that she loses all sense of herself, loses perspective on the relationship and comes to expect all sorts of satisfactions to come out of the relationship. Her expectations reach a level of need that quickly translates into insecurity, because she tends to need more than most people can provide, and certainly more than is healthy. Such a woman can come to see that she does this **of her own volition**— that is, she actually chooses to behave this way in reaction to her own tendencies.

She can learn that when she does behave this way, her partner either bolts immediately or the two of them get into victim/savior games. She can then learn how to gauge what is a more appropriate level of emotional involvement for a relationship. She will always have to keep an eye on herself in relationships; stress will tend to make her revert quickly to unrealistic expectations and an unhealthy level of emotional dependency. However, if she fully accepts responsibility for her own tendencies, she will recognize the signs that she is in too deep again, and she will be able to struggle back out of the pit, to a level which is healthier and happier.

It is always possible to accept responsibility for our own tendencies, to learn what behaviors those tendencies usually lead to in ourselves, and what results we thereby provoke in others. With such insight, we then have the chance to choose behaviors which will bring about results we would rather have. Neptune, by its house position and aspects, gives us some excellent hints about those areas of life in which the tendency toward unrealistic expectations and illusion is most likely to be acted upon, and therefore most likely to result in unhappy or destructive situations. Once we examine the chart, we may be able to see those tendencies in our own lives, and then to take charge of them. The relearning process takes time, but the sense of satisfaction gained is much greater than can be imagined.

CHAPTER EIGHT

THE LIGHT AT THE END OF THE TUNNEL

It all comes down to love. From love, all positive growth is possible. From fear comes only more fear and all the hurtful things people do in the name of protecting themselves.

Inner Strength or Inner Emptiness

Life can be difficult. No matter how wealthy or poor, healthy or ill, every person has burdens and unfulfilled needs, everyone has suffered disappointments and has seen fond dreams shattered. Those who deny it deny themselves and their own experiences.

Sometimes it is possible to point out that an individual has contributed to his own pain. Often he has set up the pattern himself, by his own attitudes and behavior, as has been pointed out in previous chapters. Equally often, it is not possible to make such a connection. Some people seem to be visited by outrageous fortune in such a way that their only fault seems to be that they were in the wrong place at the wrong time. It is often tempting to label such occurrences "fate," yet it may be that we have not yet evolved enough to see the connections which are there.

Fated or self-determined, however, life can be idyllic, re-warding and full of joy; it can also be harsh, unfair and full of pain. The Human Potential and New Age movements have awakened many people to the fact that much suffering is self-caused and can be eliminated, but the techniques and attitude changes which can turn an unhappy North American life into a rewarding one will not solve the problems of a starving African child. Like it or not, there is much of life that cannot be controlled.

Given that it is not possible to eliminate all the pain, what is to be done? What choices are available? The choices are essentially these: either grow stronger through adversity or build false defenses against it.

Those **people who build inner strength will build for themselves a lasting foundation**, a resilient foundation which will support them well when life becomes extravagantly de-manding. Those who build artificial defenses against the diffi-culties of the world will constantly spend their energies main-taining those defenses instead of developing inner strengths. They have no firm foundation upon which to build; they are haunted by their inner emptiness and they are deeply afraid of it, and of serious challenges to it.

In the broadest sense, many myths and fairy tales attempt to get this important message across. The prince, though he is handsome and wealthy, must always fight the dragon or other evil entity before he can claim his bride and his inheritance. In other words, he must face adversity and overcome it before he can claim a sense of completeness.

It is not often that the prince wins by sheer strength. Usually he wins through courage, or purity of heart, through the strength of his love and faith or perhaps through cleverness. The dragon is often a symbol of an "evil" or unhealthy uncon-scious drive, which the prince must face and learn to master. In modern versions the prince usually kills the dragon, but in older versions the dragon was simply overcome and then frequently became a meek, or at least a controllable, tethered creature. In modern life we often think we must completely eliminate those traits with which we are uncomfortable, but it makes more sense psychologically to gain mastery over those traits and then try to integrate them. All qualities have their gifts as well as their curses!

Those who will not fight their own personal dragons must forever be cowed by them, haunted by them and must busily reinforce such defenses as they can construct. They forget that dragons live forever and have a number of magical tricks which enable them to break down the defenses designed to keep them at bay.

Love Or Fear

In any situation in life, an individual is faced with a choice. That choice is to act out of love or to act out of fear. When she chooses to act out of fear, she treads the limited and limiting Neptunian path of illusion and delusion. Only a small amount of territory can be successfully defended against the encroachments of reality. Conversely, when she chooses to act out of love, she embraces the limitless Neptunian path of illumination and understanding. Energy can be turned toward growth and development rather than devoted to defense. Many times a day each person is faced with situations which demand the choice of love or fear. Love inevitably enhances us, fear diminishes; it is up to us to choose wisely.

The more frequently an individual opts for fear and its illusory defenses, the harder it is for him to stare down his inner emptiness, yet at the same time it becomes harder to ignore it. He is like an empty shell which is always on the verge of collapse; much energy must be used just to maintain the appearance of normalcy and health. If he has a mainly introverted chart, he may opt for pretense. If he is mainly extroverted, he may distract himself by blaming others for his pain. The more time he spends in these activities, however, the more self-disgust he collects and the more he believes he is too weak to handle life any other way.

The more frequently an individual opts for love and its very genuine strengths, the more she builds self-respect and an unshakable belief in her hard-won abilities. If she has a mainly introverted chart, she may opt to be a receptive and openly caring individual, much devoted to meditation or other quiet activities aimed at self-development. If she is mainly extroverted, she may choose to spend a great deal of her time going out into the world to help in whatever way she can. The more time she spends in these activities, the more she will grow in love and in enlightenment.

The person who reaches for Neptune from a base of fear warps the very themes he yearns to learn to express. His own attitudes make him too deeply concerned about himself, too grounded in defensiveness and too fearful to uplift himself to the level at which spiritual energy flows. He obstructs it, uses it for his own purposes, then often gets swallowed up by it because he has not learned to utilize it. The individual who reaches for spiritual insight out of love, and the understanding that Neptune is a major key to the realization of our Divine nature, allows the energy a pure channel through which to pour. It becomes a part of him and he a part of it; he experiences at-one-ment to the degree of his understanding.

The practical reality of life is that **most people swing back and forth between love and fear**. There will be areas with which each person deals easily and with love, openly and with acceptance. There will be other areas with which the same individual deals uncomfortably and with fear, repression, rejection or denial. Growth comes about when the individual faces her areas of fear and tries to learn how to let go of her predetermined agenda in those areas. Love has no agenda except more love. This, however, requires the ability to surrender any personal need to control, acceptance of a natural outcome, and faith that all is unfolding for a meaningful purpose. This is Neptunian love.

Acceptance, Surrender and Faith

So often, we think of "surrender" and "giving up" as synonymous. Often surrender is, indeed, a "giving up" and a loss. Someone wins; the other surrenders or loses.

In the spiritual sense, "surrender" is also a giving up; but what is given up is not lost— it is **transcended**. To give up in the sense of resignation is to learn nothing. It is abandonment of responsibility, avoidance of effort, denial of ability or desire. Nothing is gained except despair or resentment. To surrender in the spiritual sense, however, means to give up some attitude or way of seeing things which is an obstacle to further advancement. We surrender the old attitude, accept the new and we gain in understanding and insight.

On the psychological level, most of us have experienced times when we were convinced we were right about something, only to discover someone else had a different idea. It is, for example, common for young adults to think that any injustice has to be confronted immediately and vociferously. They are impatient with older adults who counsel patience and tact. The younger adult will often ignore such advice and cause a fuss, often winning the case but just as often gaining a reputation as a troublemaker. Only when the younger adult learns to bide his time will he notice that there are many benefits to patience and careful planning. He can learn how to bring the injustice up in a nonthreatening manner, that it isn't necessary to punish the perpetrator— who often wasn't fully aware of causing an injustice— and that it is a real kindness to leave another individual with his self-respect intact. The issue will get resolved, without any further animosity. Indeed, if handled very carefully, the relationship may well be improved rather than irreparably destroyed.

If the young adult has the wisdom to try this out, before he really believes it can work, in a sense he is surrendering— at least temporarily— his own impulse and convictions of rightness. This is not abandonment, but a genuine setting-aside of his own notions so that he can look at other concepts. We do this intellectually some of the time, psychologically some of the time, but spiritually we have a tendency to get locked into a viewpoint and to cling to it to our own detriment. We can only grow to the extent that we are willing to be flexible.

Neptune represents our ability to surrender in this way— the ability to actually **include another viewpoint** before we are fully cognizant of all its implications. It actually represents a desire to surrender, which needs to be carefully directed lest it seep into inappropriate areas. The ancients knew that spiritual knowledge could be dangerous if misused or misapplied. Their concern led to the development of the mystery schools, with students who had to prove themselves worthy and responsible at each level before they were allowed to go on to learn the secrets of the next level.

Surrender Attachments

Today, too many individuals are spiritually sensitive, if not actually awakened, to keep the knowledge secret. Many people intuit the secrets, and many of those do not understand what they intuit. Neptune's urge to surrender can be applied to anything, and often is. It is meant, however, to be applied to our attachments. Those who are attached are not free. We are attached to our own beliefs, our loved ones, our cultures, our countries, our economic systems and our political beliefs. We are attached to being right, to being looked up to as a parent, to being respected in the workplace and to being admired as beautiful. We may be attached to being treated certain ways, and get wildly upset when we are not. All of these are illusions, but we become very dependent upon them and expect them to continue. We often try to control or manipulate others in order to satisfy our addiction to the way we want the world to be.

All of this— all of our preconceived ideas and expectations— have to be released before we can be spiritually free. This is what surrender is about: **learning to recognize our attachments**— one author calls them "addictions"— and then learning to **let go of them**. We can still prefer the world to be that way, but we will no longer go to ridiculous lengths to ensure that it is.

Acceptance is part of the picture. We balance our preference against acceptance that another way may be better, or is just plain inevitable. We balance our preference against the advisability of letting a situation unfold without our meddling. **Faith** is also part of this, faith that there is an order and a pattern which makes sense, whether we understand it or not. This faith becomes easier as we learn more about the connection between attitudes/behaviors and so called "fated" situations. When we see the patterns which certain types of behaviors always bring about, the world begins to look logical and reasonable. Then it is easier to accept that a bewildering situation has its logic, too, which we may come to understand if we learn more, or if we surrender our own preconceived notions about that situation.

So many times people say, "Why me?" A woman who seems to meet only men who are irresponsible and weak-willed may wonder why she always gets stuck with these types. If she wonders sincerely, she may seek out advice or knowledge, and she may come to hear about life scripts and how people seem to live out certain patterns which reinforce their own unconscious beliefs. If she examines her attitudes, she may find that she tends to think men are not much better than large children. It seems a natural consequence of her experience, but it may also be the cause of it! In other words, the attitude may actually have preceded her experience with men and have determined the type of men to whom she responds.

If this woman thinks back to her childhood experiences with men, particularly those in her own family, she may find that they let her down in major ways so that she learned not to expect too much from them. It is quite normal for a child to generalize so that experiences of one or two men seem applicable to all men. This attitude becomes second nature— or semiconscious. When the child becomes a woman, it seems as if all the men she meets are the same way: they keep letting her down. In fact, if she looks at the men she actually meets versus the ones to whom she responds, she will find that she carefully weeds out those who do not fit her preconceived ideas about men. She doesn't know how to deal with them nor do they play a role which she can recognize or respond to.

If she learns to understand these experiences, what seemed like a bewildering pattern suddenly begins to make sense. She will see that she determines her own experience by her attitudes, and she can choose to change her attitudes. In fact, if she does so, her experiences will change, too. After such a learning experience, it will be easier for her to have faith that other patterns operate which she does not yet understand. This faith is part of the inner strength which can be built, with practice.

Neptune's True Gift

All of the outer planets— those beyond Saturn— awaken people to greater possibilities. Neptune's sphere is particularly spiritual in nature. The planet symbolizes our own Divine nature and its possibilities, of which we are infrequently aware. Our Divine nature is reflected in the world around us, a world rich in opportunities. We are responsible for our Divine nature, even when we do not know it is ours, or when we have a glimpse of it yet do not accept it and all that it implies.

We are creative, and we play an active part in the creation of our own world. Sometimes we accept this when we learn about creative visualization, yet forget it when we are in a black mood and think negative and even destructive thoughts. Our anger is as powerful a creative force as our love, yet in the throes of rage we fail to credit our creative ability and the impact of our thoughts. This does not mean we should not express anger, but it does mean we need to remember to do so responsibly. Ideally, we work on ourselves when we are angry, and find out what **our** problems and issues are and solve those, rather than trying to control, manipulate or punish the person we blame for our anger, or our hurt. In such a way, we accept more and more of ourselves as we are, yet as we accept, we change, we transmute.

Acceptance Heals

When we apply our minds to an unconscious "wound," an area of sensitivity, we begin to make sense out of it. We come to understand it and hopefully, to accept it. With acceptance, the "wound" is healed, as if by magic. The area of sensitivity exists only as a memory. We no longer react to it with wild emotions, but from understanding and with insight. We see, once we are able to heal and let go of an inner wound, how we created much upset for ourselves because of our own inability to handle that particular situation or subject.

Initiation

This is a difficult philosophy to understand, and even more difficult to live, although it brings incredible rewards. We speak with awe of "initiation" as if it were a secret ceremony reserved for a select few. In fact, **initiation is acceptance of responsibility** for oneself, in all areas of life. Every time we accept a little more responsibility for ourselves and the way we affect and determine our own experiences, we undergo another initiation.

Perhaps all of the outer planets are involved in the process of initiation. **Uranus indicates flashes of intellectual insight** and the freedom to make connections where none previously existed, to see situations in a new light, and to handle an emotionally "loaded" situation with detachment and lightness. **Pluto represents the force which drives deeply buried material into consciousness** where it demands our attention in a way we cannot refuse, as well as the ability to delve into painful areas and know that we have the strength to persist. In a way, Pluto and Uranus balance each other, for what Uranus takes too lightly and tends to intellectualize, Pluto will cause to erupt until it cannot be dismissed. What Pluto takes too seriously and gets involved in so intensely that perspective is completely lost, Uranus will detach from and see the funny side.

Transcendence

Neptune represents our ability to surrender to whatever we have previously denied, to accept it and then to transcend it. The transcendence does not mean we leave it behind, but that we reach a new level of understanding in which we no longer see the issue in a polarized form, where we must defend one side and fight the other. Transcendence brings the understanding that what looked like two opposing issues is actually one, of which we could accept only one half. Often the conscious acceptance comes only after the transcendence; we can only admit that we **had** a problem after we have healed it and let it go!

Most of our problems are the result of fear. Fear begets denial, limitation and lack of faith. We deny our Divine nature, we deny the existence of Universal Love, or at least our personal ability to connect to it, and we believe in many limitations. Much of this is necessary in order to live successfully in the material world, but we usually overdo it. What starts out as a lesson on the physical limits of the world may become a lesson in ever-diminishing possibilities. We may learn not to expect too much, but how much is too much? For some of us, anything is too much. Early in life we faced too many harsh disappointments and we learned to stop hoping.

Neptune is all about hope, and the vague sense that everything we ever hoped for is possible, after all. Neptune is all about compassion and the need to help others. It represents the highest spiritual goals to which we can aspire, as well as the attitudes we need to reach those goals. Applied to worldly affairs, Neptunian attitudes don't always work successfully. Applied to the world of spiritual evolution, they are the only ones which work.

A Sustaining Faith

Neptune's true gift is that of faith. It is not the certainty of personal rightness, nor the blind acceptance of one creed or religion above all others. It is the faith that there is an order to the workings of the universe, and that the order has meaning, and that we have meaning and a role within that order which is utterly "right" for us. The real Neptune is deep inside us. Call it our soul, or "the force," prana, the essence of Universal Love, Cosmic Consciousness or God; these are words which we use to describe our experience of Neptune.

All around us flows the endless spiritual love and the limitless possibilities for which some corner of our souls still yearns. We may become so mired down by earthly realities and physical laws that we disconnect ourselves from the flow of spirit, no longer believing it exists. We often close ourselves off from possibilities and the most supportive love we can ever experience because we dare not hope it is out there, or because we have become confused and expect to find it from other people. Like a lodge shuttered against the night cold, we have closed our doors and battened down our hatches, too immersed in the business of life to remember our spiritual nature and what its rules and laws are.

Neptune is always open, however. It may work poorly, or be disconnected from the rest of your personality, but Neptune is your door back to your Divine spiritual nature. You may have spent years looking in the wrong place, but Neptune is open for you. You may even have buried it under years of deceptions and illusions, which was the best way you could cope at the time, but Neptune awaits you. **If you want to reconnect, the door is open.**

As with all planetary themes, the gifts are easily misused by those with uncertain motivations. Those who live in love take Neptune's faith and make it real in their lives. They accept that everyone has a spark of Divinity, they believe in something good in everyone, without being gullible. They believe in the existence of vast and unimaginable spiritual possibilities without being escapist or getting lost in illusions. They are sensitive and receptive without being masochistic. They are kind and caring without making martyrs of themselves. They are imaginative and inspirational without being deceptive. They remain open to the flow of Neptunian energy without becoming unstable and lost in a dream world. They are mystical, not fanciful. They are introspective without being morbid, open and idealistic without becoming vague or insecure.

Neptune opens the door for us to reconnect with our own Divine spirit, with our true spiritual heritage. It is not really a difficult path to tread, but it is one that is made difficult by our addictions to the material world and the pleasures of ego, self and power. The energy which we associate with Neptune does not require us to cut ourselves off from these pleasures, but to see them for what they are and to see their limited and limiting uses, and to outgrow them.

Neptune is symbolic of a different level of reality than the one we habitually use. The Buddhists call all of life as we commonly know it *maya* or illusion. That is the message which Neptune represents— that all of the constructs, habits, conventions and laws which people create are just that: creations. They do not constitute the whole of reality. They are reality only on the level at which they are created. There are other realities, and Neptune tells us that many realities are not nearly so limiting as the one in which we habitually live.

With the insight that Neptune represents, we find we are not mere bodies, but the **keepers of a remarkable spark of consciousness which is eternal**. Neptune's true gift is the faith that this spark is "real" and it has a purpose. When we open our minds to the possibilities that Neptune symbolizes, we can experience some remarkable insights.

Many of the most liberating insights we discover have to do with ourselves and how we create our own experiences. The most painful insights occur when we see, understand and accept the many behaviors with which we have hurt ourselves and others, over which we have deluded ourselves and used to avoid real growth. These insights are painful because we have to accept some very unpleasant truths about ourselves; yet once we do so, we begin to really heal, and with the healing comes a new approach to life. This is initiation.

Most of us experience our initiations one step at a time, which is merciful. Imagine if we had to suffer, in one terrible moment, the discovery of all our mistaken ideas, delusions and self-caused pain. It is enough of a shock, for most of us, to discover one illusion at a time which contributes to our suffering, to cope with that discovery and to learn new and more constructive attitudes and behavior. In fact, most of us only manage to cope with pieces of an illusion. How many people have worked, for example, for two or three years on a single problem, such as a dominating mother? They may feel they have it solved, only to have deeper levels of the issue come up a decade later.

Each time we work through such an issue, however, we feel as if we have come out of a deep pit or a long, dark tunnel, into the warm and beautiful light of understanding. Neptune **is** the light at the end of the tunnel— the light of our own Divine nature which beckons us on to the path of self-realization.

APPENDIX

EXAMPLES OF NEPTUNE IN HOUSES, SIGNS AND ASPECTS

Because Neptune takes approximately 165 years to circle the zodiac, it spends about 14 years in a sign. Thus, we have no examples of famous people with Neptune in certain signs. The people listed here are based on birth certificate data and by Michel and Francoise Gauquelin.

NEPTUNE IN CANCER

20 ♋ 09	ALVAREZ, Luis		24 ♋ 25	MURAYAMA, Makio
21 ♋ 57	JACKSON, Henry		24 ♋ 37	CHILD, Julia
23 ♋ 42	HERMAN, Woody		26 ♋ 48	CRANSTON, Alan
23 ♋ 47ʙ	ROGERS, Roy		29 ♋ 28	RAY, Dixy
24 ♋ 23	COHEN, Wilbur		29 ♋ 44ʙ	WIDMARK, Richard

NEPTUNE IN LEO

2 ♌ 11	PAAR, Jack		13 ♌ 17ʙ	DAY, Doris
3 ♌ 12	BROOKS, Gwendolyn		13 ♌ 45	GARLAND, Judy
3 ♌ 12	MARTIN, Dean		15 ♌ 3O	EISENHOWER, John
3 ♌ 13	BOONE, Richard		17 ♌ 45ʙ	BRANDO, Marlon
4 ♌ 12	DILLER, Phyllis		17 ♌ 51ʙ	VAUGHAN, Sarah
4 ♌ 56ʙ	RIGGS, Bobby		17 ♌ 52ʙ	GARDNER, Ava
5 ♌ 24	WEINBERGER, Casper		18 ♌ O6ʙ	FOXX, Redd
5 ♌ 46	LUCE, Charles		18 ♌ 44	SAINT, Eva
5 ♌ 58	FORD, Henry		19 ♌ 58	CRAIN, Jeanne
6 ♌ 28ʙ	BRADLEY, Thomas		21 ♌ O1ʙ	HOLBROOK, Hal
9 ♌ 19	GRAHAM, Billy		21 ♌ 38ʙ	NEWMAN, Paul
11 ♌ 57	CHAMPION, Gower		26 ♌ 25	MARTIN, Billy
11 ♌ 58	BRADBURY, Ray		26 ♌ 26ʙ	TEMPLE, Shirley
12 ♌ O1ʙ	DOWNS, Hugh		27 ♌ O6ʙ	BORMAN, Frank

NEPTUNE IN VIRGO

0 ♍ 54	EASTWOOD, Clint	12 ♍ 35 CONNOLLY, Maureen
2 ♍ 31	ARMSTRONG, Neil	14 ♍ 12 KRISTOFFERSON, Kris
5 ♍ 04ʙ	BANKS, Ernie	15 ♍ 44 REDFORD, Robert
7 ♍ 32	RATHER, Dan	20 ♍ 48ʙ COLLINS, Judy
7 ♍ 55	LAWRENCE, Carol	24 ♍ 47 WELCH, Raquel
9 ♍ 13ʙ	NOVAK, Kim	25 ♍ 19 TREVINO Lee
10 ♍ 21	ELDER, Lee	27 ♍ 28 PRYOR, Richard
11 ♍ 40ʙ	AARON, Hank	

NEPTUNE IN LIBRA

1 ♎ 41ʙ	LUCAS, George	8 ♎ 39ʙ MILLER, John
1 ♎ 53	BUTKUS, Dick	10 ♎ 34 FLEMING, Peggy
2 ♎ 47ʙ	ROSS, Diana	12 ♎ 32 PLUNKETT, Jim
3 ♎ 42	KING, Billie	14 ♎ 23 SPRINGSTEEN, Bruce
4 ♎ 14	DENVER, John	16 ♎ 49ʙ FODOR, Eugene
6 ♎ 08ʙ	FARROW, Mia	17 ♎ 12ʙ SPITZ, Mark
6 ♎ 14ʙ	BERGEN, Candice	22 ♎ 16 WALTON, Bill
7 ♎ 41ʙ	MINNELLI, Liza	

NEPTUNE IN SCORPIO

0 ♏ 23	NABER, John	2 ♏ 36 BABASHOFF, Shirley
2 ♏ 24	LOPEZ, Nancy	7 ♏ 40ʙ CAUTHEN, Steve

NEPTUNE IN THE FIRST HOUSE

ALPERT, Herb	HILLER, Stanley	RALSTON, R.
BALL, William	JURGENSEN, Christi	RAY, Dixy
COLBY, William	LOSEY, Joseph	SHOEMAKER, E
COOLEY, Denton	LYNDE, Paul	SIMON, William
COWENS, David	MATSON, Oliver	SIX, Robert
CRANSTON, Alan	MATSON, Randi	TOWNES, Charles
ELDER, Lee	MUNSON, Thurman	WEYERHAEUSER,
GARDNER, Ava	NELSON, Willie	George
GREENE, Joe	OATES J C	WHITE, Jojo
GRONOUSKI, John	O'BRIEN, Parry	YOUNG, Whitney
HARTZOG, George	OTTO, James	

NEPTUNE IN THE SECOND HOUSE

ALI, Muhammad	FRANCIS, Sam	ROZELLE P
ANDERSON, Jack	GARDNER, John	SCHOLLANDER,
ASHLEY, Elisabeth	GARLAND, Judy	Donald
BLANCHARD, Felix	GRIFFIN, Merv	SHAPP, Milton
BOONE, Richard	KRAMER, Gerald	SHORE D
BROWN, Jerry	LAMBERT, Jack	SIMPSON, Orenthal
BRUBECK, David	LEWIS, David	SUMMER, Donna
CAULFIELD, Joan	LEWIS, Jerry	TAYLOR, James
CHADWICK, Florence	MAYO, Robert	TRABERT, Marion
CHAMBERLAIN, Owen	MOORE, George	WELLES, Orson
COLLINS, Judy	PARSEGHIAN, Ara	WHITE, Byron
CONIGLIARO, Tony	PECKINPAH, Samuel	WHITWORTH, Kathy
EAGLETON, Thomas	POSTON, Tom	WINTERS, Jonathan
FOREMAN, George	RICHARDSON, Bobby	WYETH, James

NEPTUNE IN THE THIRD HOUSE

ALVAREZ, Luis	GIFFORD, Frank	NITSCHKE, Raymond
BAILAR, Benjamin	GLASER D A	OLSEN, Merlin
BARRY, Richard	GOOD, Robert	PARKS, Robert
BUDGE, John	GREGORY, Cynthia	PEROT, Henry
BURKE, Yvonne	HAYES, Elvin	REVELLE, Roger
BUTKUS, Dick	JONES, Deacon	RUSH, David
CHILD, Julia	KIDD, Billy	SHORT, Bobby
DELLUMS, Ronald	KRAMER, John	SPITZ, Mark
DILLER, Phyllis	LAMB, William	WILHELM, James
DUNCAN, Charles	LOWENSTEIN, Allard	
FARREL, Suzanne	MAUCH, Gene	

NEPTUNE IN THE FOURTH HOUSE

ARMSTRONG, Neil	KEMP, Jack	STARR, Bryan
ASKEW, R	KILMER, Bill	TALBERT, Bill
BLACK, Karen	MOYNIHAN, D	TARR, Curtis
DAVIS, Miles	PEPPLER, Mary	TRAVOLTA, John
FOSBURY, Richard	RAINEY, Froelich	WALTON, Bill
GOLD, Herbert	ROBERTS, Ken	ZIEGLER, Ronald
HARRIS, Patricia	SCHLAFLY, Phillis	

NEPTUNE IN THE FIFTH HOUSE

ALIOTO, Joseph
BABASHOFF, Shirley
BAKER, Howard
BYRD, Robert
BYRNE, Brendan
DELOREAN, John
DENVER, John
FREEMAN, David
GILLIGAN, John
GONZALES, Richard
GOODMAN, Julian
GRAEBNER, Clark
GRAHAM, Billy

GRIER, Rosey
HAACK, Robert
HAVLICEK, John
HILLS, Carla
JANOV, Arthur
LOPEZ, Nancy
MAHAN, Larry
MARTIN, Dean
MAY, Rollo
MORRISON, Toni
MURRAY, Don
PATTERSON, Floyd
RATHER, Dan

SCALI, John
SCOTT, David
SEITZ, Frederick
SHAPIRO, Irving
SPRINGSTEEN, Bruce
TAFT, Robert
THOMPSON, D
TREVINO Lee
VALENTI, Jack
WAGNER, A J
WARWICK, Dionne
ZUMWALT, Elmo

NEPTUNE IN THE SIXTH HOUSE

ALWORTH, Lance
ANTHONY, Earl
ARNESS, James
BEBAN, Gary
BERRA, Yogi
BREEDLOVE, Craig
BROWNING, John
CHANDLER, Otis
CHAPLIN, Geraldine
COUNSILMAN, James
DIEBOLD, John
DULLEA, Keir
DUVALL, Robert
FAIRCHILD, John
FARROW, Mia
FEINSTEIN, Dianne

FLEISCHER, Leon
FORD, Henry
FREEMAN, Orville
GABRIEL, Roman
HADDON, William
HARRELSON, Ken
HAYES, Bob
JOHNSON, Don
KUCINICH, Dennis
LONDON, Julie
LUCAS, George
Mc ADOO, Bob
MAILER, Norman
MATHEWS, Edwin
MIDLER, Bette
MILLETT, Kate

MINNELLI, Liza
MONDALE, Walter
MORGAN, Joe
PAINE, Thomas
PERRINE, Valerie
REDFORD, Robert
ROGERS, Roy
SCHROEDER,
  Frederick
STEWART, William
TROWBRIDGE,
  Alexandre
VERDON, Gwen
WILLIAMS, Billy
YARBOROUGH, Cale

NEPTUNE IN THE SEVENTH HOUSE

BERGQUIST, Kenneth
BOMBECK, Erma
BOWEN, William
BRADBURY, Ray
CHARLES, Ezzard
DALY, James
DAWSON, Leonard
DEGAETANI, Jan
DONAHUE, Phil
DUERK, Alene
FODOR, Eugene
GILRUTH, Robert
GRAMM, Donald
HAMILL, Dorothy
JAMES, Daniel

JORDAN, William
KAHN, Madeline
KESEY, Ken
KNIEVEL, Evel
KOONTZ, Elizabeth
LAYNE, Bobby
LEWIS, Henry
LOGAN, Karen
LOVE, John
MITCHELL L
MOYERS, Bill
NABER, John
NEWMAN, Paul
NOVAK, Kim
O'NEAL, Arthur

PAAR, Jack
PREUS, Jacob
PRICE, Leontyne
PRYOR, Richard
ROSE, Peter
SEAGREN, Bob
SHEEN, Martin
SIMONE, Nina
SLAYTON, Donald
STEINBRENNER,
  George
STEINKRAUS, Bill
WARMERDAM,
  Cornelius

NEPTUNE IN THE EIGHTH HOUSE

AMECHE, Don
BENTSEN, Lloyd
CERNAN, Eugene
CHAMPION, Gower
CLIFFORD, John
CONNALLY, John
COPPOLA, Francis
DAVENPORT, W
DAVIS, Glen
DEBUSSCHERE, David
DELAVALLADE, Carme
DILLMAN, Bradford
FRIEDAN, Betty
GALVIN, Robert
GOULIAN, Mehran

GRIZZARD, George
HAGGARD, M
HOFFMAN, Dustin
HOLBROOK, Hal
HORNUNG, Paul
HUGHES, Emmet
JACKSON, Maynard
KASTENMEIER, Rober
KING, Billie
KROL, John
LILLEHEI, Clarence
LOVELL, James
LUCAS, Jerry
MAYS, Willie
MORTON, Roger

MOTT, Stewart
NEAL, Patricia
PAGE A
PERRY, James
REHNQUIST, William
RIGGS, Bobby
ROBERTS, Robin
SAYERS, Gale
STONES, Dwight
THOMAS, Michael
WARFIELD, Paul
WEINBERGER, Casper
WILLSON, Zack
WRIGHT, Mickey

NEPTUNE IN THE NINTH HOUSE

ARFONS, Art
ASH, Roy
BANKS, Ernie
BERGEN, Candice
BERGLAND, Robert
BERRIGAN, Daniel
BRADLEY, Thomas
BRANDO, Marlon
BROWER, David
BUTTON, Richard
CONNOLLY, Maureen
CROSSFIELD, Albert
CURTIS, Ann
DYLAN, Bob
EHRLICHMAN, John
ETHERINGTON, Edwin
FELKER, Clay

FRAZIER, Joe
GLENN, John
GOODSON, Mark
GREY, Joel
GRIFFIN, Archie
GROZA, Louis
HARRIS, Franco
INOUYE, Daniel
JACKSON, Henry
KIRKLAND, Joseph
KITT, Eartha
LAWRENCE, Carol
LYNN, Janet
MARIS, Roger
MATHIAS, Robert
MILLER, John
MUNSEL, P

PRESLEY, E
RAUSCHENBERG,
  Robert
REED, Willis
ROTH, Philip
SAINT, Eva
SALINGER, Pierre
SMEAL, Eleanor
STAUBACH, Roger
STEWART, Thomas
TEMPLE, Shirley
TURNER, Ted
VAUGHAN, Sarah
WARNECKE, John
WELCH, Raquel
WILLIAMS, Theodore

NEPTUNE IN THE TENTH HOUSE

BACKE, John	HOLLEY, Robert	O'NEAL, Ryan
BERRY, Raymond	IRVING, John	PAIGE, Janis
BROOKS, Gwendolyn	KAEL, Pauline	PETTIT, Robert
CARSON, J	KIRK, Claude	PHILLIPS, W
CRAIN, Jeanne	KNOWLES, John	RHODES, John
CSONKA, Lawrence	KRISTOFFERSON, Kris	RICE, Jim
EASTWOOD, Clint	LEIGHTON R B	ROSS, Diana
EVANS, Daniel	LEVINE, James	SNYDER, Gary
FLEMING, Peggy	LUCE, Charles	STEINEM, Gloria
GAGNE, Verne	LYNN, James	TETLEY, Glen
GODDARD, James	MANN, Dick	VOLCKER, Paul
GRAHAM, Otto	MEREDITH, Burgess	WHITE, Edward
HANSEN, Fred	MOTHERWELL, Robert	WIDMARK, Richard
HARRIS, Fred	NASH, Philleo	YOUNG, John
HODGSON, James	NICKLAUS, Jack	

NEPTUNE IN THE ELEVENTH HOUSE

ANDERSON, John	FOXX, Redd	MURPHY, William
BLAKE, Robert	FOYT, Anthony	NOLAND, Kenneth
BLEGEN, Judith	GIBSON, Althea	PEARSON, David
BLUE, Vida	HALDEMAN, Harry	RAUH, Joseph
BLUME, Judy	HART, Phil	RICHARDS, Bob
BORMAN, Frank	HAUGE, G	SAWHILL, John
BOUTON, Jim	HEARNES, W E	SCAMMON, Richard
CAGE, John	HERMAN, Woody	SCHLESINGER, Arthur
CHANNING, Carol	HOWARD, Frank	SCHMIDT, Mike
CLARK, Eleanor	KEATON, Diane	SEAVER, Tom
COHEN, Wilbur	KERKORIAN, Kirk	TARKENTON, Francis
DAY, Doris	LEMON, Meadow	THEROUX, Paul
DEMPSEY, Tom	LEWIS, Roger	WILLS, Helen
DINE, James	MARTIN, Billy	WYNN, Early
FABRAY, Nanette	MIKAN, George	

NEPTUNE IN THE TWELFTH HOUSE

AARON, Hank
ANNENBERG, Walter
ASHE, Arthur
BEAN, Orson
BRADLEY, Bill
CASPER, William
CAUTHEN, Steve
CHILES, Lawton
COSELL, Howard
CRONIN, Joseph
DONOVAN, Hedley
DOWNS, Hugh
DRYSDALE, Don
DUNLOP, John
EISENHOWER, John
FIDRYCH, Mark
FIELD, Sally

GABLE, Dan
HALL, Floyd
HARD, Darlene
HEFNER, Hugh
HELMS, Rich
HUFSTEDLER, Shirley
JENSEN, Arthur
JONES, Everett
KOCH, John
LEDERBERG, Joshua
LEE, Sammy
LILLY, Bob
LITTLER, Eugene
Mac NEIL,
MALDEN, Karl
MARSHALL, Burke
MASTERS, William

MILLER, Neal
MITCHELL, J
MORIARTY, Michael
MURAYAMA, Makio
OKUN, Arthur
OWEN, Nancy
PLUNKETT, Jim
RYUN, James
SAVITT, Richard
SCHIRRA, Walter
STEVENS, George
STOKES, Carl
TALESE, Gay
TYUS, Wyomia
UDALL, Morris
WELLS, Mary
WICKER, Tom

SUN/NEPTUNE

SEXTILE ✶ 3° 00′ orb

0° 04′	RATHER, Dan	1° 32′	ANDERSON, Jack
0° 05′	PLUNKETT, Jim	1° 33′	HERMAN, Woody
0° 41′	LYNDE, Paul	1° 36′	EVANS, Daniel
1° 10′	CASPER, William	2° 02′	GALVIN, Robert
1° 17′	MIDLER, Bette	2° 23′	FIDRYCH, Mark

TRINE △ 3° 00′ orb

0° 05′	DAY, Doris	2° 07′	REVELLE, Roger
0° 06′	LAYNE, Bobby	2° 09′	PARKS, Robert
0° 12′	ZIEGLER, Ronald	2° 13′	GRAHAM, Otto
0° 32′	HILLS, Carla	2° 16′	LEMON, Meadow
0° 34′	DUERK, Alene	2° 21′	LOVE, John
0° 51′	HARD, Darlene	2° 27′	NELSON, Willie
0° 57′	PATTERSON, Floyd	2° 31′	ALI, Muhammad
1° 03′	SAYERS, Gale	2° 47′	PRESLEY E
1° 04′	BRUBECK, David	2° 47′	BLANCHARD, Felix
1° 39′	FOXX, Redd	2° 53′	HEFNER, Hugh

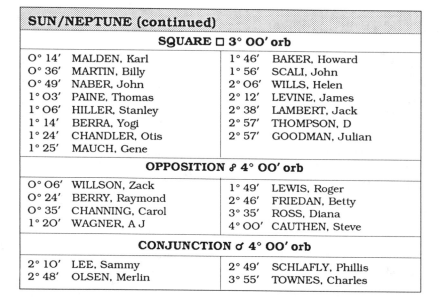

SUN/NEPTUNE (continued)

SQUARE □ 3° OO' orb

O° 14'	MALDEN, Karl	1° 46'	BAKER, Howard
O° 36'	MARTIN, Billy	1° 56'	SCALI, John
O° 49'	NABER, John	2° O6'	WILLS, Helen
1° O3'	PAINE, Thomas	2° 12'	LEVINE, James
1° O6'	HILLER, Stanley	2° 38'	LAMBERT, Jack
1° 14'	BERRA, Yogi	2° 57'	THOMPSON, D
1° 24'	CHANDLER, Otis	2° 57'	GOODMAN, Julian
1° 25'	MAUCH, Gene		

OPPOSITION ☍ 4° OO' orb

O° O6'	WILLSON, Zack	1° 49'	LEWIS, Roger
O° 24'	BERRY, Raymond	2° 46'	FRIEDAN, Betty
O° 35'	CHANNING, Carol	3° 35'	ROSS, Diana
1° 20'	WAGNER, A J	4° OO'	CAUTHEN, Steve

CONJUNCTION ♂ 4° OO' orb

2° 1O'	LEE, Sammy	2° 49'	SCHLAFLY, Phillis
2° 48'	OLSEN, Merlin	3° 55'	TOWNES, Charles

MOON/NEPTUNE

SEXTILE ✶ 3° OO' orb

O° 20'	SCHMIDT, Mike	1° 36'	DONOVAN, Hedley
O° 21'	LOGAN, Karen	1° 38'	BOMBECK, Erma
O° 21'	JONES, Deacon	1° 53'	MAY, Rollo
O° 36'	FLEISCHER, Leon	1° 54'	REED, Willis
O° 53'	OKUN, Arthur	1° 58'	RATHER, Dan
1° O6'	PEARSON, David	1° 58'	WILLSON, Zack
1° 1O'	HADDON, William	2° 12'	BROOKS, Gwendolyn
1° 17'	BROWN, Jerry	2° 25'	MOTHERWELL, Robert
1° 20'	MORIARTY, Michael	2° 33'	KOCH, John
1° 23'	WRIGHT, Mickey	2° 33'	YOUNG, John
1° 26'	GARDNER, John	2° 50'	TEMPLE, Shirley

MOON/NEPTUNE (continued)

TRINE △ 3° 00' orb

0° 05'	HAACK, Robert	2° 07'	COOLEY, Denton
0° 21'	WARWICK, Dionne	2° 19'	BLEGEN, Judith
0° 21'	WILLIAMS, Billy	2° 38'	FAIRCHILD, John
0° 24'	FIDRYCH, Mark	2° 39'	BARRY, Richard
0° 27'	ETHERINGTON, Edwin	2° 42'	GRONOUSKI, John

SQUARE □ 3° 00' orb

1° 02'	LITTLER, Eugene	1° 39'	ASH, Roy
1° 20'	RUSH, David	2° 18'	HARRIS, Patricia
1° 21'	YARBOROUGH, Cale	2° 51'	DIEBOLD, John
1° 27'	KEMP, Jack	2° 51'	GRIER, Rosey

OPPOSITION ☌ 4° 00' orb

0° 18'	LOVE, John	2° 59'	TAYLOR, James
0° 27'	HELMS, Richard	3° 00'	SCHROEDER, Frederick
0° 48'	DEGAETANI, Jan	3° 01'	MUNSEL, P
0° 53'	LEWIS, David	3° 06'	TALESE, Gay
1° 25'	CLIFFORD, John	3° 38'	WHITWORTH, Kathy
1° 41'	MARSHALL, Burke	3° 51'	PECKINPAH, Samuel
2° 36'	EHRLICHMAN, John	3° 51'	FIELD, Sally
2° 49'	CERNAN, Eugene		

CONJUNCTION ♂ 4° 00' orb

0° 36'	GRIZZARD, George	2° 24'	FOXX, Redd
0° 36'	WELLS, Mary	2° 32'	GODDARD, James
0° 36'	HOFFMAN, Dustin	2° 58'	KING, Billie
0° 39'	BLAKE, Robert	3° 18'	ASKEW, R
1° 06'	WHITE, Edward	3° 30'	REDFORD, Robert
2° 20'	STEINKRAUS, Bill		

MERCURY/NEPTUNE

SEXTILE ✳ 3° 00' orb

0° 19'	JACKSON, Henry	1° 22'	STEINKRAUS, Bill
0° 26'	BROOKS, Gwendolyn	1° 24'	BOONE, Richard
0° 39'	BEBAN, Gary	1° 47'	MAHAN, Larry
0° 56'	WELLS, Mary	1° 55'	GABRIEL, Roman
0° 56'	RALSTON, R	1° 56'	FORD, Henry
1° 00'	MARTIN, Dean	2° 02'	PAIGE, Janis
1° 13'	STEINBRENNER, George	2° 17'	MOYERS, Bill
1° 13'	SHEEN, Martin	2° 44'	WARFIELD, Paul
1° 14'	SCHLESINGER, Arthur	2° 52'	KING, Billie
1° 16'	ALWORTH, Lance	2° 53'	STEWART, William
1° 21'	DIEBOLD, John		

MERCURY/NEPTUNE (continued)

TRINE △ 3° 00′ orb

0° 16′	FOXX, Redd	2° 03′	NICKLAUS, Jack
0° 28′	STARR, Bryan	2° 06′	MAYS, Willie
0° 29′	BYRD, Robert	2° 19′	OWEN, Nancy
0° 30′	KIRK, Claude	2° 20′	JOHNSON, Don
0° 36′	HODGSON, James	2° 40′	LOGAN, Karen
0° 42′	FARROW, Mia	2° 52′	MITCHELL, L
1° 38′	DAVENPORT W	2° 56′	TEMPLE, Shirley
1° 51′	PATTERSON, Floyd		

SQUARE □ 3° 00′ orb

0° 13′	MUNSON, Thurman	1° 37′	HALDEMAN, Harry
0° 15′	KROL, John	1° 48′	SCOTT, David
0° 24′	POSTON, Tom	1° 48′	SNYDER, Gary
0° 27′	MATSON, Oliver	1° 51′	HARRIS, Patricia
0° 34′	GONZALES, Richard	1° 54′	DYLAN, Bob
0° 36′	DAVIS, Miles	2° 14′	GILRUTH, Robert
0° 46′	O'NEAL, Arthur	2° 19′	HANSEN, Fred
1° 11′	OATES, J C	2° 24′	WILLS, Helen
1° 34′	SCALI, John	2° 54′	HADDON, William

OPPOSITION ☍ 4° 00′ orb

0° 34′	WILLSON, Zack	2° 18′	THEROUX, Paul
0° 51′	BORMAN, Frank	2° 21′	HAACK, Robert
1° 20′	MINNELLI, Liza	2° 24′	DELAVALLADE, Carmen
1° 59′	STEINEM, Gloria	2° 31′	PECKINPAH, Samuel
2° 10′	HAVLICEK, John	3° 04′	CERNAN, Eugene

CONJUNCTION ☌ 4° 00′ orb

0° 01′	HARRELSON, Ken	2° 03′	GREENE, Joe
0° 28′	CHAMBERLAIN, Owen	2° 08′	SCHMIDT, Mike
0° 38′	ARMSTRONG, Neil	2° 29′	REDFORD, Robert
0° 55′	COOLEY, Denton	2° 35′	BROWER, David
1° 32′	DUNLOP, John	3° 36′	GIBSON, Althea
1° 40′	BRADBURY, Ray	3° 58′	MORGAN, Joe

VENUS/NEPTUNE

SEXTILE ✱ 3° 00′ orb

0° 11′	LILLY, Bob	1° 47′	BUDGE, John
0° 19′	SCHROEDER, Frederick	1° 54′	DONAHUE, Phil
0° 20′	HALDEMAN, Harry	2° 02′	GLENN, John
0° 21′	HORNUNG, Paul	2° 22′	WELCH, Raquel
0° 27′	SUMMER, Donna	2° 29′	DAVENPORT W
0° 39′	HALL, Floyd	2° 36′	BACKE, John
0° 49′	WILLS, Helen	2° 51′	LUCE, Charles

VENUS/NEPTUNE (continued)

TRINE △ 3° OO' orb

0° 24'	DOWNS, Hugh	1° 53'	ALIOTO, Joseph
0° 30'	LUCAS, Jerry	1° 54'	FREEMAN, Orville
0° 39'	REED, Willis	2° 10'	HAMILL, Dorothy
0° 57'	ALPERT, Herb	2° 13'	SLAYTON, Donald
1° 09'	LEMON, Meadow	2° 22'	DELOREAN, John
1° 30'	WIDMARK, Richard	2° 32'	MOYNIHAN Daniel
1° 33'	DAVIS, Miles	2° 41'	KIDD, Billy
1° 39'	KITT, Eartha	2° 50'	HADDON, William
1° 53'	O'NEAL, Arthur	2° 59'	GOULIAN, Mehran

SQUARE □ 3° OO' orb

0° 11'	BLACK, Karen	1° 55'	GREY, Joel
0° 24'	PAGE, A	2° 20'	WELLS, Mary
0° 36'	KEATON, Diane	2° 23'	HERMAN, Woody
0° 44'	MATSON Oliver	2° 42'	LOVE, John
0° 45'	Mac NEIL,	2° 45'	BROWNING, John
0° 47'	HARRIS Fred	2° 48'	GILLIGAN, John
1° 08'	LAMBERT, Jack	2° 55'	KROL, John
1° 16'	WHITE, Edward	2° 56'	MATHIAS, Robert
1° 17'	GRAHAM, Billy	2° 58'	SAWHILL, John

OPPOSITION ☍ 4° OO' orb

0° 23'	KIRK, Claude	2° 29'	MILLER, John
0° 31'	MASTERS, William	2° 52'	RYUN, James
0° 53'	BORMAN, Frank	2° 54'	TETLEY, Glen
1° 13'	FARROW, Mia	2° 55'	ARFONS, Art
1° 29'	RAUH, Joseph	3° 20'	HUGHES, Emmet
1° 54'	NEAL, Patricia	3° 28'	PECKINPAH, Samuel
2° 03'	WRIGHT, Mickey	3° 56'	RICE, Jim
2° 21'	HART Phil		

CONJUNCTION ♂ 4° OO' orb

1° 02'	LEWIS, David	2° 32'	CRANSTON, Alan
1° 39'	LEWIS, Henry	2° 51'	DUNCAN, Charles
1° 45'	REHNQUIST, William		

MARS/NEPTUNE

SEXTILE ✶ 3° 00' orb

0° 35'	BOONE, Richard	1° 41'	RICHARDSON, Bobby
0° 48'	MARTIN, Dean	1° 50'	SCHMIDT, Mike
0° 57'	KOONTZ, Elizabeth	1° 56'	STEWART, William
1° 07'	BROOKS, Gwendolyn	2° 00'	HANSEN, Fred
1° 24'	BERGEN, Candice	2° 08'	GRAHAM, Otto
1° 25'	ANNENBERG, Walter	2° 50'	SCHOLLANDER, Dona
1° 35'	HAYES, Bob	2° 58'	LEWIS, Roger

TRINE △ 3° 00' orb

0° 09'	BROWN, Jerry	2° 01'	IRVING, John
0° 24'	COLLINS, Judy	2° 07'	SIMPSON, Orenthal
0° 58'	FRAZIER, Joe	2° 10'	TETLEY, Glen
1° 12'	DENVER, John	2° 11'	ARFONS, Art
1° 46'	ASHLEY, Elisabeth	2° 20'	EISENHOWER, John
1° 52'	GOULIAN, Mehran	2° 25'	KILMER, Bill
1° 58'	BERGQUIST, Kennet	2° 26'	EASTWOOD, Clint
2° 01'	NEWMAN, Paul		

SQUARE ☐ 3° 00' orb

0° 01'	HARTZOG, George	1° 44'	MANN, Dick
0° 32'	COSELL, Howard	1° 54'	GARDNER, John
0° 44'	WILLIAMS, Theodore	2° 03'	SEITZ, Frederick
0° 55'	COHEN, Wilbur	2° 10'	DULLEA, Keir
0° 57'	BOUTON, Jim	2° 24'	RHODES, John
1° 03'	DUERK, Alene	2° 34'	BARRY, Richard
1° 05'	KROL, John	2° 57'	LITTLER, Eugene
1° 07'	LEE, Sammy	2° 58'	MOORE, George
1° 30'	PRICE, Leontyne		

OPPOSITION ☍ 4° 00' orb

0° 34'	BABASHOFF, Shirle	2° 47'	MOTHERWELL, Robert
1° 34'	GRIZZARD, George	3° 30'	GOODSON, Mark
2° 04'	HARRIS, Patricia	3° 59'	TARR, Curtis
2° 14'	RICE, Jim		

CONJUNCTION ☌ 4° 00' orb

0° 53'	ROBERTS, Ken	2° 46'	PERRY JAMES
1° 13'	LEIGHTON, R B	3° 16'	KNIEVEL, Evel
1° 58'	BROWNING, John	3° 37'	STONES, Dwight
2° 05'	PETTIT, Robert	3° 47'	ROTH, Philip
2° 39'	BERRY, Raymond		

JUPITER/NEPTUNE

SEXTILE ✶ 3° 00' orb

0° 06'	KOCH, John	1° 55'	EISENHOWER, John
0° 19'	STEINBRENNER, George	1° 56'	GRAHAM, Otto
0° 30'	BYRD, Robert	1° 59'	RICHARDSON, Bobby
0° 33'	PEARSON, David	2° 00'	RIGGS, Bobby
0° 38'	NABER, John	2° 03'	DAWSON, Leonard
0° 45'	DILLER, Phyllis	2° 22'	GOODMAN, Julian
0° 48'	DAY, Doris	2° 24'	MILLER, Neal
0° 48'	LEVINE, James	2° 24'	DINE, James
0° 58'	KEMP, Jack	2° 29'	LEWIS, David
1° 04'	PARKS, Robert	2° 36'	ASHE, Arthur
1° 14'	PEROT, Henry	2° 45'	WILHELM, James
1° 20'	LOSEY, Joseph	3° 00'	PATTERSON, Floyd

TRINE △ 3° 00' orb

0° 16'	OKUN, Arthur	1° 39'	WARMERDAM, Cornelius
0° 18'	HILLER, Stanley	1° 55'	VAUGHAN, Sarah
0° 21'	MARTIN, Billy	1° 57'	TOWNES, Charles
0° 23'	LOWENSTEIN, Allard	1° 57'	HOFFMAN, Dustin
0° 26'	SLAYTON, Donald	2° 00'	BLEGEN, Judith
0° 31'	GOLD HERBERT	2° 01'	GONZALES, Richard
0° 38'	ALIOTO, Joseph	2° 05'	BYRNE, Brendan
1° 03'	SPITZ, Mark	2° 08'	HARRIS, Patricia
1° 25'	SCAMMON, Richard	2° 09'	BRANDO, Marlon
1° 27'	ROGERS, Roy	2° 11'	NOLAND, Kenneth
1° 31'	WELLS, Mary	2° 15'	BUDGE, John

SQUARE ☐ 3° 00' orb

0° 02'	GODDARD, James	0° 46'	HOWARD, Frank
0° 05'	CONNALLY, John	0° 50'	SHAPIRO, Irving
0° 12'	KRAMER, Gerald	1° 04'	REDFORD, Robert
0° 14'	RHODES, John	2° 25'	HAACK, Robert
0° 15'	DRYSDALE, Don	2° 27'	FOREMAN, George
0° 15'	TAFT, Robert	2° 57'	SCHIRRA, Walter
0° 18'	MAILER, Norman		

OPPOSITION ☍ 4° 00' orb

1° 18'	COPPOLA, Francis	2° 57'	LAYNE, Bobby
1° 28'	HEFNER, Hugh	3° 17'	WEYERHAEUSER, George
1° 30'	YARBOROUGH, Cale	3° 39'	TREVINO, Lee

JUPITER/NEPTUNE (continued)

OPPOSITION ☍ 4° 00′ orb

0° 27′	HARTZOG, George		2° 09′	LEIGHTON R B
0° 40′	COSELL, Howard		2° 13′	JAMES, Daniel
0° 43′	DUERK, Alene		2° 23′	LAWRENCE, Carol
1° 07′	MOORE, George		2° 58′	BURKE, Yvonne
2° 05′	CRONIN, Joseph			

SATURN/NEPTUNE

SEXTILE ✶ 3° 00′ orb

0° 05′	GODDARD, James		1° 37′	PARSEGHIAN, Ara
0° 14′	FOXX, Redd		1° 53′	ARNESS, James
0° 53′	SIMPSON, Orenthal		1° 58′	GREENE, Joe
0° 55′	FIELD, Sally		2° 02′	CLIFFORD, John
1° 00′	WHITE, Jojo		2° 37′	MUNSON, Thurman
1° 05′	SEAGREN, Bob		2° 44′	HEARNES W E
1° 07′	GARDNER, Ava		2° 44′	SCHIRRA, Walter
1° 22′	KUCINICH, Dennis		2° 53′	FRANCIS, Sam
1° 26′	JENSEN, Arthur		2° 55′	CSONKA, Lawrence

TRINE △ 3° 00′ orb

0° 15′	GOULIAN, Mehran		2° 49′	GIFFORD, Frank
1° 06′	YOUNG, John		2° 49′	TRABERT, Marion
1° 06′	ROSE, Peter		2° 50′	HARRIS, Fred
1° 40′	HARRELSON, Ken		2° 55′	WHITE, Edward
2° 08′	TROWBRIDGE, Alexandre			

SQUARE □ 3° 00′ orb

0° 02′	KNOWLES, John		1° 19′	DIEBOLD, John
0° 04′	CONIGLIARO, Tony		1° 34′	THOMAS, Michael
0° 04′	HADDON, William		1° 35′	TETLEY, Glen
0° 10′	DAVIS, Miles		1° 35′	ARFONS, Art
0° 23′	NEAL, Patricia		1° 45′	LYNDE, Paul
0° 30′	NASH, Philleo		1° 46′	FARROW, Mia
0° 34′	RUSH, David		1° 46′	MATSON, Randi
0° 48′	MAY, Rollo		2° 09′	WICKER, Tom
0° 58′	KIRK, Claude		2° 45′	RICHARDS, Bob
0° 58′	HALDEMAN, Harry		2° 58′	HEFNER, Hugh

OPPOSITION ☍ 4° 00′ orb

1° 44′	NITSCHKE, Raymond		2° 07′	PERRY, James
1° 45′	DINE, James		2° 37′	KEMP, Jack
1° 47′	DAWSON, Leonard			

SATURN/NEPTUNE (continued)

CONJUNCTION ♂ 4° OO' orb

1° 12'	WALTON, Bill	3° 06'	FORD, Henry
1° 22'	DILLER, Phyllis	3° 33'	SCALI, John
1° 37'	WEINBERGER, Casper	3° 56'	BOONE, Richard
1° 53'	LYNN, Janet	3° 56'	FREEMAN, Orville
2° 22'	LEWIS, David	3° 57'	MARTIN, Dean
2° 34'	LUCE, Charles	4° OO'	BROOKS, Gwendolyn
3° 04'	RICE, Jim		

URANUS/NEPTUNE

TRINE △ 3° OO' orb

O° O4'	BUTKUS, Dick	1° 21'	WELCH, Raquel
O° O9'	BLACK, Karen	1° 31'	THEROUX, Paul
O° 12'	SMEAL, Eleanor	1° 41'	DYLAN, Bob
O° 12'	LILLY, Bob	1° 51'	WHITWORTH, Kathy
O° 14'	BLEGEN, Judith	1° 54'	MORIARTY, Michael
O° 20'	ROSE, Peter	2° O7'	GABRIEL, Roman
O° 25'	JOHNSON, Don	2° O8'	ALWORTH, Lance
O° 27'	HAYES, Bob	2° O8'	SHEEN, Martin
O° 27'	ASHLEY, Elisabeth	2° 11'	KIDD, Billy
O° 44'	KILMER, Bill	2° 20'	IRVING, John
O° 44'	WARFIELD, Paul	2° 25'	OATES, J C
O° 45'	O'NEAL, Ryan	2° 28'	WILLIAMS, Billy
O° 54'	FRAZIER, Joe	2° 39'	ZIEGLER, Ronald
O° 56'	OLSEN, Merlin	2° 51'	ROSS, Diana
O° 57'	DEBUSSCHERE, David	2° 58'	BARRY, Richard
1° 20'	DENVER, John	2° 59'	FARROW, Mia

SQUARE □ 3° OO' orb

O° O3'	NABER, John	1° 37'	GRIFFIN, Archie
O° O8'	THOMPSON, D	2° O3'	BABASHOFF, Shirley
1° 23'	FIDRYCH, Mark	2° 51'	STONES, Dwight

OPPOSITION ☍ 4° OO'orb

O° O2'	KROL, John	1° 54'	NASH, Philleo
O° 20'	MURPHY, William	1° 56'	LOSEY, Joseph
O° 22'	RAINEY, Froelich	2° O1'	ROGERS, Roy
O° 29'	KOCH, John	3° 37'	GARDNER, John
O° 30'	MILLER, Neal	3° 47'	RUSH, David
O° 55'	SIX, Robert		

PLUTO/NEPTUNE

SEXTILE ✳ 3° OO' orb

0° 15'	HAMILL, Dorothy	1° 57'	RICE, Jim
0° 17'	THOMPSON, D	2° 06'	MINNELLI, Liza
0° 19'	SPITZ, Mark	2° 08'	Mc ADOO, Bob
0° 20'	STONES, Dwight	2° 09'	LOGAN, Karen
0° 21'	ROBERTS, Ken	2° 15'	LOPEZ, Nancy
0° 26'	HARRIS, Franco	2° 16'	TRAVOLTA, John
0° 26'	FODOR, Eugene	2° 18'	CSONKA, Lawrence
0° 46'	FOREMAN, George	2° 20'	RYUN, James
0° 48'	TAYLOR, James	2° 20'	MILLER, John
0° 51'	FIDRYCH, Mark	2° 21'	PLUNKETT, Jim
0° 55'	WALTON, Bill	2° 21'	NABER, John
0° 56'	GRIFFIN, Archie	2° 36'	KEATON, Diane
1° 01'	SUMMER, Donna	2° 42'	FARROW, Mia
1° 09'	LAMBERT, Jack	2° 44'	MATSON, Randi
1° 23'	FOSBURY, Richard	2° 58'	BABASHOFF, Shirley
1° 44'	LYNN, Janet	2° 59'	GABLE, Dan
1° 51'	MITCHELL, L	3° OO'	COWENS, David
1° 51'	DEMPSEY, Tom		

Index

Notes

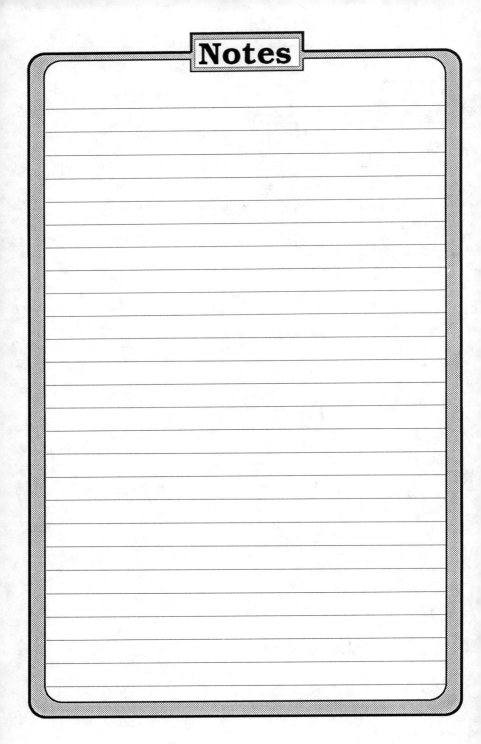

Notes

Notes

Notes

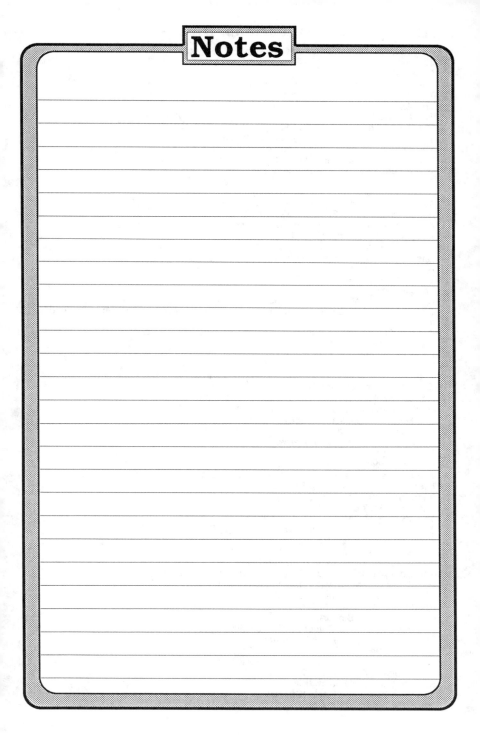

Also by ACS Publications, Inc.